The Media and Cultural Production

The Media and Cultural Production

P. Eric Louw

SAGE Publications
London • Thousand Oaks • New Delhi

© P. Eric Louw 2001

First published 2001

Apart from any fair dealing for the purposes of research or private study, or criticism or review, as permitted under the Copyright, Designs and Patents Act, 1988, this publication may be reproduced, stored or transmitted in any form, or by any means, only with the prior permission in writing of the publishers, or in the case of reprographic reproduction, in accordance with the terms of licences issued by the Copyright Licensing Agency. Inquiries concerning reproduction outside those terms should be sent to the publishers.

SAGE Publications Ltd
6 Bonhill Street
London EC2A 4PU

SAGE Publications Inc
2455 Teller Road
Thousand Oaks, California 91320

SAGE Publications India Pvt Ltd
32, M-Block Market
Greater Kailash – I
New Delhi 110 048

British Library Cataloguing in Publication Data

A catalogue record for this book is available from the British Library

ISBN 0 7619 6582 3
ISBN 0 7619 6583 1 (pbk)

Library of Congress Control Number 2001131840

Typeset by Keystroke, Jacaranda Lodge, Wolverhampton.

Contents

	Preface	vii
	Abbreviations	ix
1.	The struggle for power and the struggle for meaning	1
2.	Sites for making meaning I: the culture industry	37
3.	Sites for making meaning II: the regulatory framework	69
4.	Sites for making meaning III: commercialization and the 'death of the public sphere'	91
5.	Striving for discursive closure: the struggle for hegemony	105
6.	Moving to an informational economy: the new rules of the power game in global network capitalism	125
7.	Circulating meaning I: making news	155
8.	Circulating meaning II: the public relations-izing of war	171
9.	Circulating meaning III: making sense of distant places	189
10.	The limits of power: resisting dominant meanings	205
	References	215
	Index	223

Preface

There was a time when media production issues were central concerns within media and communication studies. It has been argued, with some justification, that this led to something of an over-emphasis being placed on the encoding dimension of the communicative process (that is, too great a focus on communicators and the medium/media), which caused the role of decoders (recipients and audiences) to be undervalued. These criticisms were to precipitate a focus-shift towards the 'active reader'. However, once the decoding dimension and 'active audience' became the 'trendy' concerns of communication studies, something of a paradigm flip-flop occurred – and not only did the issues of encoding, media production, media ownership and 'ideology' etc. tend to fall off the media studies agenda, they actually came to be dismissed as 'dated' (which perhaps confers some validity on Kuhn's hypothesis that paradigm shifts are accompanied by the active de-legitimation of earlier work). Ultimately, the turn away from 'encoding' towards 'decoding' simply generated another lopsided understanding of the communication process – instead of over-emphasized encoding, decoding was now over-emphasized.

This book wishes to place encoding issues back on to the communication and media studies agenda because this author believes that understanding communication as a 'total process' should involve a concern with both encoding and decoding. Hence this book sets out to revisit the work of those who have previously concerned themselves with media production issues. More specifically, this book attempts to re-activate a number of 'media production themes' in a way that makes this work accessible to undergraduates, an objective of this book being to produce an undergraduate text which brings together in one volume a wide range of communication studies work on media production.

Further, the book aims to introduce undergraduates to the relationship between cultural production and power – to explore how the socially powerful attempt to use the media to maintain their positions of dominance over others. It is about introducing undergraduates to an exploration of cultural and media production via the issue of power relationships. As a result, the book explores the role the media can play in the process of creating, maintaining and shifting power relations, as well as the role that the wider struggle for social power has on media practices, production and consumption. In this regard, a central theme in the book is that the socially powerful attempt to use the media in their exercise of power precisely because the media does have the capacity to 'manipulate' us. This is not to argue that the media are all-powerful, or that we are necessarily always manipulated, or that the socially powerful always get their way. Rather, this author sees the media as possessing the 'potential to influence' in a rather more diffuse way. In this regard, the book draws heavily upon Bernard Cohen's notion of agenda-setting – that is Cohen's conceptualization that the media 'may not be successful much of the time in telling people what to think, but it is stunningly successful in telling its readers what to think about' (1963: 13). This agenda-setting logic provides a useful fulcrum for exploring how the media may 'limit' what we perceive, but still allows for the conceptualization of an 'active audience' which is able to engage with what is on offer. Yet, as Cohen's logic suggests, the media has the capacity to manipulate us even if we are 'active readers'. Hence the need to pay attention to media production.

I would like to thank Trish Andrews for her useful suggestions on Chapter 1, and Rose Louw for sub-editing the book. Thanks also to James Davidson and Julia Hall of Sage for 'guiding' me to the idea of writing such a book in the first place.

Abbreviations

ABA	Australian Broadcasting Authority
ABC	Australian Broadcasting Corporation
ARD	Arbeitsgemeinschaft der Offentilich-Rechtlichen Rundfumkanstalten Deutschland
BBC	British Broadcasting Corporation
CBC	Canadian Broadcasting Corporation
CEO	Chief executive officer
CIA	Central Intelligence Agency (USA)
CNCL	Commission for Communications and Liberties (France)
CRCT	Canadian Radio-television and Telecommunications Commission
EU	European Union
FARC	Revolutionary Armed Force of Columbia (Fuerzas Armadas Revolucionarias de Colombia)
FCC	Federal Communications Commission (USA)
IBA	Independent Broadcasting Authority (South Africa)
IMF	International Monetary Fund
ITC	Independent Television Commission (UK)
MITI	Ministry of International Trade and Industry (Japan)
NATO	North Atlantic Treaty Organization
NGO	Non-Governmental Organization
NHK	Nippon Hosa Kyokai (Japan)
NWIO	New World Information Order
NWO	New World Order
OECD	Organization for Economic Corporation and Development
PAC	Political action committee
PR	Public relations

PRs	Public relations professionals
PSB	Public service broadcasting
SABC	South African Broadcasting Corporation
WTO	World Trade Organization
WWW	World Wide Web
ZDF	Zweites Deutsches Fernesehen (Germany)

CHAPTER 1

The Struggle for Power and the Struggle for Meaning

Human beings experience the world through the senses of sight, hearing, smell, touch and taste. But humans also experience the world through the more abstract phenomenon of consciousness, that is, we think, comprehend and mentally process insights. We have a capacity for understanding – a capacity for making sense of the world and our sensations. We do not simply take in perceptions, we are also conscious of these perceptions. We are 'mental' beings who try to 'make sense' of our world and of ourselves. We share our understandings, thoughts and feelings with one another through language. Our capacity to engage in this 'sharing process' has been greatly enhanced by the development of various media forms. Ultimately the human capacity for language, sharing and comprehension involves an ability to make meaning, that is we are able to take in perceptions, process them, comprehend them and then share them with others.

For many people, the meanings through which we live our lives are simply there; like the air we breathe. Meaning is taken for granted, and few reflect on how it is constructed. But meanings do not just exist – they are actively made as people encounter and think about the world, and then try to find ways to tell others what they are thinking. Meanings are also re-made as circumstances change.

In the contemporary world, meanings are frequently made within institutions called the media where meaning production has become professionalized. Such media-ized meaning-making is necessarily associated with sets of relationships between people that have been turned into institutionalized behaviours and work practices. This involves the emergence of power relationships between the people involved in such institutional settings. Unravelling the agendas, interests and struggles between such people helps give us insight into the world of meanings that we inhabit.

Understanding our 'meaning-environment' is not merely an academic exercise. After all, failure to reflect on our meaning-environment creates the potential for being manipulated by those who do reflect on this communicative process, and reduces one's capacity for engaging in democratic society. Being an active citizen and an engaged communicator requires being as conscious as possible of the nature and origins of the meanings we use.

For those interested in thinking about and unravelling meaning-environments from a critical perspective, there are two particularly useful approaches for analysing the communicative process, namely the cultural studies approach and political economy approach. Cultural studies has focused on deconstructing texts and coding systems as a way of denaturalizing the communicative process and stripping away the opaqueness and taken-for-grantedness of meaning. For example, a cultural studies examination of pop singer Madonna would look beyond the music dimension and explore also what she communicates about contemporary attitudes towards femininity. An analysis of Madonna and her fans could become a study of how the female body, sexuality and gender relationships are understood ('constructed') within conventional and alternative sub-cultures. Alternatively, the political economy approach focuses on how meaning is made by people within a productive process. This involves exploring the social positions people occupy, the relationships between them and struggles over meaning-production within organizations. For example, political economists would be interested in examining the possible relationship between the content of *The Australian* and the fact that this newspaper is part of a corporation owned by Rupert Murdoch. These two critical approaches are complementary, and can be jointly applied for maximum deconstructive effect when analysing communication processes. This book draws together elements of the work of those who have contributed to the political economy method and the cultural studies approach.

The cultural studies insight that humans swim in a sea of meanings that is the outcome of a process of semiosis provides a useful point of departure. We are born into pools of pre-constituted meanings and internalize these as we are socialized and learn to communicate. Various communication pools have emerged as clusters or structures of meaning that have congealed over time. These communicative pools are coding styles or circulation patterns that have taken on identifiable forms which we call societies or cultures. The Anglo pool of meanings has grown into a 'global culture' which incorporates various sub-pools (or societies) including the UK, the USA, Canada, Australia and Eire. In Western society the various pools have become closely associated with the production and circulation systems we now call 'the media'. As each of us internalizes the particular meaning-style that surrounds us, we are constituted as human beings and as members of various social groups/ cultures. These meanings are resources that we use to generate our personas, to negotiate with others and to position ourselves within a social milieu. But we also help to re-make these shared meanings as we proceed through life. Hence our societies and cultures are not static – they are continually being re-invented and struggled over, and every individual makes some contribution to re-shaping social meaning as we engage in the everyday process of communicating with each other. We cannot help but change the coding structure into which we were born as each individual grapples to make sense of, and shape our world. Hence the pool of meaning that shapes us, and that we in turn shape, shifts throughout our lives. Numerous, often imperceivably small shifts result in the pool of meanings becoming different for each generation. Our cultures consequently change and grow precisely because the process of communicative coding and decoding relies on innumerable, small, creative transactions between active human beings.

Contextualizing meaning-making

The pools of meaning we inhabit are not constituted by arbitrary communicative acts of randomly positioned individuals. Certainly all individuals play a role in making, re-making and circulating meaning. But some individuals or groups have more power than others within the communicative process. People are positioned differently by the power relationships into which they are embedded, and these positions impact on the access individuals have to media production and circulation systems. The positioning of people is a contextual issue. Each person who communicates is part of a context – located in a particular place and time. The meanings they consume and make are contextually-bound, rooted in a unique set of circumstances and relationships. A great strength of the political economy approach is that it stresses the need to analyse communication contextually. So for political economists, meanings need to be seen as inextricably bound to the (physical and temporal) sites in which they are made/used. Such an approach debunks the notion of universally valid meanings or 'truth(s)'. Hence, political economists find the idea that meanings can simply be transported across time and place and still retain the author's original codings as naïve. So 'meaning' is not a free-floating language game, as in the cosmology of a Derrida (1976) or Laclau and Mouffe (1985). Instead, even if 'meaning' is understood as a 'language game', it is 'language' necessarily read as being tied to specific sets of human relationships, located within concretized localities and within identifiable periods. 'Truth' is relativized by time, place and power – there are as many 'truths' as there are contextual and power relationships giving rise to such truths. For example, 'peace' and 'democracy' are signs shared by all within the Anglo pool of meanings, but (because their lived-experiences are so different) the actual meaning attached to these signs is unlikely to be the same for a Catholic in Northern Ireland, a Protestant in Ulster, a London lawyer, a US civil rights activist, a white South African, a Wall Street stockbroker, and a Malaysian-Chinese migrant to Australia. Also, the same Ulsterman would probably not attach the same 'positive' meaning to these signs during the 1999 Ulster negotiations as he did after the Second World War in 1945.

Hence, a political economist examining 'meaning' is concerned with mapping out human relationships and the way some individuals gain more power than others through their positioning relative to others, and to their positioning relative to media production and circulation systems. Implicit in this is the notion that meaning is struggled over as people work at improving their positioning. Within such a framework, meaning-making is implicated in contextually-rooted processes of struggle and power acquisition. Gaining access to the means of communicative production/circulation (and even to certain codes) is both derivative of power and a means for accumulating power. The key issue is that those with power, in any given context, will have a greater impact on meaning-making and meaning-circulation because they have greater access to the coding and code-circulation systems. Not surprisingly, sites where discourses are produced (such as newsrooms, film/television studios, parliaments, courts, universities and research institutes) and the channels through which discourses flow (such as schools, the media and telecommunications networks) are necessarily important sites of struggle. There is a constant struggle over gaining access to such sites and/or restricting the access of opponents to these sites. The pools of meaning into which we are born are the outcome of numerous past struggles (rooted in past contextual relationships), just as the results of the struggles in which we engage in our lifetimes will help to constitute the meaning-pool of the next generation. The nature and outcome of these struggles are what define the texture of each context. For political economists, such textures are not peripheral issues. Instead, it is precisely the unique texture of each time and place that provides the key insights into the nature of any 'meaning'.

For this reason power relationships between people are central variables to be mapped by anyone trying to understand why a particular set of meanings circulates at a certain time and place. But mapping power is as complex as mapping meaning because just as meanings are continually shifting, so too is the distribution of power. There is a continual struggle over power in all human groups and a constant realignment in winners and losers. And as power shifts take place, so the dynamics of meaning-production change. For this reason, mapping the mechanics of meaning-production (as with the mapping of meaning itself) is necessarily a highly contextual exercise in terms of time, place and shifting power relationships.

The power to influence meaning-making

Power does not have the tangibility of an object, yet as human beings we all intuitively recognize its presence. Like communication, it is omnipresent, yet it can be overlooked because it seems to be 'just there'. But to overlook power is to miss a crucial dimension within the meaning-making process.

Power is a slippery phenomenon with numerous definitions. For the purposes of this book, power will be seen as the capacity to get one's own way when interacting with other human beings. Weber expressed this best when saying that those with power are able 'to realize their own will even against the resistance of others' (1978: 53). Lukes added an interesting rider to this Weberian notion. For Lukes (1974), having power not only grants one the ability to have one's interests prevail over others, but is also the ability to stop conflicts from emerging by preventing oppositional agendas from even being raised. But accepting the above definition of power still leaves at least three ancillary issues to be dealt with. First, what is the relationship between power and social elites? Secondly, where does power come from? And, thirdly, what is the relationship between being 'embedded' within a power relationship and free agency?

The notion of power elites slides easily into conspiracy theory, although it need not do so. Similarly, discussions of the relationships between meaning-making and the media can easily end up sounding like a conspiracy theory in which power elites are seen to be necessarily in a position to manipulate media content to serve their own interests. For this reason, there has often been a relationship between power elite theories and those studying media ownership and control, with the political economy approach to communication being one of those theories which has lent itself to conspiratorial interpretations of media control. This occurred because theories of an all-powerful media being used to generate 'false consciousness' can all too easily be read as supporting a naïve interpretation of elite theory in which social or economic elites are seen to conspire actively to use the media to subdue or misdirect the masses. That media production can be (and often is) used by individuals and groups for the purposes of manipulation is clear. But what is less clear is whether control of the media necessarily means 'manipulation' and whether manipulation can necessarily be assumed to be the work of power elites. In part, exploring these issues requires considering the validity of the power elite theory itself.

The debate between Dahl (1961) and Mills (1959) over the existence or otherwise of power elites is useful when considering the validity of the power-elite position. Pluralists like Dahl argued that there is no unified elite because power is diffused within a democracy, while theorists such as Mills argued that ultimately power resided with a small group of people within society. In Figure 1.1 these are represented as (a) Dahl's pluralist model, in which society is seen as being made up of multitudes of intersecting (cross-cutting) interest groups (without a clear elite); and (b) Mills's power-elite model in which society is seen as hierarchially structured, with a small unified elite 'commanding' the rest of society. This book proposes a third approach, namely (c) the hegemonic-domination model in which hegemonic elites are seen as alliances of interest groups. These hegemonic alliances become elites ('rulers') who dominate the 'ruled', but their dominance is more 'messy', tentative and less 'hierarchial' than in Mills's conceptualization. Mills's and Dahl's positions may seem mutually exclusive but it is possible to see both positions as valid if power is seen to migrate and mutate, and the sites of power are seen constantly to shift in the course of struggles taking place. The hegemonic-dominance model – as seen in (c) in Figure 1.1 – is based on such a mutable/shifting conceptualization of elites. At certain moments elites might well congeal and manage to become the dominant power brokers within a particular context only later to have their power challenged and overthrown either by another (emergent) power elite or by something more akin to Dahl's pluralist-type, diffused power agglomeration. If society is conceptualized as a fluid and continually mutating entity, it becomes possible to view elite theory and pluralist theory as describing different 'moments' of a shifting continuum. Gramsci's (1971) notion of hegemonic struggle is especially useful when conceptualizing the interaction between various competing interest groups – a competition theorized by both liberal-pluralists like Dahl (1961) and

(a) Dahl's pluralist model

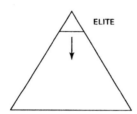

(b) Mills's power-elite model

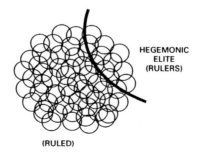

(c) Hegemonic-dominance model

FIGURE 1.1 *Pluralism, power elites and hegemonic dominance*

socialist-pluralists like Poulantzas (1980). Gramsci's notion is also useful when conceptualizing existent, emergent and decaying power elites. Hegemonies have to be built and maintained – this is the mechanism for becoming (and remaining) a ruling elite. So ruling elites are not 'conspiracies'; they are the outcome of hard hegemonic labour which can, in the contemporary era, involve coordinating the interests of millions of people.

Pluralist theory's denial that elites can (and do) emerge seems naïve. But neither is the existence of power elites a necessary condition of human existence – contexts can exist where power is diffused in the way described by pluralist theorists like Dahl (1961). Similarly, the pluralist failure to address the fact that elites can and do intentionally work to manipulate and control non-elites also seems naïve. But the notion that non-elites are necessarily powerless and perpetually manipulated seems equally dubious. It is more helpful to recognize the existence of elites and aspiring elites, as well as non-elite groups who are part of a complex pluralist competition for (material and cultural) resources and power. Within this framework the media are one of the many social sites that are struggled over as means to acquire and build power.

The question then becomes, from where does this power come? Those trying to answer this question have broadly formulated three explanations of the source of power. These are: access to resources (to implement one's will and buy others); the occupation of social positions (which enhance one's capacity to get one's will complied with, and/or to constrain the capacity of others to act); and language as a relation-structuring agent. The latter approach has become closely associated with cultural studies attempts to analyse meaning. For the purposes of this book, all three are seen as valuable – power is seen as derivative of access to resources (economic and cultural), social position and linguistic factors. And with each of these three sources, institutionalized communication is implicated. Various sites have effectively been 'licensed' to manufacture and circulate discourse such as educational institutions, the media, parliaments and courts of law. These sites are cultural resources, access to which is therefore struggled over. Access to such sites is controlled and limited, and often regulated by a credentialism. (Credentials are one of the discourses produced by communication sites as a self-regulating mechanism for limiting access.) A cultural resource that became especially important during the twentieth century was the media, because the media became a central site for defining social position and status (with publicity, for example, becoming a central resource to be battled over by politicians). The media also became important agents for positioning people (through discourse). Media discourses are necessarily battled over, because such discourses serve to legitimate (or de-legitimate) particular hierarchies of positions and the incumbents of such positions. Given the importance the media assumed as 'king-makers' and legitimators/de-legitimators from the second half of the twentieth century, media institutions have become prized possessions for those seeking power. Owning or controlling a media institution empowers the owner to hire and fire the makers of meaning. From this can emerge a secondary power – the power that derives from the capacity to make or break political leaders, and either circulate or suppress information and ideas. Whether the ownership/control of media sites does actually confer power will depend on the individuals concerned, the context in which they operate and the wider struggles taking place within that context. Rupert Murdoch (Shawcross, 1992) is a good example of how media ownership within the context of the late twentieth century has been an empowering resource when mobilized wisely within the struggles of emergent Anglo-globalism. Power is not automatic, it is the outcome of struggle. However, such struggles are not fought on level playing fields because certain players are advantaged (or disadvantaged) by having more (or less) access to the sources of power at the start of play. Pre-existent access to power is necessarily an advantage in the next round of the struggle over power. This means existent power elites are advantaged, but not in a way that absolutely predetermines their success in the next round of battle.

The notion that battles are not predetermined is an important one when considering power (and when considering meaning-production). Essentially there are two conceptions of power. In the first, people are passive and have power exercised over them – they merely inhabit pre-ordained structures. The second definition sees humans as active and part of a process in which power is struggled over. In the first, people are conceptualized as 'imprisoned' within a power relationship or structure (whether these are economic, political or linguistic). In the second, people have free agency – our lifeworlds are seen as the outcome of mutable human activity in which we make (and re-make) our own structures. In communication terms, it is a question of whether we are seen to be free to make meaning or whether we merely inhabit predetermined sets of meanings.

An examination of the shift from Saussurian structuralism to Derrida's post-structuralism will help position this book with regard to the issue of pre-determined structure versus human agency. At the risk of over-simplification, Table 1.1 attempts to summarize this shift. For Ferdinand Saussure (1974) we are socialized into a prison-house of language – a world of subjective structures (signs and codes) into which we are born. Louis Althusser (1971) took Saussure's notion of linguistic structures and used these to develop his idea of the ISA (Ideological State Apparatus). Dominant ideologies/meanings were seen as being fixed or coded into our heads via these ISAs. Within the Althusserian worldview, power derived from control of ISAs. Human agency was given little scope within this structural and subjectivist view of human communication. The shift into a post-structural interpretation of the Saussurian cosmology came with Michel Foucault (1977; 1979). Foucault also saw humans as being constituted within linguistic structures. However, for Foucault, we were constituted within discursive practices, and these practices are created by human agency within institutions. This Foucaultian shift was highly significant because it opened a space for human agency and struggle that was tied to a notion of institutionalized communication. There might be structures, but these structures, institutions and practices were mutable because they were themselves the outcome of struggles between active human beings within a particular context. The Foucaultian notion of discursive practices therefore represented a shift away from linguistic determinism. His notion of knowledge as being constituted by active human practice (within human-made

TABLE 1.1 *From Saussure to Derrida*

Saussure	Althusser	Foucault	Derrida
Linguistic structuralism	Early French structuralism	Mature French structuralism	Post-structuralism
Sign and code systems are a prison-house of *language* into which we are born.	Sign systems are institutionalized within socio-political *apparati* (ISAs). ISAs socialize us into a prison-house of language.	We are socialized into sets of discursive practices which structure meaning. But human agency struggles over these meanings. Hence they are *not fixed* structures (prison-houses).	Meanings are never fixed within structures but are *constantly shifting*.
Predetermination through linguistics.	Predetermination through an ideological apparatus.	Human agency moderates the impact of structures.	Pure human agency operative.

agencies) placed Foucault's understanding of communication within the same cosmology as that of Antonio Gramsci's (1971) notion of hegemonic struggle. For both Foucault and Gramsci, communication is the outcome of human practices that are struggled over. There may be communicative structures which set boundaries or parameters but these do not predetermine human action.

Jacques Derrida (1976) took this Foucaultian notion one stage further and explored the struggle over meaning as a process of trying to either fix meanings into place or uncouple meanings. In Derrida's cosmology there was a constant shift in meaning structures as the process of fixing and uncoupling and re-fixing unfolded. Laclau and Mouffe (1985) progressed Derrida's notion by even questioning the possibility of ever fixing meanings into place. At most, Laclau and Mouffe saw 'fixations' as partial. Within this Derridian/Laclau and Mouffe cosmology we are left with a shift into an understanding of communication as a pure semiosis – where meaning-making is understood as purely about language games. Stuart Hall (1983) noted the limitations of this extreme post-structuralist worldview. Essentially extreme post-structuralism decontextualizes meaning-making. It ignores power relationships embedded in identifiable political and economic contexts and so loses the substance and complexity that a Foucaultian or Gramscian approach has. The Laclau and Mouffe position of 'pure semiosis' is simply ill-equipped to deal with how power relationships emerge between humans engaged in struggles over resources and positions. These struggles involve symbolism and cultural resources but they are not reducible exclusively to mere battles over meaning.

The Gramscian or Foucaultian positions have the advantage of allowing for both human agency and structural limitations within the process of a context-embedded meaning-production. When making meaning we necessarily operate within pre-existing economic, political and linguistic structures, and hence within pre-existing power relations. But these existent structures and power relationships are not immutable or fixed. Rather, they simply set parameters within which the next wave of struggle for power and influence takes place. These contextual parameters may advantage certain individuals and groups engaged in the processes, but it does not imprison anyone into a predetermined outcome. Ultimately, both meaning and power relations emerge from a process of ongoing struggle. Within this process there will be those attempting to freeze certain meanings and structures if these advantage their position. And if they have sufficient power or influence they may even be successful for a while. But power is relational and messy, and is dependent upon the way humans interact in a particular location and time. There will always be gaps and contradictions in any system of control, and there will always be those who wish to circumvent, and will often succeed in circumventing, the mechanisms of control and meaning-closure. Total Orwellian control (as hypothesized in Orwell's novel, *1984*) is an impossibility because no monitor could ever be large enough. Ultimately, relational shifts cannot be prevented. Therefore power shifts are inevitable. Hence, power is always contextually-bound, transitory and slipping away from those who try to wield it. So both meanings and power relations are constantly sliding around, migrating and mutating, sometimes in sync with one another and sometimes out of sync, and this constant churning creates gaps for those who wish to challenge existent power relations and existent structures. It is relational churning that constrains the powerful because the powerful can never permanently pin down relationships that benefit themselves. Power is consequently constrained by the propensity humans have for struggle, and their capacity to find gaps and contradictions in any social structure. No structure, whether it be an economic or political structure, or a meaning-structure, is ever a permanent 'prison' – at most, structures 'channel' human agency.

The same is true for meaning-production. The process(es) of meaning-making are 'bounded' by a multiplicity of (contextually-bound) human-made power relationships and structures which may 'restrict' human agency but which can never 'eliminate' it. However, even if power relationships and structures do not determine meanings, they are part of the contextual framework within which meaning is made. Hence, mapping the structuring qualities of power relationships is a useful place to start when analysing meaning-production.

Those licensed to make meaning – intellectuals

As we enter the twenty-first century a high proportion of the meanings we individually process on a daily basis are produced and circulated by professionalized meaning-makers who work within an institutionalized set of power relationships. These people can be termed intellectuals – they make and circulate ideas.

All humans make meaning and all humans consume meaning. However, for some people, meaning-production and meaning-circulation become their full-time occupation. These professional communicators exercise an influence in society disproportionate to their numbers because they become the primary gatekeepers and regulators of the meaning in circulation. In Western civilization there is a long-standing tradition of such professionalized communicators that reaches as far back as the rhetoricians of ancient Greece. But the communication profession is one whose numbers increased rapidly, especially during the twentieth century, thanks initially to the proliferation of mass education and the mass media and more recently to the growth of the Internet. Although these mass communication forms had their roots in the late nineteenth century, it was the twentieth century that really saw the widespread diffusion of mass-schooling, the print media, radio, film and, later, television, as important social phenomena. However, it was the emergence of the global information economy in the late twentieth century that saw communication professionals become not only still more numerous, but also more socially powerful than ever before. As a consequence, intellectuals have become ever more central to the very functioning of the (globalizing) economy because flows of data, information and ideas have become key commodities within the new economy that are just as important as raw (and processed) minerals or agricultural products (see Lash & Urry, 1994).

There was a proliferation throughout the second half of the twentieth century in the variety of professionalized intellectual roles in Western society as ever-larger percentages of the work force became engaged in the work of processing ever-growing volumes of information in circulation. We now have numerous types of professionalized intellectuals, such as academics, researchers, teachers, journalists, publishers, film-makers, television producers, multimedia workers, architects, artists-cum-designers, politicians, policy advisors and regulators, economists, judges, psychologists and counsellors, the clergy and those working in fields like advertising, marketing, public relations and community development. All of these people are part of the process of making, circulating and regulating the flow of meanings within which we live. As intellectual roles proliferated, the nature of intellectual work also shifted. The traditional Western image of an intellectual as a cloistered ivory-tower academic or a member of the clergy is no longer valid for the bulk of intellectual roles. A more suitable image of an early twenty-first century intellectual worker is an employee of the Fox network who is working as part of a team creating, packaging and distributing ideas through a global (largely electronic) information network. Intellectual work is increasingly concentrated within organizational sites where creative people are employed to generate ideas. Some sites have more influence (and hence status) than others. Gramsci (1971) argued that ideas produced in such sites are ideological when they fit the hegemonic needs of the ruling order. Intellectuals are significantly implicated in the creation of social power relationships through the way in which political and economic power elites form symbiotic relationships with intellectuals – a relationship discussed by Berger (1977). Berger used the analogy of Aztec temples to describe how ruling elites sacrifice people for their dreams, and how intellectuals (like Aztec priests) are deeply complicit in such sacrifices: 'The Great pyramid at Cholula provides a metaphorical paradigm for the relations amongst theory, power, and the victims of both – the intellectuals who define reality, the power wielders who shape the world to conform to their definitions, and the others who are called upon to suffer in consequence of both enterprises' (Berger, 1977: 22).

Because of the capacity intellectuals have to both set and tweak the parameters of social meaning, there is a growing status attached to many media-intellectual roles and, as a result, a significant competition for such jobs (because they are perceived as 'influential' or 'powerful'). One consequence of this has been the emergence of sets of 'professional standards' and 'licensing' arrangements for such professions, and these are generally tied to accessing tertiary education. This in turn has led to a new growth industry in the form of tertiary-level communication programmes. Meaning-making has increasingly become a function of people working within institutionalized sites who were recruited from a training system specifically designed for the mass-production of professional communicators. The consequent proliferation of an education/training industry (linked to licensed professionalism) potentially becomes a mechanism for limiting/'controlling' both media and education content by effectively reducing the range of coding possibilities. The mass-production of intellectuals, who are needed to staff the proliferating communicative machinery, can easily lead to discursive closure and standardized banality thanks to a 'cloning-process' which can, in turn, lead to (globalized) intellectual copy-catism and trendiness among those staffing the new communication networks. Members of the Frankfurt School, such as Adorno and Horkheimer (1979) and Marcuse (1964b), were among those theorists who worried about the possibilities for producing intellectual one-dimensionality as a result of industrializing meaning-production.

Of concern to the Frankfurt School theorists was the way in which twentieth-century intellectuals had their creativity channelled (restricted?)

and had any 'oppositional' ideas curtailed by their need to work within an institutionalized media industry. The argument was that, once employed, intellectuals found themselves (necessarily?) 'tamed' by the patronage relationship into which they were embedded. The Frankfurt School produced its theories towards the middle of the twentieth century. One can only speculate how concerned they would have been to witness the banalities and discursive closures that characterized information-flows of the late twentieth century. Other theorists, such as Gramsci, while recognizing the potential for such control and conformity, did not see intellectual work as necessarily always 'closed'. Instead, Gramsci (1971) recognized the possibility for struggle and turmoil even within an institutionalized meaning-making machinery. Hence, closure could never be universal or permanent. In a similar vein, Enzensberger (1974) noted that the products of the culture industry were always going to be contradictory because this industry relied upon the one element that was ultimately untamable – namely, human creativity.

Overall, the trend has been for the processes of Western meaning-making and circulation to become increasingly organized, institutionalized and commoditized throughout the course of the twentieth century. Many meanings continue to emerge from *ad hoc* human creativity and interaction. However, the twentieth century saw the numbers of professional communicators increase. These professionals were employed in the task of deliberately constructing meaning. Hence, an ever-expanding percentage of the meanings available to Westerners became the result of the conscious construction and professional manipulation of communicative variables, rather than *ad hoc* mutations in meaning. The meanings we are exposed to are less and less likely to be the outcome of chance and are ever-more likely to be the products of intellectuals who have been trained in particular coding processes, practices and worldviews. Employers now select 'appropriately' trained communication professionals. These intellectuals plan the meanings we encounter, and generally do this as employees. This has important consequences for meaning-production because employees are not usually in a position to question seriously the wishes of their employers. Therefore, the greater the volume of institutionalized social meaning, the more one can expect to find employer pressure impacting on the available meaning-stock.

Institutionalizing meaning production – the media

The nineteenth century saw the beginnings of the industrialization of Western meaning-making. The process began with newspapers. Although newspapers originated in fifteenth-century Flemish and German states, these were not the highly institutionalized, mass circulation media that arose in the wake of the industrial revolution. The nineteenth century brought with it a number of developments which, when combined, generated the conditions for the creation of a new type of communication, initially in the Anglo-world, but soon spreading elsewhere. The invention of ways to produce cheap paper and ink, the rotary printing press and typesetting machines generated the necessary technology for mass-produced newspapers. The industrial revolution also led to the creation of large cities, growing literacy rates and improved road and rail transport, which provided expanding markets for mass newspapers. Then came advertising, which made it possible to sell newspapers cheaply – the mass circulation 'penny press' was born. Towards the end of the nineteenth century, Americans invented the 'Corporation' as an organizational form – a form that soon came to underpin the culture industry as well. From this confluence of variables grew the mass media – an industrialized production and distribution of meaning. A new set of practices (and discourses about meaning-making), which still formed the basic underpinning of newspaper, magazine, film, radio and television practices at the end of the twentieth century, emerged from this industrial crucible. (Educational practices were similarly industrialized and massified.) Only with the arrival of digital electronic networking during the 1990s did these practices show any signs of modification.

At heart, this industrialized form of communication involved institutionalizing intellectuals. Intellectuals came to work within organizations where the organizing principles were hierarchical and mechanistic, and where factories geared towards mass production were the model. The nature of meaning-making was altered by this process of institutionalization. If Figure 1.2 represents pre-industrial communication, Figure 1.3 represents the effects of industrialization on meaning-making.

FIGURE 1.2 *Unmediated communication*

THE STRUGGLES FOR POWER AND MEANING 17

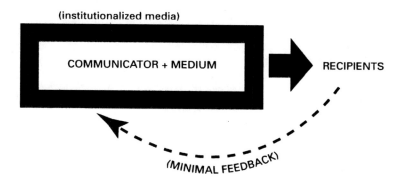

FIGURE 1.3 *Institutionalized communication*

In Figure 1.2 communication involves a process of sharing. Meaning flows back and forth between the communicator and the recipient; in fact the roles of communicator and recipient are interchangeable. Meaning emerges out of the interchange. The medium merely facilitates the process of exchange. But in Figure 1.3 the communicator works within a communication institution – the organizational form of the medium becomes a central part of the communication process and the communicator becomes a functionary of the culture industry. Importantly, the communicator and medium are 'collapsed' into one another. From the point of view of the audience/recipient, any distinction between communicator and medium becomes unimportant – s/he is now seen as part of an organizational entity: the media. In a sense the communicator (and his/her meaning) has been de-personalized; his/her individual identity and individually-held ideas have become much less important than in the mode of communication illustrated in Figure 1.3. In Figure 1.3, recipients consume meaning, and when consuming a product of the culture industry it is the 'collective' identity of the organization that is perceived. The final product is the outcome of the work of innumerable employees of the organization, making it very difficult to identify the opinions or work of a single author. So, rather than an author (as another human being), we find institutionalized roles (driven by institutional needs and practices). Such an institutionalized intellectual necessarily makes meaning within a set of externally derived 'organizational' rules which governs and controls him/her. The space for individual creativity is greatly curtailed by the requirement to conform to organizational needs, hierarchies and practices. Further, institutionalized communication changes the recipient's role within the communication process from a partner in making meaning (in Figure 1.2) to a passive audience (in Figure 1.3). The flow of messages becomes one-way, there being little scope for feedback within industrialized communication. Simultaneously, the capacity to deliver messages is greatly enhanced, with the industrialization of communication dramatically increasing the range and potency of message delivery.

By the end of the twentieth century the mass media's reach became virtually ubiquitous in the industrial (and post-industrial) world. It is now difficult to find a 'space' where one can step outside the reach of one or other media form. So the mass media simultaneously increases the reach of professional communicators, while dramatically narrowing the role of recipients, turning recipients into passive receivers of meanings made by others. For those working within the culture industry, this has led to the reconceptualization of audiences as mass recipients to be 'targeted' as anonymous 'public(s)'. Communicators effectively 'de-personalize' those to whom they deliver messages. Instead of being addressed as another human being, they become mere constructs (such as 'the public') to be reached via the techniques of professional communicators. Hence the 'human' quality of messages was reduced at the same time as its strength and potency was enhanced by industrialization (see Van Schoor, 1986: 115–20).

At heart, industrializing communicative processes (beginning with newspapers, but reaching its zenith with television) led to *mass* communication, which is inherently top-down and manipulative. Industrialization reduced the spaces for 'ordinary' people (non-professional communicators) to engage in meaning-making as anything other than audiences. Ultimately, mass communication is structured to be top-down and uni-directional, unlike popular communication which allows for multi-directional and bottom-up communication (White, 1980). Much of the Frankfurt School's concern about the culture industry was due to its recognition that mass communication lent itself to such (top-down) rhetoric, manipulation and control. For the Frankfurt School, industrializing communication created two (interrelated) negative side-effects: it increased opportunities for manipulating/controlling communication while reducing the space(s) for dialogical communication. The Frankfurt School saw this as producing 'mass society' – a society in which, it believed, the majority of people passively consumed (and so were effectively manipulated by) mass-produced meanings. From this (mass media-induced) passivity grew a 'one-dimensional' society. This one-dimensionality was seen as the 'natural' outcome of a significantly narrowed range of voices/opinions that were distributed widely and loudly by the mass media – that is an industrialized 'megaphone-effect' tended to 'silence' (or at least radically curtail) those voices that the mass media did not deem it fit to distribute.

Seen from another angle, the mass media can be viewed as having become agenda-setters. As Cohen said, the media 'may not be successful much of the time in telling people what to think, but it is stunningly successful in telling its readers what to think about' (1963: 13). It has been argued that in industrial societies the mass media have come to set the agenda for the bulk of the population, with most people only tending to think about that which the media places on the (social) agenda for discussion. If this position is accepted, it means that only a relatively small group of professional communicators (working within the culture industry) are actively involved in the decision-making processes which ultimately set the communicative agendas for the 'masses'. So industrialized meaning-making seems to imply a 'narrowing' of communicative options.

But the 1990s saw sections of the culture industry begin reorganizing as they adjusted to the possibilities offered by new information technologies – essentially post-Fordist logics have entered the culture industry. An important result has been the proliferation of niche medias. Theoretically this creates the possibility for winding back the 'mass media' because commercialized media no longer have to conform to *mass* production logics in order to be profitable (a development that would no doubt please social critics like the Frankfurt School). However, to date, post-Fordizing the culture industry has not fundamentally challenged the industrial logic underpinning media production, or altered the top-down nature of the communication emerging from this industry. It has simply seen the (single) mass audience fragmented, which means media professionals become specialists in targeting media niches. This actually increases the scope for professional communicators to manipulate audiences more effectively. The new media technologies hold out many possibilities for the growth of truly alternative (dialogical, non 'top-down') communicative forms that could fundamentally challenge the uni-dimensionality of twentieth-century industrialized culture. But to date, this has not occurred, and it is the global media corporations which have most successfully colonized the spaces offered by the new technologies; the resultant 'post-Fordizing' culture industry, far from abandoning the logics of 'industrial culture', is merely modifying, improving and intensifying these logics.

If the Frankfurt School's position is correct, industrialized communication reduces (but does not eliminate) spaces for bottom-up struggle over meaning, while it enhances the possibilities for top-down control. It also suggests that mass media have considerable power to influence opinion. If correct, one would expect to find the emergence of struggles over the control of, and access to, the culture industry, as well as meaning-struggles between those professionals staffing the culture industry.

The struggle over meaning

Meaning(s) emerge out of relationships rooted in a particular place and time. Important dimensions of human relationships are the struggles taking place over power and dominance between competing individuals and groups. These (continually shifting) competitions impact on both the circulation and production of meaning. Ultimately, meaning(s) cannot be understood outside the power relationships and struggles of a specific context. For example, 'affirmative action' means one thing in the USA, where it describes a policy of increasing the representation of disempowered ethnic minorities in certain job categories, and a different thing in South Africa, where it refers to a race re-ranking exercise favouring the ethnic majority in power. Further, embedded within the meanings that are circulating are the legacies of past social interactions/relationships within that context. For example, in some contexts Catholicism is associated with the socio-economic elites and privilege; in other contexts with membership of the working class; in some, with ethnic subservience; in some with pro-communist struggle; and in others with anti-communist struggle.

At heart, all societies have dominant and dominated groups, and dominant groups necessarily prefer to remain dominant. Dominant groups have two mechanisms for creating and retaining dominance: using violence against those challenging their interests, or creating legitimacy for those social arrangements which grant them a dominant position. In general, the more legitimacy dominant groups have, the less violence (or threat of violence) they need to employ. In situations of serious de-legitimation, ruling groups generally use overt military violence against those who will not abide by their rules, for example, Malaysia in the 1960s, Vietnam in the 1950s–70s, South Africa in the 1980s, the Kurdish lands (Turkey) in the 1980s–90s, Ache (Indonesia) and Chechnya (Russia) in the 1990s. In 'normal' situations, ruling groups do not need to deploy much (overt) violence because they succeed in 'criminalizing' those who will not 'play by the rules'. This means getting most people in society to agree that the laws are 'just', so that when the police-courts-prison system is used against 'criminals', the 'violence' of this system is seen by most people as 'legitimate'. Ruling groups generally employ a mix of violence and legitimacy to maintain their dominance, with legitimacy being seen as preferable to violence. For this reason, the processes of meaning-making and meaning-circulation are necessarily important instruments for those wishing to become or remain dominant. As Gramsci (1971) noted, a key element in building or retaining dominance involves the successful manipulation of meaning to gain the consent of the dominated. Dominant groups necessarily engage in the process of building hegemony, and central to this process is the work of intellectuals who consequently become implicated in the resultant struggles over meaning.

For Gramsci, there were two types of intellectual – traditional and organic. Traditional intellectuals are those adopting the 'ivory-tower approach' and holding themselves aloof from contemporary struggles. Organic intellectuals, on the other hand, grow organically from the ranks of the different groups in society. These intellectuals consequently produce ideas enmeshed with the aspirations of the groups to which they belong. (Within Gramsci's cosmology, this did not imply that the consciousness of intellectuals was predetermined. Rather, intellectuals could choose the groups to which they attached themselves.) Importantly, for Gramsci, struggle necessarily occurred because there were always conflicts of interest between dominant groups (the 'ruling classes') and the dominated (the 'subordinate classes'). Inherent in this Gramscian view is the idea that organic intellectuals are necessarily engaged in struggle, with some engaged in assisting the dominant group (or alliance of groups) and some whose meaning-making assists the dominated. By extension, for Gramsci, meanings are fluid because they are the outcome of a constant struggle between different sets of intellectuals. In general, socially-dominant groups are in an advantaged position within this struggle over meaning because they have greater resources to pay for the services of professional intellectuals. In this regard, the election of US presidents and legislators advantaged those with the resources to make large campaign donations (and so buy 'future influence' over the law-making process). Those able to afford the best consultants and communication spin doctors increase their chances of success by increasing the likelihood of placing their ideas on to the social agenda. Similarly, those who can afford the best legal teams are more likely to gain favourable court rulings (which also impacts on legal precedence). The capacity to buy intellectuals does not absolutely predetermine the outcome of meaning-making. At most, it skews meaning-production in favour of those who are socially dominant/powerful at any point in time. But clearly, grappling with the nature and extent of this skewing of intellectual work is important for anyone trying to understand meanings in context.

Gramsci's work on what intellectuals do is a valuable point of departure for any analysis of meaning-production. For Gramsci, intellectuals build hegemony. Hegemony is the creation and maintenance of the consent of dominated groups for their domination. According to Gramsci, this involves intellectuals engaging in three tasks. First, they help to build consent and legitimacy for a society's dominant group(s). In part, this involves organizing support for the interests and goals of the dominant group(s). It also means getting the dominated to accept as 'natural' the leadership and moral codes of the dominant group(s). This legitimacy-making work is at its most obvious in the media and education systems. Secondly, intellectuals help organize alliances and compromises. This work is most visible within parliaments, where bargains are struck between different interests groups, deals are done and compromises are identified. Thirdly, intellectuals help strategically to 'direct' political (coercive) force. For Gramsci, violence underpins all hegemonies. It may not actually be necessary to use violence against most citizens but the threat of violence is necessarily omnipresent. An example is the enforcement of a legal code by the police and judicial system. For most citizens, understanding the consequences of breaking the law is enough to deter them from doing so. Intellectuals organize (and legitimate) these deterrent 'forces'. A fourth intellectual task could be added to Gramsci's list, namely the development of technocratic knowledge; that is intellectuals help to organize the economy as well as legitimate existing relations of production. Habermas (1971) argued that technocratic ideology, which naturalized 'progress' based upon technological development, had become central to the maintenance of Western societies.

There now exists a plethora of intellectuals carrying out the above tasks, with each of the above hegemonic roles having become institutionalized in Western society. The different hegemonic institutions – political, legal and ideological – each specialize in different ideological functions within the overall undertaking of inventing and circulating 'appropriate' meanings. Gramscians argue that intellectuals working for dominant social group(s) are engaged in producing the 'dominant ideology'. By extension, it can be argued that at a particular place and time it is possible to identify a dominant discourse which 'governs' the production and circulation of ideas within that context. This ('governing') dominant discourse serves the interests of the groups dominating that society at that moment in time. Foucault contends that this dominant discourse is institutionally encoded within the key institutions regulating social interactions.

Not everybody accepts the dominant discourse. At any moment there will be individuals and groups who are unconvinced by intellectuals labouring (consciously or unconsciously) on behalf of the socially dominant. Stuart Hall (1980) argues that such ('oppositional') people reject or re-negotiate the meanings generated by intellectuals when decoding these meanings. Further, there will be intellectuals working in opposition to the needs of the socially dominant. Examples of this have been anti-communist intellectuals in the Soviet Union, anti-apartheid intellectuals in South Africa and contemporary green intellectuals opposing globalization economics, genetic engineering and greenhouse emissions. Some oppositional organic intellectuals engage in deliberately and consciously working to develop and circulate ideas that are designed to undermine existing hegemonic discourses and/or are designed to promote the interests of oppositional groups (and those aspiring to overthrow existing dominant groups). Such intellectuals are engaged in counter-hegemonic work. — more to say about this?

Ultimately, the pool of meanings within any context is the outcome of both hegemonic and counter-hegemonic work and of the engagement/struggle between these competing sets of meanings. Our cultures are built from such struggles (Tomaselli, 1986) – from the processes of hegemonic and counter-hegemonic codings, from the decodings and re-codings (of intellectuals and non-intellectuals alike), and from the hybridizations and syntheses that take place along the way. To complicate matters further, spillages will occur from other cultures because cultural sign-systems (the pattern of codes and signs employed by a particular culture) cannot be isolated from one another. Sometimes such spillages are deliberately engineered by intellectuals as a part of their hegemonic battles, but many spillages are merely the result of the ease with which information and ideas can flow globally. Hence, struggles in one context can produce meaning shifts that inadvertently spill over into other contexts. For example, the discourse of multiculturalism was originally developed to deal with a set of North American social problems but spread through intellectual copy-cattism to contexts without such problems, such as Australia.

Importantly, the struggle over meaning need not be seen as a purely subjective phenomenon because meaning-shifts have material consequences and visa versa. Valentin Volosinov (1973) pioneered the notion of a semiotic struggle which was simultaneously grounded in both a struggle over meaning and a struggle over material resources so that by changing the nature of meaning one could also change human interactions, social organization and the distribution of resources. Feminist successes in placing gender issues on the social agenda have, for example, altered human interactions, work practices and resource distribution in advanced Western societies. The converse is equally true from a Volosinovian perspective: changing material relationships shifts interactions, which then shifts signification. For example, the significant transfer of wealth into black hands in post-apartheid South Africa rapidly transformed many former pro-socialist 'comrades' into pro-'free enterprise' businesspeople. This interactivity between social/economic structures and consciousness/signification also interested Jürgen Habermas. For Habermas, the complex interpenetration of material and subjective actions and consciousness constitutes our 'lifeworld'. But Volosinov's view of this complexity included a concern with what might be termed 'linguistic struggle' – the struggle to construct and reconstruct societies, cultures and economic systems, in part, involves battles to attach, detach and re-attach meanings down to the smallest level of signification, namely, signs. But the resultant semiotic shifts change more than languages and worldviews (how we 'see' and 'talk' about the world): they can change the way we live. Our lifeworld is altered. This, in turn impacts on power relationships, which then influences the next round of hegemonic struggle and meaning-making.

Hegemonic work is consequently complex – there are constant shifts between competing interests and hence a constant mutability of human interactions. People are always being positioned and repositioned within these shifting relationships, which produce an infinite number of mutable decoding positions. So no possibility exists of ever producing a permanently stable set of dominant meanings. Instead, hegemonic work involves the never-ending task of dealing with challenges, 'aberrant' decodings, slippages, power shifts and ever-changing patterns of alliances between players. Meanings are thus only hegemonic in a temporal sense because, from the moment of their conception, they are under challenge. Despite this, there will always be some intellectuals trying to control (and stabilize) meaning. At issue here then becomes the question to what extent can meaning be controlled?

The control of meaning

There are broadly two perspectives on the control of meaning. One contends that the meanings we consume can be successfully controlled (and manipulated). Among the 'control school' would be those subscribing to the 'bullet theory' of propaganda, orthodox Marxists believing in class-determined ideology, and structuralists who believe we inhabit a 'prison-house of language'. On the other hand, there are those who argue that meaning is not controllable because recipients actively 'read, interpret and decode meanings for themselves. The latter set of approaches stresses active human creativity within the communication process and so inherently challenges the notion of gullible, passive recipients who are open to manipulation by professional communicators. The latter group – who will be looked at in more detail in Chapter 10 – includes David Morley (1992), John Fiske (1987) and the reception theorists (Holub, 1984). The two sets of perspectives are not necessarily mutually exclusive. It is possible to conceive of individuals and groups attempting to control meaning-production and meaning-distribution and being successful in certain contexts, but unsuccessful in others. It is equally possible to conceive of varying degrees of active readership/decoding within different contexts which would challenge manipulative communication. Ultimately, for most people, there will probably be a continually shifting dialectic between being susceptible to manipulation/control and engagement in active decoding. This shifting dialectic is tied to contextually-based relational variables, changing group memberships and individual differences all of which determine a person's propensity to be an active reader.

What seems clear is that there will always be some individuals or groups trying to control meaning. Underpinning this is a competition over resources (material, cultural and status). Our life-chances are set by the social parameters facilitating or hindering our access to such resources. Contexts differ with regard to how limited resources are, but in no context are there enough resources to satisfy all, and as long as there are insufficient resources to satisfy all, struggles will occur between groups and individuals. Central to the nature (and outcomes) of such struggles are the rules of governance in any context. From Gramscian and Foucaultian perspectives, a battle over meaning is centrally implicated in this, because the rules of engagement are set within meaning-structures. It would be strange not to find attempts to control the sites and processes of meaning-making and circulation – after all, any player managing control (or even temporary influence) of such sites/processes gains an advantage over the other players. The belief that some have managed to gain 'control' over meaning has generated concerns about 'distorted' communication and a 'restricted' communicative process.

The notion of 'distorted communication' necessarily assumes that non-distorted communication can exist, because the concept implies some corruption (of an 'ideal' form of communication) has occurred. It also implies some human agency must be to blame for corrupting the ideal, which raises the question: what drives such agents to distort communication-flow? Explorations of this theme have ranged from sophisticated theorizing – much of it associated with Marxist work on the (mutating) concept of 'ideology' – through to simplistic conspiracy theories of media control and ownership.

Another approach to the control of meaning explores the way communication processes are *restricted* in some way. There are two broad visions of such restriction: the 'human condition' and 'human action' views. The first involves believing that the restriction of communication processes is a 'natural' human condition. This includes the French structuralist school, initiated by Saussure, who believes that humans are born into existing linguistic structures which then govern ('restrict') our experiences and behaviour. For this category of thinkers, no 'non-restricted' communication exists because we necessarily inhabit a pre-ordained 'prison-house of language' from which there is no escape. This linguistic 'prison' is not willfully or consciously constructed by anybody and so cannot be challenged or altered. A modified version of the 'prison-house of language' model was developed by Volosinov, who accepted that linguistic structuring/restriction occurred naturally, but did not believe that such structures were permanently fixed into place. Rather, he saw human action as interfacing with natural linguistic structures so that such structures could be shifted (and evolve).

The second view regards communicative restriction not as 'natural' but rather as produced by human agency. Such restriction is deliberate when professional communicators consciously decide to manipulate or censor communication-flows. However, restrictions need not be deliberate. Instead, they may occur due to, for example, communication professionals (unconsciously) conforming to media practices which have the effect of skewing or narrowing the flow of information. But in both cases, the restricted communication can be challenged and altered because humans can choose, or be taught, to behave differently. This has the effect of undoing the restrictive practices. But as soon as one talks of 'teaching' people to behave differently, power relationships come into play – those wishing to 're-educate' people need first to acquire enough power to be able to have such an impact. This can occur by forming pressure groups and alliances of such groups, which then work to 'pressurize' discursive agencies (e.g. the media and educational institutions) to shift their discourses. This approach has been seen in North America and Australia where feminists, gays, greens and ethnic minorities mobilized enough power through the 'rainbow coalitions' of the 1980s to challenge and change dominant discourses. Alternatively, discourses can be changed by taking control of the state and using this control to change the dominant discourses in circulation. This approach has been seen in South Africa in the 1990s, where black nationalism replaced Afrikaner nationalism as the dominant discourse and where the new ruling elite is trying to 'teach' people to 'see' and behave differently.

A large body of work exists on distorted and restricted communication, albeit that some of this work – such as that associated with the concept of 'ideology' – is currently fashionable. However, even if unfashionable, it remains an intellectual resource worth exploring when considering 'control' over meaning-production. Neither 'ideology' nor 'discourse' are concepts to be sidestepped when exploring the issue of the control and manipulation of meaning.

'Ideology' is a multi-layered concept that has evolved and grown over the past two centuries. An especially useful exposition of the epistemology of this term has been provided by Jorge Larrain (1979). But if we are to find a broad 'core' meaning for 'ideology', it means sidestepping the richness that Larrain discussed. At its most simplistic, the Marxist and neo-marxist understanding of 'ideology' is concerned with the way in which some negative state of being and/or set of social contradictions are hidden from view. For Marxists, this negative state is 'class exploitation' which generates a set of social contradictions. Managing these contradictions (to prevent social turmoil) requires, in part, that the exploiters find ways to ensure that the exploited do not become aware of the extent or nature of their exploitation. 'Ideology' is thus a state of 'unknowing', in which some 'truth' is disguised/hidden by one or other distorted communicative process. This is based upon the Marxist (possibly unjustified) belief that they can identify an 'ideal' non-contradictory state of being or 'truthful' reality, where there is consequently no need to disguise contradictions. However, in Marx's model, merely understanding the contradictions ('reality') will not overcome 'ideology' because there can be no communicative solution to social problems. 'Ideology' is not merely a set of (linguistic) 'untruths'; rather, it is a set of untruths necessitated by real social contradictions/problems. Within this model, 'ideology' ('distorted communication') cannot disappear until actual contradictions disappear – that is social 'reality' (and skewed power relationships) must be changed (not understood) to 'overcome' the reasons for ideological distortion. From this basic model has arisen a large body of work examining the nature, extent and mechanics of 'ideological distortion'. A key issue arising from this model is whether a 'non-ideological' state is ever possible. For Marxists (at least up until Althusser), a Marxist re-ordering of society (and re-ordering of power relationships) would produce a 'classless' state in which 'ideology' would no longer be needed. So it became possible to conceive the 'end of ideology'. It is possible to use much Marxist work on 'ideology' without necessarily assuming that the latter 'ideal' should, or can, be brought into being. Gramsci's work, for example, makes it possible to conceptualize a perpetually-shifting struggle (over resources) leading to the ongoing need for (mutating) ideologies as ever-new sets of contradictions emerge. Marx's 'solution' can be put aside without having to also abandon his basic conceptualization (of contextually-based social contradictions, derived from competition over resources, giving rise to a need to hide these contradictions through ideology). The Frankfurt School took this one stage further and saw ideology not just as the control of meaning, but as a mechanism for actually 'taming' or blocking social contradictions.

A key feature of the Marxist concept of 'ideology' – at least up until Althusser's reformulation (1979) – was the notion that communicative distortion was not natural. Rather, distortion was regarded as the outcome of a need to disguise the negative social consequences (for some people) of human decision-making. In this regard, an important sub-concept within the Marxist conceptual repertoire was that of 'fetish', fetishness being seen to exist when social decisions (which produced a skewing in power relationships and wealth distribution) were made to appear 'natural' (i.e. 'just the way things are' rather than 'human-made', and hence changeable). For example, human relationships based on class differentials have been fetishized in Britain, and Americans have fetishized a particular form of democracy.

However, Althusser effectively redefined 'ideology' by recasting it within a semiological structural framework. This made ideology a 'natural' linguistic prison (from which there was no escape) instead of being seen as the outcome of a process for disguising contradictory social structures. In the process Althusser (inadvertently) opened the door to a host of post-structural challenges to structural thinking, including

Marxism and, by extension, to some core features of its notion of ideology. As 'ideology' went into decline as a fashionable concept (in the post-Althusserian world), so an alternative concept grew into prominence. This emergent concept – 'discourse' – offered a powerful tool for conceptualizing the process of 'restricting' communication.

Michel Foucault's (1972) notion of a 'discursive formation' came at an opportune moment – just as deploying the concept 'ideology' became unfashionable because it was unencumbered by the Marxist baggage of needing an 'ideal' utopia against which to measure 'distortion'. For those still interested in exploring how meaning-production might be 'distorted' or 'restricted', Foucault's notion of 'discursive formation' offered an alternative to 'ideology'. Foucault explores meaning-production through a concern with how authors make meaning. (In this regard, there are some interesting parallels with Gramsci's work on intellectuals.) Foucault sees the author as an historical construction. Authors are constructed by their context – an author is someone occupying a 'position' within a meaning-making machinery and so is learning to behave and work in certain ways.

According to Foucault, societies create institutions (he looked at prisons, clinics and asylums). Each institution develops its own set of practices and discourses. Those working within such institutions have to learn the (interconnected) practices and discourses appropriate to that institutional site, with practices being the acceptable way of doing things and discourses constituting acceptable 'language' within that site. So a person is unlikely to be recruited into an institutional site unless s/he is able to demonstrate a 'compatibility' with the practices/discourses already operative therein and is unlikely to remain employed unless s/he conforms to the institutionally-embedded practices/discourses.

Hence, within Foucaultian cosmology, conformity is a key governing mechanism. This implies recognizing negative consequence(s) for failing to conform – presumably based upon some underlying power relationship(s). Importantly, Foucault's cosmology does not necessitate seeing us as prisoners of 'natural' language structures. Rather, it allows space for 'active' human choice regarding conformity (or otherwise) to existing practices and discourses. But whether by choice or not, adherence to a discourse limits what one is able to say (and think?). According to Foucault, a discourse governs the knowledge and/or ideas that can appear. This is an idea not far removed from Saphir–Whorf's hypothesis that a culture's language shapes what people think and do (Kay & Kempton, 1984). Foucault explored the way in which discourses 'constrained' the emergence of knowledge and concluded that there were three ways in which parameters were set: namely, discourses only allowed for certain 'surfaces of emergence', 'authorities of delimitation' and 'grids of specification'. These set the 'linguistic' boundaries (or 'organizing fields') of what is acceptable. These organizing fields not only make certain ideas impossible and others possible, they actually make certain ideas inevitable. This Foucaultian idea overlaps with Thomas Kuhn's (1974) views on how knowledge grows (within 'normal' science) precisely because certain questions necessarily suggest themselves to intellectuals working within a given paradigm. These questions are governed by the prevailing scientific discourse (paradigm) and the context within which intellectuals work. So, implicitly, the struggle to make new meaning is enmeshed within, and is constrained by, sets of power relationships within the 'spaces' where intellectuals work.

Foucault's work on knowledge, prisons, clinics and asylums led to a conception of restricted communication based on the idea that discourses are made by authors occupying certain sites (within institutional arrangements). When looking at Western civilization, Foucault found authorship to be institutionalized. Institutions, in turn, imply codified practices; and practices govern the way authors can both 'see' and communicate about the world. The resultant discursive formations necessarily imply a curtailment of what humans can communicate about. This is consistent with the notion of knowledge being contextually-based, and hence residing within institutions that arise, grow and die in association with particular social needs. And these 'needs' are tied to power relationships that operate in a given context. So discourse – as a restrictive set of practices and meanings – becomes another way of conceptualizing the struggle either to manage or to overcome contextually-based social contradictions. There are some interesting overlaps between Foucault's work on authorship and Gramsci's work on intellectuals, with both recognizing the power implicit in the control of meaning-making.

Further, both Gramsci and Foucault recognize the contradictory nature of human existence, in which, although humans are free to act, it is a constrained freedom. Ultimately, then, Gramsci's notion of 'ideology' and Foucault's of 'discourse' conceptually overlap. Both recognize structural impediments to meaning-making. But within Foucault's cosmology humans are not imprisoned within immutable (linguistic) structures. Rather, they make (and re-make) these structures. Similarly, within Gramsci's cosmology intellectuals are not imprisoned within class structures. In both cosmologies it is possible to conceive of intellectuals as having a choice to act either as change-agents or as conservatives because, up to a point, intellectuals can chose between the institutional and discursive arrangements available within their context. Hence, fluidity and struggle are central to both the Gramscian and Foucaultian worldviews, given that intellectuals can chose how they relate to existing power relationships and that power relationships are themselves not fixed but mutate as struggles are won or lost.

Within these struggles, if intellectuals choose an uncritical acceptance of, and adherence to, existing dominant discursive practices, they function as conservatives. But Foucault's notion of 'discourse' does not propose conservative intellectual 'imprisonment' as in the prison-house of language model. It is possible to read Foucault and Volosinov in tandem so as to conceptualize intellectuals not only engaged in the conservative practice(s) of discursive reproduction, but also possibly engaged in discursive struggle and reformulation.

What Foucault offers is a means for conceptualizing how discourse is a potentially powerful hegemonic tool for social control, because discursive formations have the power to exclude from discussion certain questions or issues. This forecloses 'debate' and so predetermines what conclusions may be reached. There are many instances of discourses automatically excluding alternative perspectives. For example, the 'free enterprise' discourse can block its adherents from grappling with the notion that capitalism may disadvantage some people with merit and undermine their capacity for achievement. Similarly, socialist discourses can block adherents from confronting the view that competition may generate achievement and wealth-generation, while state interventionism may promote dependence and undermine wealth-making. Nineteenth-century imperial discourse precluded its adherents from questioning the rectitude of colonialism and the violent subjugation of natives, just as the contemporary American discourse of 'human rights' precludes a serious examination of 'other' (non-Anglo-America) value systems and excludes debate on the deployment of US military violence against foreigners. Similarly, contemporary Western 'political correctnesses' prevents open examination and debate of a range of discursive closures concerning, for example, race, gender, ethnicity, sexuality and post-coloniality.

Discursive closure is at its most effective when intellectuals find ways to naturalize and stabilize the boundaries of the discourse. Stabilization is most effective when a system of discursive self-policing, which guards the discourse's boundaries by creating mechanisms for excluding taboo terminology, is achieved. As groups (and/or individuals) vie for resources (material, cultural and status) they will try to naturalize and stabilize those relationships that benefit them – that is those relationships that grant them maximum access to scarce resources. Within both a Gramscian and Foucaultian framework intellectuals become important allies (or employees) for any group or individual trying to achieve discursive closure on its own terms (i.e. excluding points of view that upset or challenge closure).

One advantage of Foucault's perspective over Gramsci's is that Foucault's approach is able to conceptualize a variety of groups vying for closure, for example, groups based on class, race, ethnicity, gender, hereditary status or religious belief, whereas Gramsci was only concerned with class struggles. Within a Foucaultian framework, different interest groups can potentially all be simultaneously engaging in such discursive battles (for closure) within the same context. So discursive struggle is a necessarily messy and complex affair.

From a Foucaultian perspective it is also possible to view attempts at left-wing discursive closure, currently referred to as 'political correctness', as equally restrictive as those of the right (Manne, 1993). It also raises the possibility that in one context a discourse may be 'progressive' while in another the same discourse may be 'restrictive' and/or be a mechanism for discursive control (i.e. a mechanism to limit what may be discussed). For example, socialist discourse has been used to challenge exploitative social relations but has also been mobilized as a mechanism for discursive closure and repression (Bahro, 1981). Similarly, feminist discourse can be used both to challenge restrictive (patriarchal) social relationships or to close debate concerning power relationships that disadvantage some females relative to others. The discourse of multiculturalism can, in one context, empower minority groups but, in another context, serve the interests of the majority as a mechanism for co-opting and 'pacifying' the leaders of minority groups.

From a hegemonic point of view, discourses can serve two interrelated purposes: they can disguise social contradictions and/or promote the interests of one or other social group (or individual). Both purposes are enmeshed with power relationships; they either challenge existing power relationships or promote new relationships. Discourses will usually also hide their own complicity in furthering a particular set of social relationships, and hide the fact that they are themselves mutable constructs. A discourse will be at its most closed when it is so opaque that even its own intellectual practitioners accept its 'naturalness'. It then becomes a 'truthfulness' not open to scrutiny.

The work of Frankfurt School members, like Adorno and Marcuse, is especially interesting when considering the possible social consequences of such discourse closures. The Frankfurt School became concerned that the mass media that proliferated during the first half of the twentieth century was encouraging a certain type of discursive closure which they regarded as socially dangerous. Members of the Frankfurt School believed that society was at its most healthy when active social dialogue existed. This required a working dialectic in which no perspective (thesis) would be allowed to go unchallenged. The Frankfurt School (dialectical) model was based upon the view that for every thesis there always existed an antithesis (a counter argument or position), and in a 'healthy' society, the airing of antithetical positions would be encouraged (see Jay, 1973). This involved not only accepting the inevitability of conflict (because of thesis–antithesis clashes), but also seeing such conflict as a social good – because from such conflicts new syntheses would emerge. For the Frankfurt School, as dialecticians, any synthesis (new idea) was necessarily superior to either the thesis and/or antithesis from which that synthesis had emerged. This is based upon a teleological worldview in which 'rational' progress is (unjustifiably) assumed to be the natural outcome of change. This worldview led Habermas to propose an ideal society based upon dialogical communication (to which all had equal access) – that is Habermas's vision of democracy was built upon his ideal of wishing to facilitate ongoing dialectically-driven learning/change (Habermas, 1979: 186).

However, the Frankfurt School became concerned that twentieth-century industrialization of cultural production was inherently undialectical. The Frankfurt School argued that when intellectuals were industrialized they were locked into institutional arrangements and power relationships which had the effect of disallowing the airing of antithetical views. Views confirming the interests of those with power to control the media were widely circulated by these culture industries, while views that were fundamentally contradictory (antitheses) were curtailed. The result was that the social dialectic was stilled and replaced by what Marcuse (1964b) called a 'one-dimensionality' where conventionally dominant 'theses' went unchallenged. Foucault's notion that discourses (as 'organizing fields') only allow for certain 'surfaces of emergence', 'authorities of delimitation' and 'grids of specification' thus has an interesting complementarity to the Frankfurt School's view of the culture industry as a site for twentieth-century discursive closure.

Many members of the Frankfurt School – especially Adorno –

became intensely pessimistic because they came to believe that culture industry discursive closure was so complete that dialectical conflict was no longer possibile. Their extreme pessimism was no doubt overstated. However, the Frankfurt School's concerns cannot be entirely dismissed and decades after it produced its critique of the culture industry, many of the restrictive practices it attacked remain in evidence in the contemporary media. Of particular concern to Adorno and Horkheimer was the practice of creating 'pseudo choice', that is phenomena which were really quite similar (e.g. ten brands of soap powder or three political parties) were presented as being different. This generated the appearance of alternatives when no substantive choice was really available. So instead of the media facilitating consideration of (and conflict over) substantive alternatives (as in the dialectical model), they narrowed the options, presenting only a limited range of the full number of opinions/issues potentially available. The Frankfurt School saw patronage as responsible for this narrowing – it saw creative people/intellectuals as needing to work for one or other branch of the culture industry. This industry effectively acted as a form of patron. The resultant patronage relationships generated by the culture industry dramatically narrowed the discourses and practices available to intellectuals.

Noelle-Neumann (1973) developed an interpretation of the 'narrowing process' that complements the Frankfurt School's vision, but she goes further. Noelle-Neumann's idea of the narrowing process goes beyond the discursive pressures and patronage of the culture industry. She also looks at the wider pressures of social conformity. According to Noelle-Neumann, there is a tendency towards an ever-narrowing range of opinions due to the interaction of cultural industry practices and 'public opinion'. She argues that when an issue first arises there will be many opinions about the topic. However, over time media practices produce a narrowing of opinions that are heard. This happens because media workers choose to advantage some opinions over others, in accordance with their own preferred discourses, patronage-pressures and other power relationships into which they are embedded. Pressures towards social conformity mean that members of the public who disagree with the dominant (media) interpretation progressively fall silent. As a result, counter-opinions (antitheses) are increasingly not heard. This, in turn, leads media workers to conclude that there are no opposition views to report. A 'spiral of silence' results, in which fewer and fewer of the full range of opinions are heard. If Noelle-Neumann is correct, the culture industry is centrally implicated in the process of discursive closure. This raises two (interrelated) themes: (1) can one identify those exercising power within and over the culture industry so as to close social discourse?; (2) how do discourses themselves acquire the power structurally to lock alternative views out of the culture industry?

In addition to their work on undialectical communication as discursive closure, the members of the Frankfurt School were also concerned that the culture industry focused on trivia rather than substance. Presenting trivia makes it possible to avoid issues that might lead to real debate and conflict. Late twentieth-century examples of this trivialization-cum-distraction phenomenon were the (near-global) media frenzies surrounding the coverage of the death of Diana, Princess of Wales, and the Monica Lewinski affair. During the same era, the (global) Anglo culture industry displayed an extraordinary propensity to be content to mobilize uncritically the same narrowed range of discourses about conflicts in Iraq, Bosnia, Kosovo or Timor. This had the effect of foreclosing debate on these complex issues. The way in which the bulk of Anglo intellectuals globally fell into line and simply recycled these late twentieth-century dominant discourses lends some credence to a continued basis for Adorno-type pessimism. And as the twenty-first century opens, any closure in discourses circulating among Anglo intellectuals is of global significance because of the way in which the post-Cold War New World Order is dominated by the USA and its Anglo allies. The emergent global media is effectively an Anglo-dominated system. This consequently gives Anglo intellectuals a disproportionate influence on the meanings circulating in all corners of the globe. For this reason, this book will overwhelmingly focus on Anglo meaning-making in both the core and peripheries of the emergent (Anglo) global system, starting with the machineries of this meaning-making process – the culture industry.

CHAPTER 2

Sites for Making Meaning I: The Culture Industry

The culture industry grew into an important feature of twentieth-century Western society as growing proportions of the making (and circulation) of meaning were housed within institutional frameworks. Professionalized intellectuals worked within these institutions, deploying work practices that were strongly influenced by the logic of industrial production. This logic came to inform a wide range of meaning-organizations, including media corporations, schools, universities and even charismatic churches.

Although the large-scale industrialization of cultural production really took hold in the twentieth century, this communicative phenomenon had its roots in nineteenth-century newspaper production. The penny press developed rudimentary large-scale organizational forms that became the foundation of practice within the culture industry – organizational hierarchies were based on specialist division of labour, producing 'packaged meaning' aimed at mass middle-class audiences, which avoided partisan stances in order to appeal to as broad an audience as possible, and where industrial means of production set the pace (Demers, 1996: 36–41). The penny press of the 1830s was the first mass medium to be conceptualized as a means of delivering consumers to producers. This form of communication was only fully developed in the twentieth century as newspaper ownership was concentrated in fewer and fewer corporate hands and mass circulation increased (Demers, 1996: 3–4). This corporatized and industrialized mode of meaning-making was also adopted as the basis of the embryonic film industry between 1910 and 1914 when the Hollywood Film Studio system was established. It later plugged into an international movie distribution system. In the 1920s, radio was institutionalized as another form of mass media, although radio's industrial potential was not fully realized until it was enmeshed with an industrialized (and corporatized) music recording industry after the Second World War. Commercial radio, which has characterized US broadcasting, has also become industrialized, using networks for cost-cutting, and has been built around a number of standardized listening formats. Within the British Empire, public radio was developed as an alternative to the commercial model, but it was still a corporatized and industrialized production of communication. When television emerged as a mass media form in the 1950s it hybridized elements of the institutional arrangements and practices of the newspaper, radio and film industries. Early television was particularly influenced by radio production practices, so much so that early television assumed the form of 'radio-with-pictures'. Eventually it was television that developed to new heights the corporatized, industrialized mode of communication in both the USA's commercialized TV networks model and the British public service broadcasting model (PSB) (the BBC). Cable television used an alternative mode of delivery but otherwise deployed the same corporate industrial practices. The twentieth century became an era when intellectualism and meaning-making were institutionalized so that all the major communication forms – from newspapers to television – were organized in accordance with corporate industrial logic.

During the twentieth century systems of communication emerged that were to be truly 'mass' in their scope. The reach of institutional communication became ubiquitous within Western societies, so much so that it was the 'big five' mass media (television, radio, newspapers, magazines and film) that set the agenda for what people discussed. Increasingly, stepping beyond the reach of these mass media was equivalent to stepping 'outside' (Western) society. In this way 'mass publics' were created which increasingly 'lived' second-hand realities, that is these publics experienced the world in a second-hand way via the various mass media. For much of the twentieth century the boundaries of these second-hand media worlds neatly coincided with national administrative spaces. For the Frankfurt School, these second-hand (media-made) worlds generated a passivity and conformity that 'cretinized' media audiences. Some of the Frankfurt School's members, like Adorno, became deeply pessimistic because they believed conformity and 'discourse closure' had become unchallengeable and a permanent feature of media-centric Western societies. Critics of the Frankfurt School believe that this pessimism is misplaced and derives from underestimating the human capacity for creativity, resistance and active decoding. Certainly, the Frankfurt School paid scant attention to this 'active agency' dimension of communication which led to its view that 'discourse closure' was a necessary and permanent phenomenon. The Frankfurt School did not foresee the rise of the Internet with its potential for de-industrializing and de-institutionalizing communication flows. But even if total and permanent closure is seen as an exaggerated position, this is no reason to discount completely the capacity industrialized mass media systems still have for producing significant discourse closures. And there is also no reason to believe industrialized and institutionalized communication, and therefore second-hand communicative experiences, will be entirely displaced by new communication technologies. A more likely scenario is that the Internet will itself become another site for institutionalized communication.

Ultimately, Frankfurt School pessimism was derivative of agenda-setting logic; if institutionalized media curtailed the range of opinions/information available to audiences, a 'distortion' was the result. Its argument was that industrializing communication resulted in work practices which necessarily narrowed the range of voices/opinions that were heard. (Presumably, this 'narrowing process' even impacts, to some extent, upon active, creative and oppositional decoders.) The roots of this narrowing process can be traced back to the organizational power-relationships and work practices implanted into the British press by Lord Northcliffe's 'mass journalism', and into the USA by Pulitzer's 'popular journalism' (Smith, 1979: 154–160). The Northcliffe/Pulitzer revolution of media practices ultimately influenced more than newspaper journalism – it impacted on how meaning-making and consumption were conceptualized and practised within the Anglo world (and later the rest of the world).

For those (like the Frankfurt School) who believe institutionalized meaning-making (e.g. the media) is a powerful and 'corrupting' force in society, the next questions must be: who is in control of these institutions? And what is the relationship (if any) between such control, the work practices within these organizations and the meanings produced?

Types of ownership and control of the media

A twentieth-century trend was that ever-growing percentages of social meaning originated within institutionalized machinery. Broadly, such institutionalized communication meant that someone (or some group of persons) acquired a measure of control because institutionalization brought with it a hierarchy within which crucial decision-making was located at an organizational apex. Policy set at this apex impacted upon all functionaries within the organization. Not surprisingly, as mass media (especially, newspapers, radio and television) grew into social phenomena, touching virtually all lives, questions were raised about the control of this media. Studies of media ownership and media moguls (e.g. Bagdikian, 1997; Tunstall & Palmer, 1991) proliferated in the 1980s. However, once 'active audience' research became academically trendy, researching media control and ownership and those occupying the organizational apexes of media production became unfashionable.

During the nineteenth and twentieth centuries, there were two main contenders for controlling media organization apexes – capitalists and the state. Two main varieties emerged, namely private business and the public sector ownership. However, as media organizations grew larger and more complex, both the capitalist and state-owned varieties adopted similar organizational frameworks and practices. In both forms professional managers were in control. Burnham (1962) suggested that managerialism effectively removed control away from capitalist owners. However, even if managers did acquire considerable power, and (some) even succeeded in joining the power elite, the power and influence of owners (whether capitalists or the state) cannot be discounted. Ultimately, managerialist influence is a derivative power; it is derived from managers developing successful symbiotic relationships with 'owners', whether these are individual capitalist owners, key shareholders or alliances of shareholders, parliamentarians or political party leaders.

In the third quarter of the twentieth century, a new kind of media 'ownership' emerged as various actors within civil society attempted to set up media. For example, community media 'ownership' emerged as an alternative to both state and business ownership. However, this new form has not yet become a significant feature of media organization.

In all, there have been five forms of public sector influence over the media. Of these, two involved direct government control and three involved indirect forms of government influence.

Communist media

The most extensive and sophisticated system of direct government-controlled media to emerge was that created by twentieth-century communist states. This media system was built upon Lenin's (1929) interpretation of Marxism. In Lenin's model, the Communist Party represented workers who constituted a majority of the population. The Party needed to capture the state in order to advance the interest of workers in the face of (minority) capitalist exploitation and the repression of workers. According to communists, a media system owned by capitalists would necessarily portray a (minority) capitalist wordview. So Leninists argued that the state (after being captured by communists) should establish state-run media systems. In terms of this logic, (communist) government-run media would be more democratic than a capitalist-operated media system because communists controlled the state and represented the exploited majority. So the communist system produced a government that explicitly intervened in the meaning-making process. This ultimately led to the creation of enormous state-run media systems in the Soviet Union, Eastern Europe and China. But as Bahro (1981) argued, instead of representing a majority of workers, this system came to represent only the minority, *apparatchik* ruling class of the communist states who used repression and ideology to remain in power.

Theoretically, communists occupied the apex of state-run communist media systems. In reality, many in control of this system were cynical careerists who simply joined the Communist Party to further their job prospects. Ultimately, the media industries controlled by these 'nominally communist' ('nomenclature') careerists produced hyper-closed (propagandistic) discourses which served their conservative managerial *apparatchik* interests (see Bahro, 1981: Chapter 9). The *apparatchik* managers built media machines premised upon the same managerialist corporatist-industrial model of top-down, uni-directional communication that also characterized the culture industry then being constructed by their capitalist opponents. But communists constructed communication systems *explicitly* to control, manipulate and 'educate' populations. This was justified by a teleological model that argued that a 'utopian' future would emerge from the manipulative actions of an enlightened communist 'vanguard'. For the Frankfurt School, both communist-run and capitalist-run media were problematic because both were run according to the same managerialist and 'instrumentalist' logics, and both excluded oppositional ideas (antitheses). However, Marcuse (1964a) argued that he 'preferred' the communist system because it was more *obviously* repressive. For Marcuse, both the communist and capitalist, liberal varieties of Western technocratic society were 'one-dimensional' because they both excluded truly oppositional ideas. He predicted that the communist system would collapse sooner because it was more obviously repressive and so would necessarily produce (dialectical) opposition sooner.

Development elites and the media

A second form of government-controlled media arose in parts of Africa, Asia and the Middle East in the second half of the twentieth century in the wake of the decolonization process. As the colonial powers Britain, France, Portugal, Holland and Belgium withdrew, many new countries were created and power was handed over to 'Westernized', managerialist elites in these new states. These elites faced enormous problems: their countries were 'artificial' creations of the colonial powers; the elites were visibly privileged minorities within their countries; their states were economically underdeveloped and often riven with ethnic, racial and religious differences; and there was usually a deficit of skilled and experienced people to run these countries after European colonials departed. They were states with a high potential for social conflict. Consequently, a high proportion of the 'Westernized' Afro-Asian ruling elites resorted to authoritarian measures to maintain control, 'develop' their states and create 'national unity'. In many respects, they were simply a new, minority 'tribe' within a complex patchwork of 'tribalisms' in each of the new states.

Power was handed over to the 'Western tribe' because they were, after all, clones of their colonial masters. As dark-skinned Anglophiles or Francophiles, the Western powers necessarily felt more comfortable doing business with this new Western 'tribe' rather than one of the non-Western tribes. Also, the Westernized elites generally lived in the cities created by colonialism and so were close to the managerialist levers of power. As the colonial powers withdrew, it was 'natural' to hand power to these European-made elites in Africa and Asia. As Fanon (1968) noted, African and Asian bourgeoisie were only too happy to step into the shoes of their departing masters and continue managing the new states in ways that reproduced the (now de-racialized) colonial model. But the Western elites continually encountered challenges to their hegemony from non-Western tribes, and maintaining the integrity of the boundaries of their states was a constant struggle. However, the position of the Western tribe was different from the other (non-Western) tribes – their very survival as a Westernized group depended upon the survival of the (Western) state and economy that they managed. Many elites soon found that only authoritarian methods could hold their 'tentative' states together – hence the drift towards one-party or military rule.

Government control of the media also became a feature of much of Afro-Asia, with the ruling elites either 'nationalizing' the settler/colonial media or buying out the settler-owned media. These media were staffed by members of the new Western elite and were expected to apply 'self-censorship' to 'assist' the ruling elite in creating 'national unity' and to help 'develop' these states. This led to the formulation of the New World Information Order (NWIO) which justified 'development journalism' as necessary in the 'developing world' (Masmoudi, 1979). The NWIO doctrine was formulated by African, Asian and Latin American intellectuals. But whereas the Afro-Asian intellectuals were part of the ruling managerialist elites in their societies, the Latin Americans tended to be oppositional intellectuals. Within the NWIO formulation it was justified for the media to be used by the state to control, manipulate, 'educate', manage and develop their populations. Both the communists and third world managerialist elites built their culture industries using the same hierarchical, bureaucratic organizational forms, and using the practices of industrial production. There was some overlap between the communist and NWIO understandings of the culture industry – both saw the media as tools that could be used in a top-down way to bring about the hegemonic ends deemed desirable by the state. Both the communist and third world developing states placed a great deal of emphasis on building state-run education systems (as part of a wider pattern of deliberately manipulating their cultural industries) to re-mould the discourses and practices of their populations. In Afro-Asia, 'education' and 'development' were managerialist tools by which ruling elites (forcibly?) Westernized their populations, thereby increasing the numbers of their own Western tribe. But by the end of the twentieth century a number of 'developing' countries, especially those in Africa, had become 'failed states'. Manipulation and control of their culture industries had not helped them to maintain their hegemonies or develop their countries.

State-licensed media

Some forms of public sector involvement in the culture industry have not entailed direct ownership or control of the media. The oldest of these are the state-licensing of newspapers, stamp duties and governmental censorship. State-licensing and censorship were the forms of governmental interference that Milton's *Areopagitica* complained about. Licensing/censorship involves governments trying to curtail and channel the communication flowing from non-government-run media. This form of control was widely used by European governments until well into the nineteenth century (Smith, 1979). This media control regime was also exported to European colonies in the Americas, Australia and Southern Africa. The licensing/censorship model was born of the rise of a European middle class. Initially this new social group of 'free citizens' was a minority, confined to the emergent urban areas of Western Europe. As their numbers grew and their trade networks expanded and spread, they emerged as a possible threat to the European ruling elite – monarchies and aristocracies with their roots in the feudal system. The entrepreneurial middle classes (bourgeoisie/burgers) soon began communicating with each other via owner-operated printing presses, and so the earliest newspaper ventures catered to the small, but growing, literate population of Europe and its colonies. For the monarchs and princes of Europe (and their ally, the Catholic Church) the printing presses represented sites from which potentially destabilizing discourses could emerge. On the other hand, European rulers found the emergent middle classes economically useful. Their solution was to allow middle-class printing presses to exist, but to circumscribe what they could disseminate. A state-run licensing/censorship system was the result. The French Revolution, American Revolution and the revolutions of 1948 all contributed to the process of challenging these restrictions. From the 1820s to the 1870s such restrictions were gradually overthrown in Europe and its colonies as the ever-expanding middle classes came to challenge successfully the power of the European monarchies and assert their own hegemony.

Public service broadcasting

A second form of indirect government involvement in meaning-making has been the public corporation, such as the British Broadcasting Corporation (BBC). The BBC/Lord Reith's broadcasting model (Briggs, 1961: 229–49) was replicated in corporations all over the former British Empire. It was also transplanted to occupied Germany after the Second World War where it has mutated into the public service broadcasting (PSB) system of the ARD and ZDF. Reith saw broadcasting as a vehicle for educating and 'uplifting' people – his was a middle-class paternalism drawing upon Mathew Arnold's (1957) vision of using schools and the media to 'civilize' (and tame?) the lower classes. Although these corporations were state-owned and received operating revenue from the state, they were not directly government-run as was the case in the communist model. Governments appointed members of the boards of control; the corporations were accountable to parliaments; and broad policy guidelines were set by parliamentary legislation. However, the boards (theoretically) provided a mechanism for blocking direct government interference in the meaning-making process. The degree to which these corporations were actually autonomous of governments, however, varied from country to country. At one extreme, the BBC retained a fair degree of autonomy, while at the other extreme broadcasting corporations in Africa effectively became government mouthpieces. Irrespective of the extent of actual government control, all the public corporations drew upon productive practices based on hierarchical managerialism and specialist 'division of labour' practices. All produced industrialized, top-down communication. This served the hegemonic needs of state bureaucrats who were trying to create administrative-economic units (such as 'Australia', 'Canada' or 'South Africa') during the first half of the twentieth century. It also suited the (top-down) 'nation-building', hegemonic needs of development bureaucrats in places like India and Zimbabwe in the wake of decolonization because it provided the ruling elites with a means for uni-directional communication with those they were trying to organize into nation states. So in much of the decolonized British Empire, the public service model merged with the 'development'/ NWIO model.

The PSB model has the advantage of not being subject to the same market pressures as the commercial media (although this began changing during the 1990s). This means that at its best – as in the case of the BBC and the Australian Broadcasting Corporation (ABC) – PSB is able to provide quality programming that is not driven by the twin needs to cater to the broadest possible audience and to produce the most cost-effective programming. As such, PSB became a media system beyond the reach/ pressures of the business sector, and so is able to produce 'alternative' material. But it is not an 'uncontrolled' media. Autonomous boards may provide breaking-mechanisms which limit direct government interference in operational decisions. In the broader sense, PSB is built upon a two-step model of hegemonic control that has the effect of making these organizations conform to a general 'mainstream' discursive consensus (not far removed from the consensus also found within the commercial media). Governments are unlikely to select board members who do not conform to the dominant discourses of their society, and 'appropriately' selected board members will, in turn, select 'appropriate' managers. Increasingly, the pattern in advanced Western societies is that governments alternate between two mainstream political parties, whose policies increasingly 'overlap'. Public service broadcasting in Britain, Australia, New Zealand and Canada has consequently tended to discursively occupy this 'overlapping' space. From a Frankfurt School perspective, PSB thus also serves to confirm the dominant social 'theses' while excluding the 'antithetical'. Hence, the BBC remains the same under Thatcher (Conservatives) or Blair (Labour), as does the ABC under Keating (Labor) or Howard (Liberals).

State-subsidized media

A third indirect form of government involvement in meaning-making is the state-subsidy model. This model has been implemented in a number of social democratic states such as the Netherlands, Belgium and in Scandinavia. These states decided that market-driven media systems skewed meaning-making because some demographic categories (e.g. isolated regions and the poor) were not serviced. Also, in terms of the Dutch *verzuiling* system, an attempt was made to ensure that all the main voices ('pillars') of society had their own media – that is, political 'difference' was subsidized. In these social democratic societies, governments created subsidy systems to fund media which was deemed 'socially valuable' but which would not survive if left to the market. Parliaments allocate funds to media subsidy boards. Board members are appointed by parliament. These boards allocate the funds available. The result is an indirect state intervention into the meaning-making process wherein the boards are technically autonomous of the government of the day. However, as with PSB, a two-step model of control exists in which the state exercises influence in a mediated way. Ultimately, these subsidized media broadly conform to the social consensus, as mediated by the parliamentary systems within which they function, because those at the apex of the subsidized media must necessarily work within the dominant discourses of their society in order to be acceptable to the subsidy boards.

An interesting form of state-subsidized media arose in parts of Latin America during the 1960s and 1970s where alliances developed between authoritarian governments and local capitalist elites. The Latin American trend was for privately-owned commercial media to predominate. However, forms of state-directed capitalism arose in which the state poured capital into the development of the media infrastructure. Commercial media systems (which supported their governments) could then piggy-back on these government-owned infrastructures. Brazil's Globo TV developed in this way. The Brazilian state paid for a huge media infrastructure that was owned by the state telecommunications company EMBRATEL. By the 1980s the privately-owned Globo TV had grown into the fourth largest television network in the world on the back of the EMBRATEL infrastructure (Fox, 1988: 127). These state-subsidized private media companies produce meanings that are compatible with the interests of the governments subsidizing them.

Privately-owned media

Media have also operated outside public sector influence, namely capitalist-owned media systems. These media have their roots in the small presses developed by the emergent middle classes of northwest Europe during the seventeenth and eighteenth centuries (Smith, 1979: Chapters 2 and 3). From these small beginnings grew the huge, capitalist culture industry that straddles the globe today (Herman & McChesney, 1997). From the 1990s these privately-owned media industries emerged as central players in the production and circulation of global meaning. The dominance of these players coincided with the emergence of neo-liberalism as a globally dominant discourse, with the collapse of the communist media system and with the survival of PSB looking ever less likely.

During the twentieth century a culture industry grew up that looked upon its audience as consumers. This industry was driven by a commercial desire to attract advertisers. It meant collecting and packaging readers, viewers and listeners and then selling these packaged audiences to advertisers (Smythe, 1981). The proliferation and the refinement of commercialized media techniques was overwhelmingly a twentieth-century phenomenon, although it was rooted in the 1880s when the practices and logics of industrialized capitalism seeped into the processes of meaning-making. Today's commercialized culture industry can be traced back to the innovations of Joseph Pulitzer in the USA and W.T. Stead in the United Kingdom (Emery, 1972: Chapter 17; Smith, 1979: Chapter 6). These two men developed 'New Journalism' practices that were designed to attract the widest possible audience – an audience that could then 'be sold on' to advertisers. The sites of these innovations were Stead's *Pall Mall Gazette* in London and Pulitzer's New York *World* magazine. These were both highly capitalized ventures because large amounts of capital were required to buy the latest print technologies. As capitalist ventures, they were driven by the logic of profit derived from mass consumerism. The new technologies made the production of millions of the same article (e.g. a newspaper story) not only possible but 'necessary'. It was necessary because not using one's capital to its fullest capacity was illogical by the rules of capitalism – within the discourse of capitalism, one would 'go bankrupt' if one failed to exploit adequately the full potential of one's capital. This meant that building mass audiences of the sort that appealed to advertisers became the primary goal of such media.

This changed the nature of the meanings being produced because industrialized work practices were introduced, and mass production meant moving away from catering to specialized, niche groups. In its place emerged 'sensationalism' – a form of 'exaggerated' and 'generalized' meaning designed to appeal to 'everybody' (and hence to 'nobody' in particular). The result was the building of a media machine that, the Frankfurt School argued, produced a monologue. With sensationalism came a formulaic focus on crime, violence, sport, sex and 'entertainment', while opinion, debate and dialogue were deemed counter-productive to producing profit. Sensationalism, of course, pre-dated Pulitzer's press. However, Pulitzer's press came to *depend* on sensationalism as the key means to attract 'mass' audiences. It was the Stead/Pulitzer model that Alfred Harmsworth (later Lord Northcliffe) deployed and refined when creating the *Daily Mail* – the first half-penny morning newspaper of the 1890s (Clarke, 1950). The Northcliffe revolution produced a truly mass circulation, commercially-driven press which grew into the norm for Anglo presses around the world, a norm that also spread to the non-Anglo world and to other media forms as they emerged in the twentieth century.

By the 1970s the Stead/Pulitzer/Northcliffe print model had evolved into mass commercial television in the USA, Australia and Latin America. Ultimately, it was American network television that arguably developed the 'mass' media model into its 'highest stage'. Over time many features of the productive practices and genres of US television seeped into most global television production, including PSB television. Some societies, such as Australia, Brazil and Canada, offered especially fertile ground for the replication of the US network television model (see Audley, 1983;

Cunningham & Turner, 1997; Guimaraes & Amaral, 1988). At the same time mass television became the main fulcrum for late twentieth-century Western meaning-making and meaning-circulation (Abercrombie, 1996: Chapter 1).

As a 'mass' medium, the meanings produced were necessarily designed to offend as few people as possible, so as not to drive away any potential audience segment. The result was a uni-dimensionality that was constructed (by 'industrial' formula) to privilege titillation and sensational entertainment. In essence, a form of market censorship emerged – meanings that offended the people advertisers were interested in would be avoided. So meaning-making tended to be skewed in favour of those with disposable income. This created a tendency to produce and circulate meanings that would appeal to the middle classes, while shunning meanings that would appeal to disadvantaged sectors or groups on the margins of the mainstream. So privately-owned media tend to produce discourses that are appropriate for a middle-class hegemony. In some societies skewing meaning-making towards those with disposable income is more serious than others. For example, in societies demographically characterized as containing large middle classes (such as Australia), a market-driven media system does not disadvantage the majority of the population. However, in other contexts (e.g. South Africa or Brazil) market censorship can effectively exclude the majority of the population from having their views aired because disposable income is concentrated in the hands of an elite (Louw, 1984).

The Northcliffe revolution had one other important consequence; it resulted in a dramatic reduction in the number of private owners. Throughout the twentieth century the number of media owners has shrunk as ownership of the culture industry has been concentrated in the hands of ever fewer individuals and organizations. The dynamic of a concentration of media ownership can be observed across the globe, but has perhaps been most clearly observed (and documented) in the USA. As Bagdikian (1997) noted, at the end of the Second World War 80 per cent of US newspapers were independently owned. By 1989, 80 per cent were in corporate hands. By 1996 Bagdikian reported that the bulk of the USA's media were in the hands of only ten huge media corporations. This dramatic shrinkage in ownership is the outcome of a propensity towards monopoly within a capitalist system geared towards mass production. The drift in media ownership from multiple ownership to oligopoly, and then to monopoly, is caused by two factors. First, taking advantage of scales of production can decrease the relative cost of each item produced and so improve profit margins. This requires major capital investment to create mass-production machinery. The result is that existing large capitalists tend to be advantaged, while entry to new small players is restricted by lack of access to capital. Secondly, success tends to breed success. Once one player accumulates more wealth than the others (often due to luck), s/he has the capital to out-manoeuvre others and buy out the smaller, less successful players. Gradually, fewer players remain until all that is left is a monopoly or duopoly. The tendency towards the ever-greater concentration of media ownership within the capitalist culture industry has given birth to media moguls and the media corporations.

Among the first wave of newspaper moguls were the innovators Northcliffe and Pulitzer. But others followed, men who built newspaper empires which they used to wield considerable power in their societies. Among these were William Randolph Hearst (USA), Alfred Hugenberg (Germany), Max Aitken or Lord Beaverbrook (Britain) and Maurice Bunau-Varilla (France). These men created vertically and horizontally integrated newspaper organizations, thereby increasing profitability and efficiency. After the Second World War a new type of mogul emerged – the media mogul. These were also 'own-and-operate' men who used their communication empires to wield socio-political influence (some even entering active politics, such as Robert Hersant, Silvio Berlusconi and Robert Maxwell). But the post-Second World War moguls tended to diversify into a number of different media forms and to build media empires that simultaneously reached into a number of different states (Tunstall & Palmer, 1991). The Australian Rupert Murdoch has been the most successful of these, building his News Corporation into a global media giant. Others have been Canadians Roy and Kenneth Thompson, and Conrad Black, Britain's Robert Maxwell, Italy's Silvio Berlusconi, Germany's Axel Springer and Leo Kirch, and France's Robert Hersant and Jean-Luc Lagardere. But even where media moguls have interests in a number of different states, they still tend to be identified with one country where they mobilize their media holdings to exercise political influence. The exceptions to this rule have been the Thompson family whose influence straddled Britain and Canada, and Rupert Murdoch who built up influence in the USA, Britain and Australia.

As media empires have become huge global entities, the amounts of capital involved have become astronomical. Raising capital for such media empires has required spreading the net wide so as to attract as many investors as possible. With this has come a shift away from individual media moguls towards media corporations with complex ownership structures. Thus it becomes increasingly difficult to identify an organization with a single individual or family. In the process, even media organizations that are strongly identified with single individuals (such as Ted Turner's CNN) have been swallowed up by larger media agglomerations (CNN, for example, has become part of the Time Warner/America On Line (AOL) stable). And even media corporations with narrow ownership bases, such as Bertelsmann, are not run as mogul properties. The Mohn family, for example, do not use Bertelsmann for private political aggrandizement and, in the way it operates, Bertelsmann is not easily identified as the property of a specific individual or family. The Bertelsmann Group is run by professional managers. The shift from control by bourgeois owners to control by professional managers became a feature of media organizations from the 1950s onwards.

An exception to the rule is News Corporation, which is closely identified with the private interests of its owner, Rupert Murdoch. Murdoch has been a visible, hands-on owner and is not shy in using his media assets to intervene into the political processes of the Anglo world. Rupert Murdoch has managed to retain significant control of News Limited as it has expanded into a global organization by skillfully avoiding diluting his shareholder-stake in the company. And, like Hersant, Murdoch has been highly successful in raising capital to expand his ventures. But whereas Hersant plays the game on a European scale, Murdoch has succeeded in doing so globally. Significantly, though, Murdoch relies on a mix of professional managers and professional networkers. This is perhaps one of the reasons for Murdoch's success: he has constructed a communications empire that hybridizes a range of organizational modes and practices, including a nineteenth-century capitalist entrepreneurialism, managerialism, post-managerial networking, Fordism, post-Fordism, and even (some might argue) touches of feudalism. It seems that Murdoch's creative, eclectic hybridizing approach places News Corporation at the cutting edge of global media development, the Murdoch style seemingly representing the harbinger of a post-Northcliffe, post-managerialist media style. Murdoch's approach captures much of the essence of what seems to be a new form of (post-managerialist?) global network capitalism.

To date, however, both the mogul and multiple-shareholding media corporation models have employed Northcliffe-type 'culture industry' practices. These produce communicative uni-dimensionality derived from the logic of 'market censorship'. What is significant is that an ever-growing percentage of our meanings now derive from fewer but larger global players. These players have grown into enormous organizations with international interests in a wide array of media forms (Herman & McChesney, 1997: Chapter 3). In 2000 the top ten global media corporations were:

- America On Line (AOL)/Time Warner (Internet, books, magazines, comics, movies, cinemas, cable TV, music, theme parks and sports teams).
- Vivendi-Universal (Internet, television, pay TV, mobile phones, radio, movies, cable TV, PC games, books, music, theme parks).
- Disney (theme parks, television, cable TV, radio, movies, newspapers, magazines, books, sports teams and music).
- Bertelsmann (books, music, television, newspapers, magazines and radio).
- Viacom (movies, music, radio, cable TV, television, video rental stores and theme parks).
- News Corporation (newspapers, magazines, television, cable TV, satellite TV, movies and sports teams).
- Tele-Communications Inc./TCI (cable TV and satellite TV).
- Sony (music, movies, television programmes and video games).
- Philips/Polygram (music, movies and television programmes).
- General Electric/NBC (television, cable TV and radio).

Significantly, the largest media corporation in 1999, Time Warner, was taken over in 2000 by a ten-year-old Internet provider, America On Line (AOL), a take-over which served to underline the speed with which Wall Street ownership structures are being transformed by the arrival of the global network capitalists. Similarly, Vivendi (a French Internet provider) merged with Universal-Seagram in 2000 to become the world's second largest communications corporation.

Nine of the above corporations operate globally. (TCI is essentially a US operator, although it does have international interests via share ownership in some of the other global media corporations.) Five have their headquarters in the USA (AOL, Disney, Viacom, TCI, General Electric). Vivendi-Universal's headquarters is in Paris, although it has an additional corporate centre in the USA. Bertelsmann's headquarters is in Germany, News Corporation's is in Australia, Sony's is in Japan and Philips's is in the Netherlands. What is significant is that the global media system has come to be dominated by this small group of ten privately-owned, vertically-integrated media conglomerates, with another 30 to 40 supporting media firms filling out the meaningful positions within the global media system (Herman & McChesney, 1997: 194). As Herman and McChesney argue, these inter-meshed media corporations have become key players in making and circulating those meanings advantageous for emergent global corporate capitalism. Capitalist-owned media have come a long way from the days of the small presses founded by the emergent European middle classes during the seventeenth and eighteenth centuries

Community media

The twentieth century saw the industrialization of meaning-making and meaning-circulation within three main institutional forms, namely, capitalist corporations, public corporations and communist bureaucracies. The 1970s saw a growing unease with the top-down, uni-directional communication produced by these industrialized media machines. As a result, a new kind of media player emerged as activists began to set up community media which specifically attempted to generate bottom-up communication in Europe (Nigg & Wade, 1980), Latin America (Fox, 1988; Mattelart, 1986; White, 1980; 1983) and South Africa (Louw, 1989). These community media projects attempted to create communicative spaces for non-government and non-business voices, or what we now call the voices of civil society. The collapse of communism in Eastern Europe in 1989–90 demonstrated the value of empowering civil society. Stalinist *apparatchiks* had crushed grassroots voices in Eastern Europe so when Stalinist states collapsed, a social void was found to exist because so few active organs of civil society remained through which people could re-energize and re-invent their societies. The social impoverishment of these ex-Soviet societies greatly strengthened the position of those who argued for participatory communication and community media forms to facilitate giving voice to grassroot needs and aspirations. In the 1990s participatory communication notions even spread to sections of the US business community (Deetz, 1995).

As yet the development of community media has remained sporadic and has not yet become a significant form of media organization. However, with the collapse of the communist system and the decline of PSB, community media is a way of organizing widely-disseminated communication that is not conceptualized as a privately-owned commercial media form. If this community form fails to grow (possibly by colonizing Internet spaces?), we might be left with only a commercially-driven culture industry, proliferating its essentially uni-dimensional discourse into an ever-expanding array of new niches.

The shifting nature of institutionalized meaning-making

The contemporary, global culture industry's roots lie in the institutions created by the West European bourgeoisie/burgers between the seventeenth and nineteenth centuries. Having gained control of Western Europe and North America, the bourgeoisie used their industrialized North Atlantic power base systematically to spread their socio-economic order to much of the rest of the globe during the nineteenth and twentieth centuries. The New World Order, deemed to have come into being by the end of the twentieth century, effectively represents a globalized bourgeois/burger-world order.

A characteristic feature of bourgeois meaning-making has been its location within an institutionalized framework where meaning is media-ized and media-ted. In its media-ized/media-ted form, meanings are made by intellectuals specializing in making and packaging ideas and information for mass consumption. The *Gutenberg Galaxy*, as McLuhan (1962) called it, was precisely born of Gutenberg's printing press – a mechanism facilitating the industrialization of meaning-making. However, bourgeois/burger meaning-making has mutated over time, passing through two main stages to date – and is now seemingly poised to enter a third stage.

During its first stage, media-ted communication was located in small organizations. Until well into the nineteenth century, bourgeois media took the form of small owner-operated firms. In part this was because, until the arrival of steam-powered printing presses, media technology only allowed for the limited mass production of messages. Consequently, early mediated communication remained a relatively small-scale affair, staffed by multi-skilled individuals. A typical newspaper owner, for example, wrote, edited and printed the copy and administered the business. Hence it was not communication made within hierarchically organized 'meaning-factories'. It was also pre-'mass' communication. Early bourgeois mediated communication was generally targeted at relatively small groups of literate middle-class people – either activists

— somewhat independent & autonomous.

agitating to end residual feudal/aristocratic privilege which blocked the growth of bourgeois/burger power or traders needing information to improve their business prospects (examples of 'traders news letters' are provided by Von Klarwill, 1924).

Three developments were to change the nature of institutionalized meaning-making and bring about a decline in the small owner-operated media form. First, technological developments made it possible to produce ever-larger quantities of identical products (at a declining cost). Secondly, as true mass production took hold, American organizational innovation produced 'the corporation'. Within corporations, bureaucratized hierarchical practices emerged as a means of organizing growing numbers of employees. Over time, corporations learned to use industrial 'division of labour' practices, which Fordism deployed to radically cut production costs. So corporatist bureaucracy, Fordist division of labour and mass production became features of the second, corporatist, phase of institutionalized meaning-making. Thirdly, the middle classes grew demographically, expanding their trade networks and accumulating wealth (and power), and so grew their potential media audience.

The second phase of bourgeois/burger meaning-making saw small owner-operated media swallowed up by larger managerialist companies and the emergence of corporatized media. Over time, corporations emerged which ran both horizontally and vertically integrated (mass) media operations. The second phase of media-ized communication saw the emergence of a culture *industry*. Identical messages were produced and distributed in ever-growing quantities, so that mass audiences became a central feature of the corporatized culture industry. The production of newspapers, magazines, music and films were structured as industrial enterprises using Fordist logic and hierarchical, corporate managerialism. Further, individual productive units were tied together into chains that facilitated the sharing of resources and cost-cutting. This process was seen in the shift from the situation where each small town would have at least two small, competing owner-operated newspapers to a situation where large newspaper chains took over and radically reduced the number of newspaper titles. Over time, even the number of newspaper groups shrank as large corporations swallowed up the smaller ones. So corporatized and managerialized meaning-making saw the growth of larger chains, such as the Gannett Co. and Knight-Ridder Newspapers in the USA, Associated Newspapers and the Mirror Group in Britain, the Fairfax Group and News Limited, in Australia, the Argus Group and Nasionale Pers in South Africa, and the Southern Newspaper Group and Thompson

Newspapers in Canada. In time, these corporatized chains reached mass audiences of millions each day and so accumulated considerable social influence. This process was repeated in all media sectors. Corporatism and managerialism, as organizing principles, also spread to public sector media with the British Broadcasting Corporation (BBC) structuring itself as a large, corporatized industrial producer of meaning. This model was then exported around the British Empire where it led to the creation of some sizeable BBC replicas in Australia, South Africa and Canada.

These corporatized media organizations became important national institutions. This was part of a wider pattern in which a symbiotic relationship developed between industrialization and nation states, with nation states becoming key vehicles for demarcating, organizing and managing populations (and resource flows) during the industrial era (see Gellner, 1983: 35). European empire-builders tried to implant nation-state imitations across Asia, Africa and the Americas as a means of replicating their model of organizing, managing (and 'Westernizing') local populations. Corporatized, industrialised communication became an important tool in the process of building nation states and organizing populations to service the needs of industrial capitalism (and also Soviet industrialism). This was most clearly seen in the BBC/Reithian, corporatist-industrial model of broadcasting. Within Britain itself, the BBC was used to help 'organize' and 'educate' the population to become useful citizens of an industrial society. A similar process took place in the Empire. For example, the Australian Broadcasting Company was deployed to 'organize' and 'educate' Australians in the process of creating a nation state that provided resources for Britain. A privatized version of this process was also developed. In the USA, privately-owned media corporations (for example, running networked television systems or print chains) operated nationally. These coast-to-coast media networks helped to 'unite' Americans into a US 'imagined community', a process initiated earlier by nationally-circulated magazines. These media were also crucial for creating the national markets that were required to absorb the flood of goods flowing from industrial mass production methods. The US privately owned, corporate media model was replicated in much of Latin America. Some societies (e.g. Australia and Canada) developed dual systems where public and private media corporatism grew side by side. Ultimately, media corporations, in both their private and public forms, played key roles in building national markets, nation states and the accompanying nationalist 'imagined communities' (Anderson, 1983). The second 'managerialist' phase of bourgeois/burger meaning-making was characterized by being overwhelmingly 'national' in character, being the outcome of hierarchical, industrialized production methods, and being geared towards mass audiences.

Bourgeois/burger meaning-making is seemingly poised to enter a third stage – global network capitalism. The shifts in meaning-making have their roots in the information technologies that emerged in the 1980s and 1990s, of networked computers, telecommunications and the convergence of all forms of communication through digitization. Such technologies make instantaneous global communication a possibility and have also undermined the cost-effectiveness of Fordist 'mass' methods of production, national markets, corporatist managerialism and hierarchical organization. In consequence, the 1990s have seen the proliferation of post-Fordist organizational practices, global networked corporations and the growing fragmentation of 'mass', nation-based societies into globally based 'taste' niches. Socio-economic relationships are mutating, and the production, circulation and flow of communication are also showing signs of shifting. But whether this represents the beginning of a radical socio-economic (and communicative) break is not completely clear. Are we witnessing the birth of a new social order? Or are we merely witnessing another modification of capitalism? Revisiting power-elite theory may offer some clues in thinking through these issues.

Shifting elites, organizational practices and meanings?

Power elites are born, mature and die. When in power they struggle to retain their positions of privilege, which includes attempts to use the media for their own interests. Each elite will develop its own preferred organizational style, practices and, discourses, and to some extent, the survival of each elite hinges upon maintaining its own preferred organizational and discursive style (and persuading the non-elite to accept and use them).

For Burnham (1962), elites emerge because they establish control over the salient institutions of a society. By the 1940s the salient Western institutions were the instruments of industrial production. Those who succeeded in gaining control over these instruments became the social elite. Burnham also looked at how elites change. He argued that change from one mode of production to another would shift the salient institutions in society and, over time, change the nature of the elite through a sort of mutation process. For example, changing technologies and modes of production will alter the rules of the game, thereby altering the sorts of people taking advantage of what becomes the dominant game in each era. Different sections of the elite will respond differently, and with varying degrees of success, to the challenges of the new arrangements. Those responding most successfully become the new winners and so emerge as the new elite.

This thesis led Burnham to describe how a shift from what he called the old capitalist mode of production to a managerialist mode of production had altered the relationship between what had been the core of the old elite (the bourgeoisie) and what had been the elite fringe (their managers). Burnham argued that the old elite fringe (the professional managers) transformed themselves during the 1940s into the new core elite. Whether Burnham is correct is a moot point. It is probably more accurate to say that, under managerialism, professional managers negotiated relationships with the owners of the means of production. The 'owners' took many forms – individual capitalists, shareholders in joint-stock companies, parliaments (as in Western state-owned enterprises) and political parties (as in the communist system). Managerial elites therefore acquired power that derived from successfully negotiating relationships with the owners of the means of production.

At any rate, Burnham argued that professional managers replaced owners as the new elite. He went on to note that this process of change had occurred previously when the bourgeoisie had replaced feudal lords in a similar fashion. For Burnham, the emergence of a new elite therefore happens through a process of intra-elite struggle over organizational structure, practices and the 'appropriate' accompanying discourses. Burnham noted that intellectuals, rather than elite members themselves, engaged in discursive struggles. He suggests that these intellectuals often failed to understand how they served particular factional interests, believing instead that 'they are speaking in the name of truth and for the interests of all humanity' (Burnham, 1962: 75). At a certain point in the struggle, a critical mass was achieved and the new elite was able to consolidate its hold over society by having its 'game plan' and 'rules' naturalized as the dominant way of doing and seeing things.

A change of productive mode will presumably alter the saliency of various sites. Currently this seems to be happening due to the impact of the new information technologies on work practices. Entry to a newly forming elite is therefore presumably, in part, a function of being quick off the mark in identifying and colonizing new salient sites in an emergent mode of production. Bill Gates and Rupert Murdoch are contemporary examples of this. It would appear that a process of intra-elite struggle and manoeuvring is once more underway. The managerial elite that Burnham saw consolidating its position between the World Wars is now itself under threat from a new group of usurpers – the global networkers. In a sense, the old managerial Fordist 'winners' are now in danger of becoming the 'losers' in terms of the new globalized, post-Fordist game. The old rules of the game, which served the interests of what the Ehrenreichs (1979) called the professional-managerial class, are now being daily de-legitimated and a new set of global-networking rules are being naturalized. For example, intellectuals and media workers tied to creating and circulating the discourses favourable to the old managerial elites' needs are being increasingly marginalized and starved of funds. It seems that the new networking elite has reached the critical mass needed to achieve hegemonic dominance in the key global cities of the USA, the European Community, Japan, Canada and Australia. However, the old managerialist elites, and their intellectual supporters, are still offering resistance. The struggle is not over yet. But shifts in the funding of media and academic infrastructures are already pointing to a new set of winners and losers – the winners look set to be those promoting the discourses of networking, teams, outsourcing, change management, e-commerce, e-communication, e-service delivery and the de-regulation/re-regulation discourses of downsizing managerialist infrastructures.

Burnham offers a way to map out a holistic view of society – a way of conceptualizing shifting patterns of social organization. If read with the Frankfurt School, Burnham's questions reveal some interesting insights concerning the relationship between cultural shifts and elite change. Burnham's work complements the Frankfurt School, which identified continuities between the supposedly 'different' social formations of Soviet communism, liberal capitalism and fascism/Nazism. The Frankfurt School argued that, at a deep structural level, each of these three social formations shared the same managerialist assumptions because the elites in each were, in many ways, interchangeable managers, whether they were Soviet *apparatchiks* or Keynesian bureaucrats). The managerialist era was, in the final analysis, a socio-economic formation built upon the principles of hierarchical (pyramid-type) organizations, a Fordist technocratism and the notion of 'mass' (mass production and mass consumption). Both Burnham and the Frankfurt School were concerned with this self-same organizational style, with the nature of the elite that emerged from this style and with the legitimation mechanisms accompanying managerialist society. The culture industry, as described by the Frankfurt School, was predicated upon top-down communication, manufactured by a hierarchically-structured intellectual-managerial elite which targeted its messages at an audience conceived as a (passive) mass. Both the BBC's Reithian broadcast model and the USA's network television model encapsulated this mass communicative style, based as it was upon a managerialist corporatism and industrial-production logic. So too was the communist media system.

Asking the sorts of question raised by Burnham and the Frankfurt School provides a way of generating a holistic picture of the relationship between elite shifts, organizational shifts, discourse shifts and cultural shifts over time. Specifically, asking these questions in today's context offers us some interesting insights into today's transformations. By asking these questions one can identify the relationship between key Western elite shifts, and shifting organizational and communication patterns (see Table 2.1).

Burnham and the Frankfurt School examined the emergence of the managerial era between the two World Wars, which produced managerial capitalism, Soviet managerialism and Nazi managerialism. After the defeat of Nazism, the remaining two managerialisms vied for world hegemony for four decades (that is, during the Cold War). Ironically, the Cold War helped generate the global information technology and communications network that has spawned what seems to be shaping up as a new elite – the networkers. So the defeat of the Soviet managerialists in 1989–90 has not proved to be a victory for the managerial capitalist elite. Instead of the New World Order becoming the era of an expanded (globalized) managerial capitalism, something else appears to be happening – capitalism (and the capitalist elite) is mutating into a new form that is not controlled by the managerialists.

A new form of capitalism – global network capitalism – seems to be shaping up around a new set of winners. It appears that a new elite is emerging from a mixture of members of the old elite (quick off the mark in shifting to the new practices and discourses) and a group of new players who can be called 'global networkers'. Clarke and Newman (1993) have called this shift a 'second managerial revolution'. This helps draw attention to the continuities with the former managerial era. The shifts (from early capitalism to managerial capitalism to global network capitalism) should not be seen as clean breaks but rather as mutations in which some past practices and discourses are abandoned, some are

TABLE 2.1 *Elite shifts and dominant forms of communication*

	Ruling elite	Power located in:	Power structured by:	Dominant form of communication
Feudal era	Hereditary Lords	• Familial networks.	Loyalty	Ritualized communication (e.g. pageantry and ceremony).
		• Decisions taken in the private domain (behind closed doors).	Birth (rank and land tenure-linked)	
		• Pre-state patchwork of principalities, and overlapping jurisdictions (with blurred boundaries).	Theology	
Capitalist era ('Early Capitalism')	Bourgeoisie	• Parliaments. • Decisions taken in public forums (externalized debate where fractions bargain in the public sphere). • Limited state.	Control of capital	'Elite communication' (produced by small owner-operated media (e.g. early Reuters).
Managerial era ('Managerial Capitalism' and 'Soviet Managerialism')	Professional managers	• Boards and Bureaux. • Decisions taken in public and private domains (e.g. parliaments and board and cabinet rooms). • State and private corporations.	Bureaucratic hierarchy	'Mass' communication (produced by a culture industry).
Global networking era ('Global Network Capitalism')	Networkers	• Information networks. • Growing privatization of decision-making (especially in private companies). • Re-feudalization of jurisdictions.	Cultural capital and access to information. 'Networked' teams.	Fragmented 'niche' communication (produced in a multiplicity of 'networked' sites).

mutated and some are retained. The 'new rules' of the 'new game' of global network capitalism have their roots in the computing and telecommunications revolutions which have transformed organizational and work practices. The result has been a shift into post-Fordist, flexible production modes using the 'just-in-time' management approach (i.e. Toyota's *kanban* principle) (Crook et al., 1992: 185). The Fordist hierarchical company therefore breaks down and is replaced with a confederated network or global 'web'. Ultimately, economic networking holds together a 'confederation' of sub-contractors, each producing an 'outsourced' component of the whole. It is these post-Fordist confederations or webs that are throwing up a new elite – the professional networkers who have learned to take advantage of the new information and computer technology to build up their own power bases.

The new elite of networkers that has been shaping up since the late 1980s is trying to outmanoeuvre the old managerial elite (which does not preclude working with the old elite on projects). The emergent elite is attempting to ensure that the new agenda (serving the interests of the networkers) replaces the old managerialist agenda.

According to Burnham, when the managerial elite went through its 'struggle phase', capturing the state was central to achieving the victory of their managerialist agenda(s). For the emergent global elite, however, the state appears to be less central (though not completely unimportant). Instead, a number of transnational bodies have emerged as key fulcra which the networker elite is using to promote its own agenda(s), for example the World Trade Organization, the World Bank, the International Monetary Fund, the Organization for Economic Cooperation and Development, the North American Free Trade Agreement, the European Union and the Asia Pacific Economic Cooperation. The emergent global networker elite is not acting in a conscious (conspiratorial) manner when it seeks to advance its interests in these global fora. Rather, a pool of shared interests tends to emerge. The emergent elite is daily learning how to colonize the new organizational spaces opening up to it. As it does this, common interests and strategies suggest themselves, and so an evolution of new, global fulcra and globalized rules take place. Intellectuals serving this emergent elite have successfully portrayed a globalized New World Order as 'inevitable'. Hence, increasingly opposing 'globalization' is to be regarded as a nay-sayer serving narrow (conservative) sectional interests, whereas to argue for 'globalization', GATT, and neo-liberal structural reform has assumed the mantle of serving 'universal' interests rather than the interests of one particular elite faction.

The networkers have adopted a different organizational style from the managerialists. Whereas managerialists deploy a uniform organizational model across all sectors, the global networkers do not. In general networkers prefer federal arrangements which allow the individual components autonomy. Where managerialists tightly integrate all functional units into a hierarchical structure where top-down command structures are facilitated, the networkers allow each unit to organize itself in ways deemed appropriate by those *in situ*. In other words, networkers deconstruct the huge bureaucratic corporations built by the managerialists and weaken top-down command chains of communication. Such organizational deconstruction became a feature of the late twentieth century as the global networkers began challenging managerialist assumptions and practices. As a result, one saw large bureaucratic corporations like AT&T broken up into the 'mini-Bells'. To some extent the collapse of the Soviet Union can be seen as iconic for the wider late twentieth-century deconstruction of the bureaucratic organizational model predicated upon central control, central planning and top-down communication. Lipnack and Stamps (1994) have described this shift from an industrial era 'bureaucratic mode' of organization to an information era 'network mode'. The new organizational model they identify broadly concurs with the societal changes described by Castells (1996).

Lipnack and Stamps argue that four organizational styles have emerged to date small group, hierarchical, bureaucratic, and the network organizational style. Interestingly, the network organizational style does not replace the previous three. Instead, it incorporates them because, as Lipnack and Stamps argue, the networkers merely add a new organizational layer on top of the older forms. In a sense, the networkers 'capture' the previous organizations but retain the old organizational forms and practices, which are merely 'networked' into a new complex, hybridized amalgam. What transpires is a mutation, not a radical break with the past. In terms of this conception, the networkers 'only connect' (Lipnack & Stamps, 1994: 41) what is already there, thus creating a new synergy. The rules that operate the emergent global networked corporation consequently allow space for earlier organizational practices and forms. What changes, however, is that the professional managers (of the hierarchical, bureaucratic structures) are displaced from the centre of power. Power now shifts to the professional networkers. Lipnack and Stamps describe the emergent style as the pepperoni pizza organization (see Figure 2.1). This organizational style combines teams, hierarchy, bureaucracy and networks (Lipnack & Stamps, 1994: 13–14).

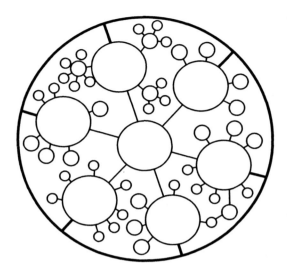

FIGURE 2.1 *The pepperoni pizza model of organization*

The pepperoni pizza organization has a coordinating nodal site of control in the form of CEOs. The CEOs look a lot like feudal lords from the middle ages in that they are located at the centre of multiple, overlapping 'territories' and jurisdictions. Rupert Murdoch's corporation has been cited as an example (Price, 1995: 56). The global networking era actually shares some characteristics with the feudal era, with decision-making being increasingly privatized (de-*public*-ized), personalized and centralized. To some extent, this is a continuation of a trend with its roots in the managerial era which saw the beginnings of the rolling back of the pubic domain by the private domain (McGuigan, 1996: 24). Further, the new style of organizing people is becoming more ill-defined and 'messy'. Indeed, it is somewhat analogous to the feudal 'patchwork' of overlapping powers. We find multiple (and proliferating) styles of control and decision-making being tolerated in different parts of the network, so long as those at the centre of the web can gain some benefit from allowing a particular practice and/or organizational arrangement to exist in a part of their networked 'empire'. In addition, the various pepperoni empires are not discrete – they can simultaneously overlap, intersect, cooperate, or even be in conflict with each other in an ever-shifting feudal-like *mélange* of networked power relationships.

If a global networker elite succeeds in displacing the managerialists, a shift in the patterns of media control, practices and content is likely to follow. Rupert Murdoch's News Corporation encapsulates the new pepperoni style of network. Although it is a style that in no way dominates all global media production, the Murdoch style is one that best fits the needs of globalized network capitalism. Murdoch is the nodal CEO. However, News Corporation is a complex global patchwork of different styles. In part, Murdoch's success derives from allowing for 'difference' – the components of Murdoch's pepperoni empire specialize in catering for the needs of different communication niches. Each component adopts a style appropriate to its niche. In the place of a closely integrated, hierarchical, bureaucratic culture industry which is organized to produce a uniform product for a single mass market, Murdoch's more feudal approach is niche-based – his media empire produces multiple forms of communication, each aiming to attract a different target group. Significantly, the Murdoch approach does not replace the Northcliffe type of mass culture industry – and mass culture continues to be produced by some sectors of Murdoch's networked empire. However, mass culture has been supplemented by niche-based and fragmented communicative forms. In some instances, these niches can involve substantive numbers of people when gathered together globally, and because News Corporation's reach is global, it can gather together such global niches. To some extent, News Corporation is learning to network 'differences' (niches) globally, but without losing the capacity to service the 'mass' sector at the same time. It is a style of fragmented communication that the other global media corporations are also learning to use.

The result is communicative complexity, different from the uni-dimensionalism of the era of pure mass communication. However, not everyone has access to niche (non-mass) communication. The pattern that began to emerge at the end of the twentieth century was the growth of a two-tier system – the 'information rich' and 'information poor'. The information rich tend to be concentrated within certain regions (especially North America, the European Union and Australasia) and in particular in the emergent hearts of global networked society, namely the affluent neighbourhoods of global cities. Niche communication is increasingly only available to those who can pay for it. Mass communication, as derived from the Northcliffe model, was precisely made available to all because it was predicated upon attempts to build mass markets (and/or related nation-building exercises). However, as mass industrial capitalism has mutated into post-Fordist network capitalism, mass markets have declined in importance, while niche markets have become more significant. This brought with it niche communication which, significantly, can be delivered on a user-pays basis (to the information rich).

Similarly, information technology has to be purchased to access the communicative channels of the global networkers. In consequence, an information-rich elite now has access to enormous quantities of information as well as to the possibilities of actively sharing ideas and information on the Internet. The information rich use a wide range of communication vehicles, including the 'mass' products of the culture industry, specialist 'niche' communication products, as well as the more 'individualized' networked channels of the Internet. The networkers have access to, and understand how to mobilize, the multiple potential of an increasingly fragmented communication system. The information poor, on the other hand, remain passive and dependent and tend to draw on only one part of the total communication system, namely, the (mass) products of the culture industry. So the information rich have greater possibilities for escaping the culture industry's uni-dimensional fare (so bemoaned by the Frankfurt School) than do the information poor.

So, as with both the feudal and capitalist eras, the global networkers' era appears to be producing growing disparities in access to cultural capital. Those with access to the information-rich networks are dispersed geographically, yet are 'connected' (networked) to each other via the new information technologies. For the emergent elite, active networked participation (within a globalized co-creation process) is a possibility, plus it has access to a wide range of communicative sources. The information poor, on the other hand, are either virtually excluded from the global communication system (as is the case with most rural Africans) or only have access as passive recipients to mass-produced messages (in the form of free-to-air television or radio). The range and quality of communicative sources available to the information poor is restricted. For these people, the culture industry remains their window on the world as well as an increasingly important vehicle for socializing their children. A global mass media machinery is emerging but it is concentrated in fewer hands, while its reach and influence becomes more global. It is a proliferating machine, circulating meanings that suit the needs of global networked capitalism as consumerism, Coca-Cola and CNN become globally ubiquitous. The way in which, from the 1990s, consumerism, market economics and electronic communication players (like Murdoch) even penetrated China – initially from a Hong Kong-base – is instructive in this regard.

The mass meanings being created and circulated by the emergent global culture industry are increasingly characterized by a genre with its roots in multicultural southern California – homogenized meanings that emerged from a process of cultural hybridization, but nonetheless built upon a solidly Anglo foundation. From this has grown a concern that global culture is being 'Americanized'. But, although this global mass culture has geographical roots in southern California, it is simplistic to call it 'American'. Rather, it is a hybrid ('partially' American) cultural form that is colonizing the 'mass sector' in other regions of the USA at the same time as it is colonizing Australia, Brazil or Malaysia. If it appears to be a 'Los Angeles-type' culture, this merely replicates a wider New World Order pattern of dominance. The New World Order represents a global hegemony that is, at heart, an Anglo alliance. The emergent global hegemonic alliance is being built upon US power, but elite membership is not restricted to Americans. Anglos have dispersed themselves globally through two waves of Anglo colonization: British and American. The New World Order appears to be re-forging the links between these scattered Anglo communities and to be building a global alliance between the now globally-dispersed Anglo elites. In this sense, 'globalization' is an 'Anglo' phenomenon (although the 'Anglo-ness' is seemingly obscured to many inside the process). Significantly, Anglo-American culture is assimilationist. Hence, membership of the global Anglo elite is not derived from having roots in an Anglo 'ethnos'. Rather, it is derived from having adopted (or having been assimilated into) Anglo culture. These processes of assimilation, which are occurring globally, are modifying Anglo cultural forms. Los Angeles has become one of the key sites for the production of this new culture of Anglo assimilation, which is then disseminated throughout the global culture industry.

So the shift towards global networking has not seen a winding back of a culture industry geared towards the production of mass communication. Rather, it sees the emergence of a multi-layered and fragmented communication system within which mass communication becomes the primary vehicle to deliver meanings to the globe's non-elites. Not only do the information poor fail to get access to the full richness of available meanings in circulation, but more significantly, they remain mere consumers of a restricted uni-directional communication system delivered by a globalizing culture industry. However, it is a culture industry with global reach. Consequently, the emergent global culture industry now has the potential to set agendas – at least for the information poor sectors – on an unprecedented scale. The question is, will the global media corporations ultimately gain control of and use the various communicative niches for their own interests? Presumably, members of the emergent network elite, like Rupert Murdoch and Bill Gates, will be doing their utmost to network as many communicative niches into their pepperoni pizza empires. In the process, they will help invent the style of communication that will come to characterize the era of global network capitalism.

CHAPTER 3

Sites for Making Meaning II: The Regulatory Framework

Gutenberg's printing press provided the means for the multiple reproduction of identical messages. For ruling elites the resulting 'Gutenberg Galaxy' (McLuhan, 1962) created opportunities for communicating with mass populations but also potential problems. Print technology increased the circulation of ideas deemed inappropriate by feudal ruling elites. Policies soon emerged in Europe and its colonies in the Americas, Australasia and South Africa to control the new media born of the Gutenberg revolution, especially to regulate the use of the Gutenberg technology by the emergent middle classes ('free citizens') who were using this new media to further their bourgeois interests. Regulation was also imposed to curtail reformist threats to the established Church. The earliest media policies regulated the new threats (to the political and religious elites of the day) through print licenses, stamp duties and censorship. Consequently, print media's pioneers worked within highly regulated environments, and much early print history is enmeshed with the struggles of editors, printers and journalists trying to wind back feudal controls on their 'right to publish'. During the early stages of the struggle, much of the printing that was deemed inappropriate by feudal elites was located in those areas first 'captured' by the emerging bourgeoisie (such as the Dutch Republic), from where it was exported to the rest of Europe. This pioneering bourgeois print media spawned reading societies and discussion groups during the eighteenth and early nineteenth centuries. This produced the dense network of public communication that Habermas (1974) has called the 'public sphere'. The public sphere played a crucial, facilitative role in sparking the bourgeois revolutions that were to eventually dislodge feudal hegemony from Europe. The nineteenth century witnessed a progressive winding back of feudal media licensing/censorship as bourgeois hegemony spread across Europe and its colonies. As capitalists asserted themselves during the nineteenth century, so access to capital (rather than state intervention) became the key 'regulatory mechanism'. The USA emerged as the cutting edge of this laissez-faire form of regulation, given that, from 1788, the USA was unique within the area of 'European' settlement in having virtually no remaining feudal residues. Outside the USA the mix between emergent capitalism and residual feudal influences varied between states, which necessarily impacted upon the speed with which feudal media restrictions were lifted and replaced by capitalist laissez-faire 'regulation'.

The twentieth century saw the laissez-faire approach rolled back and state-interventionist media regulation re-emerge in the Western world. Regulation reappeared once the bourgeoisie had consolidated their power and discovered a need to regulate the media in ways compatible with their interests. Also, in the 1920s, the arrival of radio broadcasting provided an impetus for formulating a new media regulatory framework. Simply put, a laissez-faire approach to radio would have meant airwave anarchy, making the development of any radio industry impossible. Effectively, electronic message delivery, that is the 'Marconi Galaxy' (Collins & Murroni, 1996: 182), created new media forms that sat uneasily with the laissez-faire approach. However, the new regulatory framework that emerged was unlike the earlier feudal system for two reasons. First, the bourgeois/burger struggle against feudalism had left a belief that state intervention into media affairs was unacceptable – a position most strongly spelt out in the First Amendment to the US Constitution. Those Western ruling elites which traced their inspirational roots back to the American and French Revolutions found it difficult to justify (to themselves) the re-imposition of state control over the media. Secondly, twentieth-century media (radio) regulation was born just as managerialism was emerging as an organizational form. Hence twentieth-century media regulation became enmeshed within a bureaucratic and managerialist approach to policy-making. Again, as with the early laissez-faire regulatory approach, the USA became the cutting-edge of managerialist media regulation.

The new (twentieth-century) regulatory regime grew from four main concerns. Most important was a powerful managerialist need to prevent anarchy on the radio airwaves. Secondly, the birth of mass media/'mass culture' generated unease among conservative sections of the intellectual elites of Europe and its colonies. Thirdly, agitation began for developing decency/taste frameworks to ensure the media promoted 'civilized standards'. A range of twentieth-century positions on 'standards' emerged, including those of Mathew Arnold, who wanted to ensure 'high' culture was not swamped by 'low' culture, and those who feared that the mass media would promote 'inappropriate' sexual practices and/or violent behaviour. (Sex and violence has tended to dominate the minds of advocates of media censorship.) As the twentieth century progressed, those agitating for such 'standards' encompassed a range of positions. Generally, the decency/taste activists were more readily heeded outside the USA, because for much of the twentieth century the First Amendment acted as a strong anti-censorship measure within the USA. This situation began to change in the 1980s (Demac, 1990). Finally, mass media ownership was seen to deliver social power into the hands of media moguls. This concerned a range of people who feared that this power might be used against them. Hence, over time and in various contexts, arguments have been raised in favour of regulation to 'hem in' moguls.

Media regulation in the Anglo world

The Anglo world entered the twentieth century with a largely laissez-faire media policy in place, within which capitalist owners had largely secured the right to regulate themselves. This approach served the interests of those owning the print media and the newly emerging film industry. However, with the advent of the radio, the laissez-faire approach proved to be a problem.

The arrival of radio in the 1920s threatened to produce an airwaves anarchy. At its birth, radio became the preserve of amateur broadcast 'clubs'. Once a number of clubs existed within the same region, they began to interfere with each other's signals. The military also became concerned that 'their' radio space was being interfered with. Both broadcasters and the military realized that a laissez-faire approach would not work and that some regulatory mechanism was needed to allocate the limited amount of radio spectrum available. So the fledgling radio industry called for an independent 'policeman of the airwaves'. In the USA this led to the creation of the Federal Radio Commission in 1927, which became the Federal Communications Commission (FCC) (see Krasnow et al., 1982: 10–16). The FCC has grown into the world's largest machinery for allocating airwave spectrum, and has served as a model for much of the rest of the world. The FCC system has regulated spectrum to promote a privately-owned radio (and television) industry. Effectively, this meant advertisers came to set the parameters for American media taste.

The US regulatory system effectively served to entrench and proliferate Joseph Pulitzer's commercial media model, a model that was designed to attract the 'mass' audiences that would appeal to advertisers. Ultimately, the FCC became a vehicle for spreading the practices and worldview of the capitalist elite that consolidated its hold over the USA after Unionists won the Civil War. This elite's origins lie in the middle-class values and practices of seventeenth- and eighteenth-century northwest European bourgeois/burgers, a group whose values achieved their most spectacular success after their socio-economic revolution migrated to, and entrenched itself in, North America. (Eventually, the US branch of the Western bourgeoisie became dominant, resulting in American practices and values then flowing back to Europe.) Pulitzer's personal career as a European migrant taking advantage of the opportunities of post-US Civil War capitalist-industrial expansion encapsulates the story of this transatlantic bourgeoisie. Under FCC regulation, the Americans built a particular kind of media system wherein spectrum was overwhelmingly allocated to a profit-driven 'mass' industrial media machine, producing sensationalist meanings favouring those with disposable income. The result was a privately-owned media sector which produced discourses that suited a capitalist hegemony.

However, many in the rest of the Anglo world developed a distaste for the popular culture emerging from this commercialized US media industry. Many Canadians, in particular, felt great unease about US mass culture which began spilling over the border into Canada. This disquiet also filtered into the rest of the British Empire, informing key decision-makers, such as John Reith, the first Managing Director of the BBC. British Empire media regulation took a different trajectory from the US model. The British model ultimately generated a dual media system in the United Kingdom, Australia, Canada, South Africa and New Zealand with a strong state-owned media sector operating alongside privately-owned media. The airwaves in Commonwealth countries have been explicitly regulated so as to allow space for both state and private broadcasters. In part, the greater complexity allowed for by Commonwealth media regulation systems reflected the more fragmented nature of the British Empire ruling elite(s). In the USA, feudal residues were effectively obliterated, producing a 'pure' middle-class, bourgeois-derived elite which was free to produce a society governed by 'pure' bourgeois commercialism. In the UK, however, the emergent capitalist elite had to contend with residual feudal elements who used the state to 'hem in' bourgeois aspirations. British (and by extension Commonwealth) media regulation reflected this 'hemmed in' commercialism. However, the 1990s saw this British model come under sustained attack, especially in the UK, Australia and New Zealand. Effectively, the American commercial media model grew in influence as state-subsidized PSB was increasingly questioned and many Commonwealth regulators moved towards the notion of allowing the 'market' to allocate spectrum. The notion that state intervention should 'hem in' commercial excesses and provide non-commercialized alternatives became increasingly unfashionable as Thatcherist neo-liberalism, economic rationalism and globalization became dominant discourses within the late twentieth-century Anglo world. This trend, if continued, will see Commonwealth media regulation move closer to the US model which favours commercially-driven media.

However, there was one countervailing trend within media regulation at the end of the twentieth century, namely the deliberate creation of space for non-commercial community media. During the 1970s, people began to campaign for the allocation of spectrum for community radio. This was especially successful in Australia where it resulted in the growth of a community sector alongside Australia's commercial and state-owned media (Moran, 1995). Similar campaigns in favour of community media in South Africa (Louw & Rama, 1993) saw the post-apartheid media regulator, the Independent Broadcasting Authority (IBA), actually foreground the creation of a space for community radio (IBA, 1997). That both Australia and South Africa developed lively community media sectors is partly due to the nature of the ruling elites in those societies at crucial historical moments. The Australian Labor Party (ALP) created a ruling 'rainbow coalition' in the 1980s which included ethnic minorities, aboriginals, greens, gays and a left intelligentsia. Not surprisingly, under the ALP, the Australian Broadcasting Tribunal (ABT) opened up community media spaces for these 'rainbow' groups. Similarly, in South Africa in the 1990s, the IBA served the interests of an African National Congress (ANC) government by promoting community radio stations which empowered important sectors of the ANC's urban black constituency. On the one hand, regulating to promote non-commercial community media spaces flies in the face of a global trend towards 'market-driven' spectrum allocation. On the other hand, 'localism' and the politics of 'civil society' are ascendant – a trend highly advantageous for the community media sector. However, if the community media sector is to take advantage of this trend towards localism and survive in an Anglo world increasingly driven by economic rationalist ideology, it will need to transcend its non-commercial roots. Otherwise community media is in danger of fading into a marginal footnote within the overall story of media regulation.

Overall then, the Anglo world has produced two approaches to media regulation. In the USA, FCC regulation has promoted an overwhelmingly commercial media system, where the state is not seen to have any legitimate interest in media content and where access to capital is the key 'regulatory' mechanism. Commonwealth countries, on the other hand, tended to adopt an estatist position and regulate in favour of, and even actively promote, state intervention into the media sector so as to encourage voices other than commercially-driven operations. This can be seen in the policies of Australia's ABA, Canada's CRTC, the UK's ITC and Radio Authority, and South Africa's IBA. But it is an approach most apparent in Canada where state interventionism into the media sector is advocated explicitly to demarcate Canada from the USA. Not only does the CRTC deliberately reserve airwave spectrum for a non-commercial broadcasting, but, the Canadian state also places great store in subsidizing the Canadian Broadcasting Corporation (CBC) as a nation-building vehicle. The CBC's task is to provide a Canadian cultural counterweight to 'Americanized' commercial fare which is delivered by Canada's commercial sector and by US programming spilling over the border (Collins, 1990: 66–9). This desire to ensure 'non-American' programming is available, derives from the Canadian Anglo-elite's origins as American-monarchists who fled from the newly established USA republic and then found themselves in the shadow of their stronger southern cousins. Laissez-faire media 'regulation', based purely on access to capital rather than state intervention, would not serve the interests of this Canadian elite because it would empower American commercial voices over the voice of the state-managerialist elite which administers Canadian (nationalist) 'difference'. So although the CBC (like many other BBC clones) suffered major funding cuts in the 1980s and 1990s, it remains a large and important Canadian enterprise (Raboy, 1997).

The Commonwealth media regulatory system has grown up within a symbiotic (even intertwined) relationship with the British notion of public service broadcasting (PSB). Effectively, PSB is an outgrowth of the perception held by sections of the British elite that the state can (must?) intervene to 'tame' commercial broadcasting. Britain's Reithian PSB model was originally a BBC invention, but it has strong resonance in the BBC clones in Australia (ABC), Canada (CBC), South Africa (SABC) and New Zealand (NZBC). The Reithian model was born of early twentieth-century intellectual-elite fears that the newly enfranchised British masses would 'lower standards'. Hence the BBC implemented an Arnoldian-vision of cultural intervention to educate and 'civilize' the 'lower' masses in order to preserve 'British cultural standards' and inculcate appropriate high-culture 'taste'. This Reithian/Arnoldian vision grew out of a negative reaction to the mass commercial media. Some European critics believed that the mass media amounted to commercial exploitation of the ill-informed and gullible masses, which produced cultural debasement. Among the most influential mass culture critics have been Mathew Arnold (1957), F.R. Leavis (1930), T. Adorno and M. Horkheimer (1979) and J. Ortega y Gasset (1961). For these critics, the commercial mass media constituted a catastrophic threat to (European) 'high culture' because it circulated 'low-taste' meanings that brought culture down to the lowest common denominator.

Broadcasting and compulsory education were chosen as excellent vehicles for implementing the Arnoldian mission of civilizing and 'taming' the masses. The Arnoldian/Reithian worldview became very influential among those who built Britain's media regulatory system and PSB. In Australia, Canada, South Africa and New Zealand, Anglo colonial elites adopted modified versions of this worldview. Anglo colonials often suffered from what Australians called a 'cultural cringe' – that is, they saw their derivative (colonial) cultures as less worthy than Anglo culture 'back home' in the UK. This produced a need to try to live up to 'British standards'. Hence, colonial elites became more 'British' than those in Britain. For this reason, PSB in the colonial Dominions was used (in a modified Reithian way) as an educational tool to 'uplift' colonial cultural standards. For example, the early ABC only employed announcers with 'British' (not Australian) accents. In Canada and South Africa, the Reithian BBC model was adjusted because Anglo elites in these contexts had to accommodate non-Anglos (the Quebecois and Afrikaners). Once Afrikaner nationalists captured the South African state, the South African Broadcasting Corporation (SABC) was even further transformed into a vehicle for promoting apartheid within a modified, Reithian, cultural interventionist model, with the SABC eventually trying to promote 11 separate 'nationalisms' through 11 language/cultural services.

The South African mutation of British PSB shared much in common with how the BBC model was deformed in many third world contexts.

As the British Empire collapsed, so the BBC clones left behind were seized by Westernized elites taking control in these emergent states. In one Afro-Asian country after another, PSB become a vehicle for state propaganda. The ruling elites of most of these states justified their propagandistic use of radio and television by deploying the arguments of 'development journalism' and the New World Information Order. British Reithianism/Arnoldianism changed and was attached to a new (Afro-Asian) 'educational task' of promoting 'developmental modernization' and 'nation-building'. This educational task served the interests of the indigenous (Westernized) bourgeois minorities who stepped into the shoes of the departing colonials (Fanon, 1968). There was a surprising uniformity in the post-British Empire practices adopted by Afro-Asian broadcasters such as the Voice of Kenya, All India Radio and Doordarshan (Indian television), the Rhodesia Broadcasting Corporation (and the follow-up Zimbabwe Broadcasting Corporation), the Nigeria Broadcasting Corporation (and the Nigerian Television Authority and Federal Radio Corporation of Nigeria), Radio Television Malaysia, Israeli Broadcasting Service and the South African Broadcasting Corporation. The state was seen to have a right to intervene in media production.

Key assumptions underpinning media and cultural regulation

Within the twentieth-century Anglo world there has been an ongoing tension between those advocating a minimalist (laissez-faire) approach and those believing that the state should intervene to regulate cultural production and/or even to change culture. The laissez-faire approach advantages those with access to capital. Consequently, those favouring minimal regulation are usually conservative and wealthy, while interventionists tend to be those with limited access to (material) capital, who consequently wish to use the state to alter resource distribution. Those advantaged by state interventionism are capital-poor people seeking access to resources and those administering regulation systems. The regulators are generally intellectuals possessing cultural rather than material capital. They are usually left-leaning managerialists who constitute an aspirant (alternative) elite and acquire power (and careers) by administering state interventionist policies. In the Anglo world those favouring state interventionism (estatism) have advocated a capitalist managerialism or 'liberal corporatism' (Lehmbruch, 1977). Corporatist logic grants the state an important role in directing/regulating/ orchestrating a socio-economic system which remains mostly privately owned (Winkler, 1976). The liberal variant of corporatism – capitalist managerialism – has being more benign and successful than the fascist model of managerialism. Capitalist managerialism also proved to be more successful, and benign than the Soviet form of managerialism.

Within Britain and her colonial offshoots, the struggle between minimalists and interventionists was largely resolved in favour of the interventionists from the 1930s to the mid-1980s. The failure of laissez-faire capitalism during the Great Depression legitimized Keynesian interventionism and managerialism. Early capitalism was unable to solve systemic problems through a laissez-faire approach. Keynes (1942: Chapter 24) proposed reforming capitalism, to save it from collapse, by introducing state intervention and bureaucratic management to resolve the problems. Managerial capitalism grew out of this Keynesian reformist discourse. The outcome was a regulatory state interventionist discourse which also spilled over into the cultural and media sectors.

The idea that the state should actively intervene in the media sector underpinned the British regulatory system and also saw the birth of state-owned broadcasting. The British model came to inform the media policy of innumerable states (such as countries formally part of the British Empire and post-1945 Anglo-occupied Germany). This British model has been constructed upon four legs. First, the purely pragmatic notion of regulating to avoid airwave anarchy provided the original impetus for state intervention. However, the British considerably widened this original spectrum-allocation idea beyond purely pragmatic managerialist considerations. Effectively, British media regulation, imbibed of the Keynesian notion that the state should be a proactive manager, working to anticipate and avoid, if possible, potential future problems. So the second leg of the British model allowed for strong managerialist state involvement. The state came to see itself as a legitimate cultural intervener. Cultural interventionist logic turned the British state into society's main broadcaster, allocating to itself large blocks of the airwave spectrum. States following the British model also implemented various censorship regimes (in ways that would have been inconceivable under the US model). Britain's cultural interventionist model was exported to the rest of the Empire where, at the end of the twentieth century, it still informed a range of media policies (albeit in mutated forms). In the USA, Keynesianism state interventionism was less influential, although Roosevelt's New Deal was a form of economic state managerialist interventionism, and intervention into the media and cultural sectors was far less pronounced.

The third leg of the British model derived from an elitist disdain of the masses which led to Arnold/Leavis notions of cultural interventionism to raise 'standards'. This was ultimately built upon a 'mistrust of the masses' who, it was feared, were too inclined to approve of 'low taste' (Americanized?) commercial media fare. Interestingly, both the conservative and leftist wings of the Anglo intelligentsia apparently shared a similar disdain for mass culture. For example, when social democrats were influential within the BBC (or the ABC) they continued to espouse an Arnoldian vision of 'standards'. This media policy model worked to ensure the existence of a 'space' for middle-class taste. In Britain, Canada, Australia and New Zealand, the state actively subsidized this space in the form of PSB.

The fourth leg of the British model was the creation of a whole class of managerialist regulators with a vested interest in maintaining (and where possible expanding) state regulatory regimes. This state-managerialist class (and the intellectuals training them) advance their careers, status and power by operating both a media regulatory mechanism and a PSB system built upon a state interventionist logic that is derived from a curious mix of Keynesian (social democrat) and Arnoldian (conservative-elitist) principles. Ultimately, the British approach was to create a particular cultural mix (of commercial and non-commercial cultural forms) within which a state-subsidized cultural elite played an important productive role. For those advocating a 'free market' laissez-faire approach, this was seen to produce a state-induced skewing of media production.

In the USA, media regulation was more circumscribed – as a managerialist means for promoting orderly commercialization of the airwaves rather than intervention to 'improve' cultural production. So in the USA a minimalist model was adopted. State mediation was seen as a necessary evil to prevent airwave anarchy. But the US state never saw itself as having a legitimate (corporatist or estatist) interest in media production, that is by becoming a broadcaster, imposing an Arnoldian 'taste regime' or setting up censorship bodies. Within the USA there were 'administrative' interventions (e.g. US Post was forbidden from carrying pornography) and the judiciary were empowered to rule on media content issues, albeit in the context of a First Amendment which protected 'free speech'. But overall, US government involvement in media production was limited compared to the rest of the Anglo world. If the British (and their clones) saw themselves as having a legitimate interest in taking decisions about media content and production, in the USA such decisions were not seen to be the legitimate concern of a state-managerialist class. Instead, they were seen to be the concern of those owning the means of media production, that is they were commercial not political decisions. The US approach ignored the fact that its legitimization of rampant media commercialism was itself a 'political' decision that empowered a particular form of cultural elite, and skewed media production in favour of those sectors deemed 'profitable' by business elites.

But the US and 'British' regulatory models should not be seen as mutually exclusive. Rather, they have informed each other and grown in tandem. Certainly for many decades, the US and British media systems differed with regard to the level of state intervention (differences which began to narrow in the 1990s). However, underpinning the differences were shared concerns and debates as to the nature of media regulation and the media–society interface. In all, four key themes infused media regulation in both its US and British variants.

First, there was the question of how to divide up the available airwaves spectrum (after the military, police and emergency services had taken their slice). By the start of the twenty-first century there were four main contenders claiming allocations: commercial broadcasters, public service broadcasters, community broadcasters and (rapidly expanding) mobile telephone networks. These claims were further complicated by the various potential commercial uses of the spectrum could be used for. This required policy-makers to make choices – for example, between high-definition television (HDTV) and a dual system of television plus (Internet) data delivery. (HDTV requires a lot of spectrum, which leaves less space for data.)

The way the spectrum has been divided varies from country to country. The USA traditionally and disproportionately favoured commercial broadcasters. However, towards the end of the twentieth century the USA allocated larger proportions of its spectrum to commercial mobile telephone operators. This is merely a continuation of the way US policy formulation has been traditionally geared to service business sector needs. Many Afro-Asian Commonwealth states, on the other hand, leaned to the other extreme and allocated the bulk of their spectrum to the PSB sector. These Afro-Asian regulators privileged the BBC clones in their states. When coupled with NWIO policies, this produced media environments bolstering existing governments, and restricted oppositional voices. In other Commonwealth states, such as the United Kingdom,

Australia, Canada and post-apartheid South Africa, the spectrum has been regulated to create mixed systems, wherein both PSB and commercial operators were allocated spectrum. The mixed approach also characterized Japan's regulatory framework because, although the USA tried to impose an FCC type of system upon Japan in 1950, they had to leave a sizeable space for Japan's pre-war BBC clone, Nippon Hosa Kyokai (NHK). The Japanese also 'modified' the FCC model by instituting the practice of 'coordinating' rival commercial bids for spectrum into joint media ventures, thereby effectively eliminating media competition. During the 1980s, the mixed approach also characterized the media policies of European Union states (Dyson et al., 1988). Many mixed systems have allocated spectrum to community broadcasters. However, from the 1990s onwards, there has been a tendency within the mixed systems for PSB to face growing pressure, due to the rise of economic rationalism (advocating market regulation and cuts to state subsidies).

However, by the end of the twentieth century, the whole question of airwaves regulation was up for grabs. Technological developments such as cable, satellites, digital convergence and mobile telephony radically altered media landscapes. Some have gone as far as suggesting the airwaves will eventually only be used for applications that have to be delivered without wires (such as mobile telephony), that is services that can be delivered by cable or satellite (e.g. television and Internet data delivery) may be removed from the broadcast spectrum to free up space for these other services. This predicted shift from wireless to wired delivery has been called the 'Negroponte switch' (Collins & Murroni, 1996: 43). This would be a complete revision of the logic that has underpinned broadcast policy since the 1920s.

A second question regulators have had to address is whether they have any role in the building of a national culture. What role can, or should, media have in generating collective identities like 'the nation' or 'community' (i.e. the local), or even an international, supranational or global identity? At its birth, the British regulatory model contained both national (British) and supranational (Empire) elements. Ultimately, the British media policy model, and its Commonwealth derivatives, contained the assumption that regulators (and their PSB colleagues) had an Arnoldian/Reithian role to develop media frameworks that helped build 'national identities'. These identities served to confirm and stabilize a particular set of socio-economic administrative units. These units (i.e. states often bringing antagonistic groups together) were originally created to help administer the Empire's populations, for example, Australia, South Africa, Malaysia and Nigeria). They were administrative entities highly suited to organizing populations in the era of industrial capitalism. Some specialized in food production (New Zealand), others in mineral production (Zambia) and others in processing these raw materials (England). Some have argued that the end of the twentieth century saw a shift into a post-industrial era, and 'national units' are no longer helpful for organizing post-industrial populations (Lash & Urry, 1994: Chapter 11). In its place has emerged the organizational logics of marketization, globalization (as seen in the World Trade Organization (WTO)), regionalization (as seen in the European Union) and localization (as seen in Scottish devolution) – organizing principles more suited to the needs of the global networker elite. Not surprisingly, media regulators have found it increasingly difficult to regulate 'national' media spaces in the face of pressures towards global meaning flow on the one hand, and towards 'niche' and local (community) identity on the other. To some extent, downsizing PSB and interventionist media regulation in the 1990s mirrors the wider failure of the (corporatist) state to maintain itself (Janicke, 1990).

In many ways the US media regulatory model has adjusted to the globalization era with greater ease than the British model because the US model never allocated a 'nation-building' role to FCC regulators. The FCC was always a laissez-faire regulator with no room for Keynesian or Arnoldian 'big brother' interventionism. On the other hand, regulators in Britain, the Commonwealth, France and Japan have endured a painful transition as their former roles as, among other things, the guardians of 'national culture' have increasingly been called into question. Ultimately, the FCC model slides easily into serving the regulatory needs of the global networkers, providing commercial media spaces, regulating media niches (and localism) and facilitating global meaning flows within a global media market. The British interventionist model, on the other hand, cuts across many of the needs of the global networkers, who have a vested interest in seeing the old nation-based regulatory mechanisms and protectionisms deconstructed.

A third issue regulators have to address is the question of media ownership. Media owners face a number of perceptual problems (not faced by other members of the business elite). First, their power is *visible* because of the nature of their assets. Media moguls can be 'seen' as able to manipulate politicians, whereas influences and manipulation exercised by other business sectors takes place covertly. Because of its visibility it is relatively easy to create social 'panics' around the idea that a media owner wields influence. Secondly, politicians are dependent on a symbiotic relationship with the media. The denial of access to media coverage could effectively terminate a politician's career. Hence, politicians personally fear a concentration of media ownership because this reduces their own room for manoeuvre. Politicians consequently have a vested interest in preventing a concentration of media ownership. Further, when symbiotic relationships between politicians and media owners go sour, retribution will often be the result for both sides, with owners using their media to try to discredit a political party, and ruling parties altering media policies to 'punish' owners who have been unhelpful.

Those working in the media regulation industry have constantly to navigate such a milieu, with a range of pressure groups and politicians wanting to construct regulatory regimes that curtail the power of media owners. Arguments in favour of intervening into media ownership arrangements have been many and varied. There have been calls to prevent owners from accumulating too many media assets in one city (i.e. preventing the creation of local monopolies). On other occasions it is to prevent the accumulation of assets across too many media sectors (e.g. press and television). Some calls have been 'national' in scope, motivated by a desire to stop a mogul becoming too powerful in a particular nation state. Other calls have been 'politically' motivated, for example, when a new media mogul is regarded as being too conservative, which might threaten leftist opinion. And there have been arguments mounted on racial grounds, as in post-1994 South Africa, where media regulators intervene in favour of black owners. A growing concern at the dawn of the twenty-first century was the emergence of transnational (regional and global) media moguls such as Murdoch, Berlusconi and Hersant and this has led to pressure being asserted on some 'national' regulators to hem in these players.

Ultimately, ownership policies are always contextual and tied to the ever-shifting struggles being waged between factions (and individual members) of the political and business elite. Consequently, policies over ownership are changing depending on the state of play in such intra-elite struggles. What is clear is that regulatory decisions about media ownership are important in setting the framework within which media production occurs. Such decisions do have a significant influence on the meanings that are consequently made available.

A fourth theme is the issue of censorship. Cultural interventionists have never had a problem with creating state regulatory bodies charged with disallowing the reproduction and distribution of certain forms of media material. The only issue for the interventionists has been the question of parameters, that is deciding what can legitimately be censored. To a great extent censorship policies are highly contextual; they are dependent upon the relative strengths and weaknesses of the 'pro' and 'anti' censorship groups in a particular state at a particular point in time. Not surprisingly, the boundary between acceptable and unacceptable material continually shifts depending on the state of play in each context. However, within the Anglo world, pressures in favour of censorship have become partially decontextualized due to the emergence of transnational 'moral panics' which are now dispersed by a global media network. To some extent there is now a tendency for 'global' moral panics in the USA, the UK, Australia, etc. to feed off each other (see Dwyer & Stockbridge, 1999). Examples are events such as the 1999 Denver school massacre, or Jamie Bulger's murder in 1993, events which created transnational moral panics which contributed to anti-violence censorship across the whole Anglo world.

Overall, censorship questions have involved deciding how much the state should be allowed to interfere in determining media content with regard to protecting the interests of the state and matters of public decency. Censorship to protect the state has generally involved proscribing or publishing and disseminating state secrets and the disclosure of matters relating to intelligence-gathering. This form of censorship becomes more intense during periods of warfare. Overall, the British and Commonwealth governments have been more inclined to use media regulation to protect the state's interests than has the USA. When it comes to public decency, three themes have dominated the debate: violence, sex and hate speech. Different societies have produced different sets of criteria to measure what is deemed to be acceptable. Hence, Scandinavian countries tend to have a high tolerance for sexually explicit media material, but a low tolerance for violent material. The inverse is true in South Africa. Further, censorship criteria changes over time, as public mores shift. For example, nudity and sexual explicitness became more acceptable in Anglo society over the second half of the twentieth century. On the other hand, 'hate speech' (pertaining to race, ethnicity, gender, homosexuality, disability, etc.) is becoming increasingly unacceptable, and so is increasingly subject to regulation in Anglo societies – a form of censorship that has come to be called 'political correctness' or 'PC-speak').

Ultimately, those advocating censorship subscribe to a similar worldview as the Arnoldian cultural interventionists, believing in the rights of a cultural elite to decide what media content the non-elite can receive. They believe there are occasions when 'social good' (as defined by the interventionists) takes precedence over individual freedom. Civil libertarians, on the other hand, regard censorship as a curtailment of the individual's right to chose for him/herself, and equate censorship with authoritarian behaviour. Similarly, civil libertarians are disinclined to trust the politicians' definitions of 'state interests' because of the danger that ruling elites will conflate their own interests with those of the state. Alternatively, those advocating censorship have generally used the argument that freedom has boundaries, and beyond a certain point the collective has a right to prevent a 'social evil'. The definitions of 'social evil' that are enforced, shift over time as pro-censorship pressure groups emerge, form alliances, or decay and die. For example, in the 1950s anti-pornography advocates were generally conservative religious wowsers, but in the 1990s feminists were more likely to rile against pornography. It has also been argued that children are especially susceptible to 'bad influences' (associated with, for example, media violence) and are sexually vulnerable (with regard to, for example, paedophilia). These arguments of susceptibility and vulnerability are used to justify the intervention of censors to keep 'undesirable' (sexual and violent) content out of the media. Regulation is also justified by a belief that the media *are* able to exercise powerful influences over audiences. Pro-censorship arguments pertaining to violence and sexual content have a tendency to be recycled each time a new media form emerges. As a result, arguments that have previously been used to regulate films, and then television, are simply reactivated to justify regulating video games and the Internet.

The last part of the twentieth century saw the differences between the media and cultural regulatory regimes of the USA and Britain visibly narrowing as US pro-commercial (FCC) assumptions infiltrated the Commonwealth model, while the British propensity towards censorship began to infect the USA. These hybridized US/UK regulatory assumptions also spilled over into other contexts, such as the European Union, Australia, New Zealand and South Africa. The new hybrid model facilitated a globalization of both media hardware (delivery infrastructure) and software (content), therefore serving the interests of the global networkers.

Deregulation and re-regulation

The 1980s saw the beginning of a reappraisal of many assumptions underpinning media regulation. This shift was partly precipitated by a seachange that swept across the Anglo world when a New Right ideology (initially associated with Margaret Thatcher and Ronald Reagan) advocated a return to laissez-faire market regulation and the winding back of state interventionism. The 1980s and 1990s saw this post-Keynesian logic grow to a position of dominance in the Anglo world. This logic necessarily impacted on media and cultural regulation. The position of the interventionists and state regulatory managerialists became increasingly unfashionable. In the face of a spreading Thatcherism, media regulators operating in accordance with the 'British' (Keynesian/Arnoldian) model learned to bend in the face of the new discursive pressures. As a result, media sectors as far apart as Europe and Australasia were deregulated, with shifts towards 'market-driven' spectrum allocation and a winding back of state subsidies to PSB. By the mid-1990s an era of minimalist-deregulation had dawned regarding media production. However, there was one countervailing (and perhaps contradictory) trend, namely a growing propensity towards censorship, especially regarding sex and violence. These pressures towards heightened censorship were associated with a growing social conservatism within the same societies which were otherwise moving towards the winding back of state regulation and the 'nanny state'.

However, the deregulation (re-regulation?) of media sectors across the globe was not exclusively driven by the rise of the New Right in the US/UK heartland of the New World Order. Regulators do not only respond to political pressures; they also respond to technological developments. The global shake-up of media and telecommunications regulatory systems had much to do with the rapid diffusion of new media technologies, especially fibre-optic cable, satellites, new telephony switching systems and the digital language of computers. By the 1990s instantaneous global communication was possible via a digitized network, marrying cable, telephony, satellites and personal computers. What is more, as the 1990s progressed, the new technology facilitated a convergence of previously separate media forms – personal computers, television, film, video, photographs, print (newspapers, books and magazines), data-bases, telephony and audio-recordings could all be digitized and integrated into a single, globally networked communication system. This system facilitated the rise of the global networkers. Powerful politicians, such as US Vice President Al Gore, did much to help shift the regulatory framework to promote what Gore called the 'information superhighway', that is the digitized communications network facilitating the global exchange of the 'converged' media formats. Gore directed Clinton's administration into actively promoting 'the Net' on the assumption that, once built, people would use it (Pavlik, 1998: 240–41).

However, ultimately, the communicative changes that occurred involved more than merely a rapidly proliferating Internet and more than the promotional (PR) boosterism of those, such as Alvin Toffler (1990), who heralded the future advantages of a coming 'information age'. The technological impacts were actually deep and profound, shifting work practices into post-Fordist formats (Murray, 1990), facilitating the growth of new global media empires such as News Corporation (Herman & McChesney, 1997), creating truly global (multidirectional) flows of information, news and entertainment (Cunningham & Jacka, 1998), creating a new economy and a new set of lifestyles built upon the consumption of signification (Lash & Urry, 1994), and leading to the birth of a new underclass (Lash & Urry, 1994: Chapter 6) and a new elite of global networkers. Each of these technology-led impacts changed the environment within which the regulators worked and so helped set the parameters of the decisions they took. Hence, if radio gave birth to a second form of regulation, the digital revolution and globalization appears to have driven the birth of a third phase of media regulation seems to contain both deregulatory and re-regulatory imperatives.

The new media technologies made deregulation possible. The arrival of cable and satellites undercut the original 'airwaves policeman' reason for regulation in the 1920s. Broadcasters now had alternative modes of delivery, and the scarcity of airwaves was no longer an issue by which one could justify the state intervening to make allocative decisions. However, in the new media era, infrastructure development (building and launching satellites and laying cables) did become an issue, an issue which ultimately heralded the emergence of the notion of user-pays media (i.e. providers of satellites and cables wanted a return on the capital they invested). Eventually, satellite orbital spots filled up (a new form of 'scarcity'), requiring another (global) regulator – this time to allocate orbital positions. However, cable delivery knew no such scarcity. Cable made it (technologically) possible to side-step the allocative limitations imposed by broadcast regulators. This necessarily undercut the power media regulators had acquired. The disempowering of media regulators coincided with the rise of New Right governments. The coincidence of new technologies (making it possible to deregulate) and politicians wanting to deregulate sealed the fate of the regulatory interventionists.

Not surprisingly the 1980s and 1990s saw interventionists on the back foot and their institutional bases progressively wound back. The interventionist regulators were simply in no position to resist the downgrading of their roles as 'spectrum auctioning' replaced political decision-making. Similarly, PSB previously shielded by state subsidies and limited competition (thanks to spectrum allocation decisions) faced an increasingly uncertain future as 'market-based' regulation and commercial competition became the new mantras of media policy-makers. The old purist (Reithian) PSB model seems unlikely to survive. However, the Germans may possibly have found a model offering PSB a survival route in the form of the 1987 State Treaty on the Reorganization of Broadcasting. Effectively, both the German PSB sector (ARD and ZDF) and commercial broadcasters created a 'bouquet' (mix) of programming. They also share a joint satellite and a terrestrial delivery system (Dyson et al., 1988: 148). This acquiesces to the pressures of commercialism but preserves a space for PSB. It also institutionalizes the blurring of media boundaries generated by the arrival of the new media technologies.

In essence, digital convergence has eaten away at the media boundaries that long underpinned the regulatory framework. Those investing capital in satellites and cable sought ways to maximize profit, and hence had a vested interest in speeding up boundary-blurring and a winding back of regulatory interventionism so they could get into the multiple businesses of television, pay-per-view video, audio delivery (radio/music), data delivery, Internet services, etc. This coincided with pressures to deregulate telephony. At the start of the twentieth century, the economics of telephony made monopoly-carriers the most rational delivery vehicle. Throughout the British Empire, state-owned telephone corporations built the infrastructure needed to tie the Empire together. British Empire telephony regulation created regional monopolies in order to facilitate the subsidization of infrastructure development in non-economically viable areas (such as the Australian outback). Similarly, US regulators allowed the development of a (non-state) telephony monopoly on the understanding that cross-subsidization took place from economically profitable areas to non-viable areas. But with the arrival of the new communications technologies and digital convergence, telephony became massively profitable, given that it lay at the very heart of the new 'information economy'. Not surprisingly, pressure mounted to break up the old telephony monopolies and give new players access to the profitable, infrastructural 'heart' of the information revolution (Cohen, 1992: 69–77). The pressures for media and telephony deregulation coincided and intersected. And given the growing convergences between telephony and other media forms, a merged process of re-regulating the media and telephony has became commonplace during the third wave of media regulation. An excellent example of this was the creation of a new French regulator in 1986, the Commission for Communications and Liberties (CNCL). The CNCL represented a major shift in French regulatory thinking because it involved implementing an FCC-type commercialism and a winding back of the powers of the regulatory interventionists (Dyson et al., 1988: 122–3). The CNCL was also given powers over both telecommunications and broadcasting, including cable, satellite and programming standards.

If a defining moment for the third phase of media regulation is sought in the Anglo world, it is perhaps best exemplified by the British 1990 Broadcast Act which was introduced by the Thatcher government and encapsulates both the deregulatory and re-regulatory imperatives of the third wave of media regulation. The Act represented a key moment in the Thatcherist drive to 'deregulate' the British media system by introducing an auction system for commercial television licences. Access to capital, rather than 'political' decision-making, would henceforth drive the allocation process. Yet at the same time the 1990 Act granted the Independent Television Commission (ITC) and the (new) Broadcasting Standards Council the powers to regulate public 'decency'. This effectively constituted a 're-regulatory' imperative and so ran counter to the Thatcherist drive to deregulate and wind back the state. Overall, the Thatcherist notion of 'market' (laissez-faire) regulation, as contained in the 1990 Act, entailed a radical winding back of the powers of British media regulators. This 'deregulatory' notion spread. Other Commonwealth states quickly followed Britain's lead in winding back the powers of cultural interventionists (within both the broadcast regulatory machines and the PSB sectors). Interestingly, this shift was not only implemented by New Right ideologists. In Australia, for example, the shift to a 'market-driven', auction-based regulatory model (institutionalized when the Australian Broadcasting Authority (ABA) replaced the Australian Broadcast Tribunal (ABT)) was actually implemented by a Labor government.

Why deregulation?

The emergence of a third (deregulatory) wave of media regulation demonstrates the complex pattern of the interrelationships between media technology, media forms and power elites when it comes to setting policy. The process of media deregulation was intimately bound up with the rise of the New Right and their ideological commitment to wind back state interventionism in the economy. However, the New Right was simply responding to the contextual possibilities emerging from the new information technologies and growth of global information capitalism. Emerging computer, satellite and cable technologies were quickly exploited by (post-managerialist) entrepreneurs who created the new global communicative networks, new (post-Fordist) work practices and new sites for the generation of wealth. By the late 1980s these networking entrepreneurs were already coalescing into a new business elite which was able to influence the political machineries of the OECD countries. Rupert Murdoch is a good illustration of the global reach of this new elite, given his considerable influence in Washington, London and Canberra. These global networkers necessarily had a vested interest in policies which helped speed up the development of global networking infrastructures and policies facilitating a removal of tariff barriers and regulatory machineries, given that the existing national regulatory regimes generally restricted their entry into new markets and protected their (managerialist) competitors. Throughout the 1990s the elite driving global information capitalism was immensely successful in re-working regulatory agendas across the world in accordance with the principles of commercialization, free trade, de-bureaucratization, and the promotion of media convergences. Also, notions of regional and global regulation, rather than nationally-based regulation, were successfully promoted. All of this helped to create new spaces and opportunities for the emerging global networker elite, while winding back the spaces available for managerialists and Keynesian interventionists.

As the parameters set by the regulatory machinery changed, including media regulation, so the culture industry also changed. And as the industry shifted, so to did the content.

CHAPTER 4

Sites for Making Meaning III: Commercialization and the 'Death of the Public Sphere'

Thatcherism and Reaganism promoted a winding back of Keynesian state interventionism and a return to laissez-faire market regulation. The 1980s and 1990s saw this post-Keynesian logic grow to dominance in the Anglo world. In the media sector, deregulation also became fashionable, with a shift towards a 'market-driven' allocation of spectrum and a winding back of state subsidies to PSB. An ascendant New Right promoted commercialization of the cultural sphere, contending that commercialization resulted in 'choice' and 'consumer sovereignty' over media content. The argument was that media operating according to commercial principles were compelled to deliver the products demanded by audiences, or face bankruptcy. Those opposing this commercialism argued that these shifts were undermining the public sphere and threatened democracy itself.

The 'public sphere' notion has been a feature of the Anglo media policy debate since the mid-1980s. It was introduced into the debate by a British left-wing intelligentsia demoralized by the rise of Thatcherism and the resulting commercialization and privatization of cultural production. The 'public sphere' notion, borrowed from Habermas, developed into something of a knee-jerk catch phrase, effectively meaning a 'social democratic' alternative to New Right-driven deregulation/ regulation of the media and telecommunications sector. Habermas's notion became Anglicized and reworked by cultural interventionists concerned with Thatcherist moves (initially in Britain, but spreading to other Commonwealth contexts) to deconstruct mechanisms for state intervention in the media sector. Four issues especially concerned the interventionist intelligentsia: shifts towards 'de-politicizing' media regulatory decision-making (as seen in the 'auctioning' of spectrum); the winding back of state subsidies to PSB; the drive towards commercializing the culture industry; and the emergence of global media corporations, which was seen to facilitate global 'commercialized' media flows which undercut 'national cultures'. These developments undercut the influence, power and employment prospects of the left-wing intelligentsia and the professional managers, as PSB was downsized and media regulation mechanisms wound back. Social democrats argued (correctly) that Thatcherist commercialization of cultural production undercut the 'spaces' available for 'public' debate and social (democrat) control over media content. Commercialization and globalization were seen to produce the 'death of the public sphere'. This was equated with a de-democratization and re-feudalization of social decision-making since decisions were removed from 'public' scrutiny (parliaments, boards, bureaux and state corporations) and placed within the realm of 'private spaces' (private commercial businesses).

The intellectual most responsible for introducing the 'public sphere' notion into the media debate was Nicholas Garnham. He argued that a market allocation of cultural resources, combined with the destruction of public service media, threatened 'public communication', which he suggested, lay at the heart of the democratic process (Garnham, 1986: 37–8). Garnham pointed to a string of negatives associated with this process of commercialization, namely, a growing focus on privatized domestic consumption built around the television set, the creation of 'information rich' and 'information poor' sectors and the replacement of 'national' cultural spheres with an international media market (Garnham, 1986: 38). Garnham suggested that Thatcher's winding back of PSB narrowed the national public space for debate. This policy, he argued, served the emergent global capitalist elite, that is 'it is in the interests of the controllers of multinational capital to keep nation-states and their citizens in a state of disunity and dysfunctional ignorance united only by market structures within which such capital can freely flow, while at the same time they develop their own private communication networks' (Garnham, 1986: 52). So, for Garnham, killing national 'public sphere', and fragmenting the 'social', was a precondition for creating the 'international space' needed by those building the new form of capitalism associated with the global information economy (and globalization).

Within Garnham's cosmology, there seemed to be an almost deliberate (elite-directed 'conspiratorial'?) dimension to the process of destroying democratic 'public spheres' and the state interventionist bureaucracies built up under Keynesian social democracy. Garnham's (1986) solution was to defend, at all costs, public spaces such as PSB in order to facilitate collective political decision-making (where a vision of the 'public good' could be constructed). In the mid-1980s, Garnham wanted to defend *national* public spaces. In effect, his project was defensive and even conservative; it was a call to return to the earlier 'national' and 'managerialist' logics of Keynesian and Reithian interventionism. However, a few years later, Garnham's position had shifted to a call to construct a *global* public sphere as a means of building a 'global community' and of creating the mechanics for this community to make the global (capitalist) elite accountable to public scrutiny (Garnham, 1992: 371–2). Effectively, Garnham took the (social democratic) notion of 'state-managerialist' intervention as a means of hemming in commercialism at the national level, and transposed it to the global level. He aimed to build mechanisms for a supranational democracy by creating a global public sphere which could potentially be made up of a 'federation' of 'local' public spheres (Garnham, 1992: 371).

What is the public sphere?

Habermas introduced the concept of 'the public sphere as a sphere which mediates between society and state, in which the public organizes itself as the bearer of public opinion, accords with the principle of the public sphere – that principle of public information which once had to be fought for against the arcane policies of monarchies and which since that time has made possible the democratic control of state activities' (Habermas, 1974: 50). The public sphere was a communicative fulcrum for a small revolutionary minority, namely, the emergent European middle classes ('free citizens'). These bourgeoisie/burgers used the new Gutenberg-inspired media to further their interests and mobilize against the then ruling feudal elites. The result was a print-mediated public sphere (Habermas, 1992: 406), with bourgeois print media giving rise to reading societies and discussion groups during the eighteenth and early nineteenth centuries. This produced 'a relatively dense network of public communication' (Habermas, 1992: 423) in Germany, France and Britain – that is the bourgeois 'public sphere'. This public sphere played a crucial, facilitative role in sparking the bourgeois revolutions that eventually dislodged feudal hegemony from Europe. The public sphere was thus a communicative fulcrum within which the bourgeoisie/burgers learned to constitute themselves into a counter-hegemonic force and generate collective (public) power. Significantly, the public sphere was not mass communication; it was active communication by and for a small revolutionary minority:

> Early bourgeois public spheres were composed of narrow segments of the European population, mainly educated, propertied men, and they conducted a discourse not only exclusive of others, but prejudicial to the interests of those excluded. Yet the transformation of the public sphere that Habermas describes required its continual expansion to include ever more participants (as well as the development of large-scale social organizations as mediators of individual participation). He suggests that ultimately this inclusivity brought degeneration in the quality of discourse. (Calhoun, 1992: 3)

So, once the bourgeoisie overthrew feudalism and created early capitalist society, they reorganized governance in such a way that public debate produced social decision-making instead of governance being the prerogative of a monarch. Hence the exercise of bourgeois capitalist power became public (regulated by a public debating forum), instead of the property of a feudal elite (who had exercised power through private decision-making). But in the process, the public sphere, as dialogical communication, was lost. Over time, the public sphere enmeshed with 'representivity' and managerialism, becoming merely a means to legitimate managerialist ruling elites. Habermas bemoaned the resulting 'pseudo' democracy which, he said, effectively constituted a 'depoliticized public realm' (Habermas, 1976: 37). Hence, by the late twentieth century, although there was the appearance of political participation in Western democracies, the effects of offering voters 'pseudo' choices meant that politicians faced increasingly cynical electorates. In Western, two-party systems, the 'choices' began to look increasingly similar, with both parties in societies like the USA, the UK and Australia effectively offering only marginally different versions of the same elite-directed managerialism. One consequence has been that Keynesian interventionists found themselves unable to muster enough voter support to block the processes of winding back the (managerialist) social-democratic state.

Habermas contended that this bourgeois public sphere went into decline after the consolidation of the bourgeois hegemony (Habermas,

1989: Parts IV and V). This Habermasian perspective derives from the Frankfurt School. To understand this position one needs to recognize the importance of 'the dialectical imagination' in Frankfurt School thinking (Jay, 1973). The 'mechanism' of dialectical conflict lay at the heart of Frankfurt School thinking. It regarded change as inherently socially 'good'. Society progressed because for every idea (thesis) there was necessarily an alternative perspective (antithesis). Hence, dialectical conflict (the thesis–antithesis clash) was, for the Frankfurt School, both 'natural' and socially 'useful' since it prevented social stagnation and was the driving mechanism of human 'progress', with 'progress' being equated with the 'syntheses' emerging from conflict. Adorno, the Frankfurt School's founder, regarded the bourgeoisie/burgers as the key 'antithesis' of eighteenth- and early nineteenth-century Europe, the feudal order being 'the thesis'. These middle classes drove progressive change in Europe and its colonies, for example the American and French Revolutions. However, once the bourgeoisie were in control, they became a conservative force (becoming the new 'thesis'). In other words, when the bourgeoisie were a (minority) progressive force struggling against the feudal order, their public sphere was a dynamic and exciting communicative space in which antithetical ideas were produced and circulated. However, once the bourgeoisie achieved hegemonic control, their public sphere(s) became a communicative fulcrum for generating and circulating ('conservative') ideas which helped to regulate their hegemony. Adorno and Horkheimer (1979) and Marcuse (1964b) regarded this conservative public sphere as 'affirmative culture', that is culture necessarily affirming the existing hegemonic order. This pessimistic vision underpinned the Frankfurt School's critique of the culture industry, an industry they believed produced a 'one-dimensional' culture precisely because oppositional (antithetical) ideas were absent. In essence, once the bourgeoisie became rulers, an undialectical public sphere resulted. This was especially so after bureaucratic managerialism emerged and much capitalist-bourgeois power slipped into the hands of professional managers. But, even if under 'managerialist capitalism' social decision-making (within parliaments and public boards) was subject to 'public scrutiny' (as opposed to the 'private' decision-making of feudalism), the Frankfurt School had a jaundiced view of both social-democratic 'managerialist capitalism' and 'Soviet managerialism'. Both managerialisms effectively represented post-bourgeois, post-revolutionary 'public spheres'. And although both systems claimed to be accountable to the 'people', both constituted manipulative forms of communication. From a Frankfurt School perspective, no 'dialectically active' public sphere existed under managerialism in either its capitalist or Soviet forms.

This 'dialectical' dimension appears to have been missed by Garnham and other cultural interventionists when they used Habermas's notion in their attempts to defend a 1920s–1970s' model of 'social democratic' media regulation and PSB against Thatcherist laissez-faireism. The problem is that the public sphere, as discussed by Habermas, was 'progressive' only in a particular context – during the struggle against feudalism. From a Frankfurt School perspective, it is problematic to regard Reithian/Arnoldian PSB or the media regulatory machinery developed by Keynesian capitalism as a 'progressive' public sphere in the Habermasian sense.

Commercialization – a critique

Certainly, the Frankfurt School and Habermas would, like Garnham and other cultural interventionists, be deeply concerned at the growing commercialization of the media. In fact, there are compelling reasons to look again at the Frankfurt School's critique of the commercial culture industry given the way in which commercialism is emerging as the key organizing principle of the media and cultural production under post-1990s global capitalism. Despite the fact that the Frankfurt School produced its critique of the commercial culture industry many decades ago, it retains surprising explanatory power.

The Frankfurt School was highly critical of the twentieth-century culture industry. If the public sphere of the eighteenth century constituted 'good' communication (because of the bourgeoisie's 'revolutionary' credentials at that stage), then the commercialized culture industry is the exact opposite (because those who drive this industry are no longer a 'progressive' social force. Instead, they are part of a ruling group concerned with maintaining its rule). For the Frankfurt School, 'good' (dialectical) communication involves debate and dialogue because this constitutes the 'machinery' of an ongoing process of social change. There needs to be a 'communicative space' for the expression of oppositional ideas and 'negation', that is, a space for 'the antithesis' to emerge. Following Adorno and Horkheimer's lead, the Frankfurt School argued that the culture industry was inherently undialectical and one-dimensional, producing 'mass culture' made by an elite group of professional communicators. This mass culture is presented 'ready-made' to audiences.

The Frankfurt School regarded this as 'bad' communication precisely because it encourages audiences to be passive, uncritical and dependent on professional communicators. (This is the opposite of 'popular culture', which is the organic culture people produce for themselves.) So mass culture results from top-down, planned communication geared towards producing 'distracting', non-dialogical communication. The Frankfurt School, using Freudian notions, argued that mass culture was a form of reverse psychoanalysis. If Freudian therapy involves encouraging a people to 'confront' themselves and their circumstances, the culture industry does exactly the opposite; it encourages people not to think about themselves or their circumstances but rather to immerse themselves in the 'pre-arranged harmony' of 'distractions', 'escapism' and manufactured leisure. Adorno and Horkheimer lamented the way in which the culture industry removed real choice, so that people were only offered the 'freedom to choose what is always the same . . . [and inducted into an advertising-led world of] . . . shining white teeth and freedom from body odor. The triumph of advertising in the culture industry is that consumers feel compelled to buy and use its products even though they see through them' (Adorno & Horkheimer, 1979: 167). Under this system, news becomes 'infotainment'. Commodified culture makes people feel comfortable because it requires no effort and does not challenge them to think. It is a culture designed to relax, pacify and provide easy answers and ready-made opinion. The audience is, in effect, 'cretinized'. Instead of participating in an active dialogue, commodified culture immerses people into one-dimensional, 'affirmative culture', where they are offered a pre-arranged 'false' reconciliation of social contradictions, that is reconciliations serving the interests of the hegemonically dominant. Pre-arranged harmonies precisely involve confirming the existing order (the 'thesis') and avoid antithetical ideas that might fundamentally challenge this order. The Frankfurt School believed that a commercialized culture industry effectively closed off the possibilities for dialogue (dialectical conflict) because intellectuals (such as journalists), including those with oppositional ideas, are forced to sell their skills to the culture industry.

For the Frankfurt School, the culture industry is a huge 'patronage system' which turns intellectuals into 'cultural workers' within culture-making bureaucracies. In the process intellectuals are 'tamed' – given that they are paid to produce products 'appropriate' to the needs of their employers. The 'alternative' is unemployment. If one opts out of such employment because one harbours 'oppositional ideas', 'antithetical' ideas are thereby rendered voiceless anyway. Alternatively, if one works for the culture industry, one necessarily abides by the discursive rules and 'managerialist' practices of commercialized cultural production. Either way, discursive closure is the result. Hence, the commercialization of cultural production results in 'distorted communication' when measured against Habermas's dialectical notion of the public sphere. Enzensberger (1974) disputed this logic, arguing that it was not possible to 'tame' all intellectuals: creative people would always find a way to promote oppositional ideas.

In similar vein, Frankfurt School logic can be used to challenge the notion of consumer sovereignty, a notion used to justify the enhanced commercialization of late twentieth-century cultural production. Those within the culture industry who mobilize the notion of consumer sovereignty argue that professionals running commercial media simply provide the public with what they want (as consumers). However, when operating a commercial *mass* media system, it is necessary to deliver to advertisers the largest possible audience of those with disposable income. This skews media content in two, interrelated ways. First, the middle classes are the 'ideal' audience for advertisers seeking a general mass public with disposable income and a propensity to consume. Consequently, mass media managers will seek to maximize the production of content appealing to these middle classes, so as to attract these people and thereby attract advertisers. Hence, commercial media systems tend to 'avoid' content that alienates these audiences. Secondly, when conceptualizing the 'mass consumer market', professional communicators use the notion of 'the public'. Effectively, 'the public' is a shorthand means of conceptualizing 'the average' person being targeted. There is no such average person. It is a pure intellectual construct. But it is a construct with enormous consequences for media content because it produces the myth of an 'audience-type' that journalists believe they are writing for. In broad terms, it tends to result in media content catering to a 'bland average' – content designed to avoid offending anyone. This eliminates 'difference' in favour of a 'uniformity' geared towards 'middle of the road' opinion. Ultimately, this reduces the range of ideas in circulation. Hence, commercial media content has a propensity towards a middle-class sameness which conveniently confirms the discursive needs of managerialist capitalism. From a Frankfurt School perspective, this is socially problematic because commercialized mass media are seen to be closed, uni-dimensional and unable to provide the sort of open dialogical space which can help generate dialectically-driven social change.

However, the last decades of the twentieth century saw the rapid growth of niche media – for example, proliferating cable television channels – precipitated by both new media technologies and post-Fordist production methods (which shifts the emphasis away from production geared towards mass markets and towards niche marketing). In this regard post-Fordist niche media appear to hold out at least some potential for de-massifying media/cultural production and to provide some potential for a culture industry that facilitates multi-voicing. At first sight this might appear to create the conditions for the re-emergence of small dialogical spaces (such as Habermas's public sphere, or a Platonic dialogue). However, this is not what is emerging, for at least three reasons. First, there is the propensity for audiences to only pay attention to 'their' niche. Hence, post-Fordist commercial media do not provide the sort of 'shared' dialogical communicative space the Frankfurt School requires for its dialectically-driven 'public sphere' model of social change. Secondly, it is a communicative form that is part of what has been called a 're-feudalization' process – as public spaces, whose regulation was previously subject to public scrutiny (through parliaments, public boards, etc.), are shifted into private ownership. The growing privatizing of public space has spread to a number of sectors, ranging from airwaves spectrum and education sites to shopping malls. These privatized spaces are designed for commercial profit, not the facilitation of public debate, and the new owners have no vested interest in ever allowing their private spaces to be used for social dialogue. Thirdly, because the new niche media are mostly part of a network of privately-owned enterprises, most niches are still run according to the logic of top-down, manipulative communication, produced by professional communicators who target that niche to generate profit for their employers. Increasingly, these employers are global media corporations. The logic of a commercialized culture industry remains in place but is now deployed in a more sophisticated way. Instead of producing a single 'mass' message, multiple 'niche' messages are now produced. Murdoch's News Corporation has emerged as something of a model for this new form of neo-feudalistic cultural production. Various (privatized) niches are part of a single networked entity, manipulated and commercialized communication predominates and the whole network 'revolves' around a nodal 'coordinative' fulcrum of the 'Head Office', which has a similar networking role as that previously played by feudal lords in the pre-bourgeois era. Murdoch is happy for each of his empire's niche components to run autonomously. He uses communication professionals, who understand each sector, to 'work' that niche for him. His power derives not from top-down control of each niche of his empire, but rather from the accumulative influence of reaching into so many different spheres. Allowing for 'difference' becomes a source of strength, just as it was for feudal lords in the middle ages. It is an organizational-style that is neo-feudal rather than managerialist. It also remains 'distorted' communication from a Habermasian perspective because it involves 'the manipulative deployment of media power to procure mass loyalty, consumer demand and "compliance" with systemic imperatives . . . [as opposed to dialogue concerned with] . . . the communicative generation of legitimate power' (Habermas, 1992: 452).

Alternatives to commercialization

For those concerned about the commercialization, globalization and neo-feudalizing of the culture industry, it is doubtful that viable alternatives can be found by looking backwards to dated managerialist approaches to communication. Twentieth-century managerialism does not have a good record when it comes to producing communicative spheres which allow for an unrestricted dialogical sharing of ideas. Managerialism produces manipulative communication. Communication produced by managerialist elites is inherently one-dimensional because it is skewed in favour of whichever section of the managerialist elite is driving that communicative system.

Twentieth-century managerialists have created five major forms of manipulative, one-dimensional communication: commercialized mass communication (produced by business elites); Soviet state propaganda (produced by the communist *apparatchiks*); fascist propaganda (produced by far right corporatist alliances); 'development' communication' (produced by third world Westernized elites); and 'social democratic' communication (run by intellectual elites motivated by Reithian, Arnoldian and Keynesian interventionist logics). The latter has spawned a variety of 'political correctnesses' within PSB and educational institutions. So the idea that PSB represents a Habermasian public sphere (Garnham, 1986: 49) seems rather dubious. Social democratic interventionism produced just another form of managerialist one-dimensionalism. Habermas himself says: 'the basis and sources of an informal formation of opinion in autonomous public spheres now can no longer be answered with reference to the status guarantees of the social-welfare state and with the holistic demand for the political self-organization of society' (Habermas, 1992: 452).

At heart, the 'public sphere' issue seems to be about creating alternatives to one-dimensional, narrowed, manipulated or closed communication. The New World Order that emerged in the 1990s appears to be bringing in its wake a shift to a globally commercialized communication network, which represents a particular form of one-dimensionality. Whether communicative alternatives to this new closure can or will be built remains to be seen. An alternative model would presumably entail some form of institutionalized dialogue which facilitates a free exchange of ideas (and conflict between contending positions) and a process whereby collective decisions can be made on the basis of alternatives thrown up by the debates and conflicts. The dialogical/dialectical process would also need to be seen as ongoing, that is all decisions need to be seen as temporal, contextually-bound, 'tentative' and open to ongoing challenge and re-evaluation. No participant or interest group can be allowed to freeze any past decision into a 'permanent fixture' or 'truth' because this would imply the curtailment of dialogical engagement. Such dialogical spheres appear to have existed. One is the bourgeois 'public sphere' as described by Habermas. Another is the *ecclesia* or assembly of citizens of Athens in ancient Greece. Athenian citizens were expected to participate directly in governing their city-state by attending public gatherings (where issues were discussed and voted on) and to take on any office that was allocated by drawing lots. Plato's ideas on governance, as set out in *The Republic*, were developed from this Athenian model of a 'dialogical' *ecclesia*.

But significantly, both the bourgeois public sphere and Greek *ecclesia* were not mass communication forms. And both were based on exclusionary logics. Hence, the public sphere was the creation of a revolutionary middle-class minority (of urbanized, educated, propertied men). All other social interests were excluded, including plebeians, peasants, women and, of course, the feudal aristocracy and clergy. Similarly, only Athenian citizens could participate in the *ecclesia*. This excluded the bulk of Athenian residents because most were slaves and therefore not citizens. A quorum in an *ecclesia* was a mere 6,000 citizens. Further, both the public sphere and *ecclesia* had limited life-spans as functioning 'social dialogues'. Ultimately they became 'deformed' by, among other things, the development of professional, manipulative communicators ('rhetoricians' in ancient Greece), politicians skilled in swaying mass opinion ('demagogues' in ancient Greece), politicians skilled at setting the agenda so as to limit what was discussed (the 'boule' or steering committee set the *ecclesia*'s agenda), and the power of patronage (in terms of which wealthy people could manipulate key players).

It is possible that social dialogues (public spheres) that facilitate an unmanipulated sharing of ideas and the formation of citizen-driven decision-making may be a pipe-dream. Contemporary notions of citizenship involve non-discriminatory access to membership, democratic participation in social decision-making for all members and reciprocal rights and duties that are equal for all members. But this raises a number of problems. First, today's societies are demographically huge, (involving millions of citizens), making it difficult to see how one could organize real, unrestricted dialogical participation (as opposed to pseudo-participation). Today's societies have also become extremely complex, involving a plethora of interest groups, ethnicities, creeds, etc. Homogeneous populations are increasingly hard to find. This raises a number of issues. For example, if decision-making is by way of majority-voting, how is 'difference' accommodated? How are minorities (at best) given a real 'voice'? And how (at worst) are they protected from the tyranny of majoritarianism? How does one create the spaces for 'difference'? How are individual liberties protected against infringements generated by collective decision-making and/or surveillance which has been legitimated by collective decision-making? Is it realistic to expect that manipulation of communication flows and decision-making fora by elites (especially wealthy elites) can be prevented or even tamed?

If these sorts of issues were difficult to solve when nation states were the norm, they are even more difficult to solve now, as globalization gains momentum, because 'publics' are swelling to enormous sizes and the new (networked) elites are learning to build global power bases that 'defy' regulation in a world that is 'feudalizing' globally. Perhaps 'managerialist regulation' is simply no longer possible given the new complexities? And could it be that our societies have simply grown too big for us to even entertain the pretence that citizens can any longer participate in social dialogues in which they can exercise real influence? Perhaps the notion that public spheres can be built within global information capitalism is a myth? Maybe population size and complexity now preclude anything except pseudo-participation, and that we are now left with only elite decision-making and elite manipulation of communication flows?

But to accept this would be to slip into a Frankfurt School pessimism of the sort that Habermas, for one, tried to escape by proposing to build an 'ideal communication' situation. Perhaps one should instead be reminded of Hans Enzensberger's (1974: 5) insight that as information and communication become more central to the economy, the possibilities for dialectical social change actually increase because the information economy depends upon creative productivity. Any attempt to block this creativity will undermine the information economy itself. In essence, communicative openness becomes necessary for economic growth, which means the potential spaces for possible antithetical thinking may actually increase. From an Enzensbergian perspective, a networked neo-feudal system may actually be a progressive development because it potentially adds new spaces where change-agents can operate. If it seems increasingly difficult to regulate (nationally) so as to hem in the commercial networking elite, perhaps it is equally difficult to hem in those who would seek to challenge global information capitalism and the New World Order?

Global information capitalists will be compelled (by their need to produce profits and coordinate their global interests) to continually expand the world's digital communication networks. The sheer size of the network makes it too large to control or to monitor or limit its uses fully. So just as the old bourgeois revolutionary 'public sphere' grew out of the Gutenberg print revolution, so too may new 'human interactivities' grow as a by-product of using the (as yet unimagined) possibilities inherent in the evolving digital networks. For those who wish to challenge the power of the emerging networker elite, there is no need to look backwards to past communicative interventions such as the bourgeois public sphere, the social democratic managerialist regulation or the 'Reithian', 'nation-building' logics of PSB. Instead, Enzensberger would propose looking forward and seeking out the new 'communicative spaces' and potential contradictions as they emerge.

CHAPTER 5

Striving for Discursive Closure: The Struggle for Hegemony

One approach to media studies posits communicative 'ideals' and then measures existent communication against these ideals. Within the Western tradition, the ideal has generally involved striving for communicative 'openness' and the facilitation of 'sharing'. This intellectual tradition's roots stretch back to the Socratic/Platonic notion of dialogue which emerged in ancient Greece in the fifth century BC. Not surprisingly, existent communication is found wanting when measured against such ideals. Habermas's public sphere represents a contemporary idealism. However, there is another way to explore the nature of communication, namely, by focusing on real communication flows. Real communication flows involve an ongoing struggle between those who wish to 'restrict', 'narrow', 'close' and 'manipulate' communication flows and those who have a vested interest in resisting such closures and manipulations. There is no need to privilege one of these as 'better'. Rather, both those striving for 'closure' and 'resistance' can simply be viewed as the 'necessary' and 'inevitable' outcomes of humans organizing themselves. If one adopts the 'trying for closure' versus 'resisting closure' approach to analysing communication, six questions emerge as a systematic way of unravelling the nature of cultural and media production: (1) What is the nature of the context within which the communication is taking place?; (2) Which group(s) is socially and politically dominant?; (3) How did it get to be the dominant/powerful group?; (4) How does it stay dominant/powerful?; (5) How does it manage the discourse(s) within its society?; and (6) Who is resisting the managed discourse(s)? Together, these six questions provide a basic route-map for unravelling the struggle for hegemony.

A first concern when trying to understand any communicative actor (and his/her discourses) is the context within which s/he produces discourse. Any attempt to analyse the role of communication within hegemony-building must necessarily start by locating the contextually-bound variables impacting upon the actors involved. Essentially, communication does not happen in a vacuum. Actors in the struggle for hegemony (and counter-hegemony), and their discourses and practices, are borne of a specific set of material, subjective, historical and demographic circumstances, and these circumstances are continually shifting. Because human actions and ideas are not free-floating but rooted, any attempt to understand communication (and its residues) out of context will produce only a partial understanding. Mapping out the context as the first step helps to focus attention on the 'lived' details of human interaction, which necessarily adds richness. It also acts as an inoculation against 'idealism', and against seeing communicative products (e.g. a theory or idea) as 'universally' valid instead of as a particularistic construct, created in a specific time and place to deal with a specific set of circumstances.

A key contextual variable is power. For anyone concerned with exploring the relationships between power, communication and context, Gramsci's notion of hegemony becomes invaluable. In this regard Gwyn Williams's definition of hegemony is useful.

> By 'hegemony' Gramsci seems to mean a sociopolitical situation, in his terminology a 'moment', in which the philosophy and practice of a society fuse or are in equilibrium; an order in which a certain way of life and thought is dominant, in which one concept of reality is diffused throughout society in all its institutional and private manifestations, informing with its spirit all taste, morality, customs, religious and political principles, and all social relations, particularly in their intellectual and moral connotation. An element of direction and control, not necessarily conscious, is implied. (Williams, 1960: 587)

Seeing social communication as embedded in a struggle over power draws attention away from 'ideals' and (contextually-specific) 'morality', and locates attention instead on the impact that 'lived battles' over hegemony have on communication. The notion of hegemony helps remove moralism ('idealism') from the picture because hegemonic analysis recognizes that, for those in power, striving to close discourse (whether conscious or unconscious) is sensible, just as for those not in power it is often (but not always) sensible to resist such closures. To some extent, then, Gramsci's work is an extension of the 'non-idealism' found in Machiavelli's *The Prince*.

Becoming hegemonic

Becoming hegemonic means becoming the dominant or 'leading' group (or, more likely, becoming the dominant alliance of groups) in a society. This entails becoming the 'ruling group' (or elite) whose 'concept of reality' then sets the tone. Hegemonic groups are effectively able to set the over-arching intellectual agenda in a given society and manipulate dominant discourses. Becoming the ruling group appears to require being simultaneously successful in three spheres: first, building and maintaining a working set of political alliances (i.e. constructing a 'ruling group'); secondly, successfully generating consent among the ruled (i.e. ruling group 'legitimacy'); and thirdly, building coercive capacity (e.g. policing, courts, prisons and possibly a military force) to generate 'authority'. The more legitimacy rulers have, the less coercion they need to employ. However, even the most legitimate systems rely on some coercive underpinning, even if it is only the *threat* that the police/legal machine *can* use if individuals break the law. Each of these three hegemonic functions relies on communication and intellectual-organization, but since the process of acquiring legitimacy and consent is entirely communicative, it is the function most obviously associated with media production. Ultimately, becoming politically and socially dominant means that ruling groups must successfully learn, organize and mobilize two key skills: the art of coercion and the art of communication/negotiation. (The latter is used to both 'politic' alliances and build 'consent'.)

Significantly, the fulcrum for hegemonic-communicative labour has become increasingly media-ized (and 'public relations-ized') over the course of the twentieth century. By the start of the twenty-first century, becoming socially and politically dominant required an ability to play the 'media game', ranging from the print media, to radio and television. More recently, the Internet has become a feature of this media game. Not surprisingly, professional communicators ('spin doctors', PR people (PRs) and communication advisors) are now key people in the political machinery ruling groups must build. Smith (1989) has discussed the central role of the media game within US politics. In some senses the very art of ruling has become 'media-ized' (and televisualized) and dependent upon successful image-making and discourse management. This has necessarily impacted on the nature of those staffing (OECD) hegemonic groups. To join the ranks of the socially dominant it has become increasingly important to be able to play media-ized politics, or at least to know how to get others to play it for you.

If sketching out the broader social context is a good starting point for analysing media production, then the next useful questions when studying social communication are: What is the nature of the socially dominant group within the context under examination? And how did it get to be dominant?

Industrial (and post-industrial) societies are highly complex entities, involving the interactions of millions of individuals and many interest groups. Taking the lead (becoming hegemonic) in such complex entities requires constructing alliances that draw together players from a range of social sectors (e.g. business, law, media, health, security, education, labour, etc.) and demographic or belief 'groupings'. Becoming a ruling elite is hard work.

Effectively, a political elite, whose job it becomes to coordinate the various sectoral interests of the wider ruling elite has to be constructed and then be held together through a process of 'politicking', negotiating and bargaining. This political/negotiating task has become professionalized and institutionalized within a range of sites, including parliaments, boards, bureaux and, more recently, transnational fora such as the World Trade Organization (WTO). It is an intensely communicative occupation, with those specializing in hegemonic politicking continually alternating between cooperative communication (where compromise is negotiated) through to various forms of conflictual communication (civil warfare is the most extreme form of conflictual communication because negotiated compromise has not been reached). In part, alliance construction involves producing and circulating successful, internally-directed discourses, that is discourses which hold teams together and keep such teams focused on a particular vision of 'governance' and collaboration. So the birth of a successful hegemonic group needs to be understood as a contextually unique creation emerging from good leadership and good communication skills. Hegemonies also emerge from contextually unique sets of synchronic and diachronic interactions with other groups, and often from sheer good luck. Once formed, hegemonies constantly change because the 'leading group' must continually adjust and make new compromises to survive. This makes hegemonies highly contextual organisms which are tied to a particular location and moment. The actual composition of a hegemonic alliance is seldom the same for very long because the membership and patterns of influence are ever-changing. But, in addition to small ongoing shifts (through which hegemonic groups continually renew themselves), huge cataclysmic hegemonic shifts also occur, often at those moments when the hegemonic 'rules of the game' are fundamentally altered. Such revolutionary changes usually transpire when dominant groups have failed to renew sufficiently their composition and/or their discourses, and so lose their ability to lead and organize a (changed) society. The collapse of the Soviet system in 1989 represents such a revolutionary hegemonic shift. At such moments the organizing discourses of a society are rendered transparent and the collapsing hegemonic discourse will no longer have the capacity to 'normalize' the old order's 'way of life' and 'worldview'. However, the new hegemonic order will not yet be in a position to 'normalize' its preferred vision. It takes a new order some time to dislodge fully old hegemonic discourses and practices and entrench (and close) its own preferred discourses and practices. In post-apartheid South Africa, it took the whole of the 1990s to make black nationalism hegemonically dominant.

The processes of 'becoming hegemonic' have altered over time. Such processes first emerged in the post-feudal world because, under feudalism, power was simply located in hereditary families which did not have to 'become' dominant, because they were born dominant. The bourgeoisie had to find new mechanisms for creating and organizing their power, regulating differences between themselves and taking decisions. The result was the creation of bourgeois public forums (parliaments). Within these sites, bourgeois individuals and factions learned the (communicative) art of becoming dominant (i.e. hegemonic) by forming alliances, discursively promoting their interests and negotiating. After bourgeois parliaments were widened to also include non-middle-class representation, the hegemonic arts of becoming dominant became necessarily more complex. However, to some extent, widening representation was rendered less significant by the emergence of managerialism, which saw the locus of power effectively taken away from public fora. Essentially, the managerialists used boards, bureaux and government executives (e.g. cabinets) as their key decision-making sites. The role of parliaments declined.

Not surprisingly, under managerialism the differences between parliamentary groupings (e.g. labour parties and conservative parties) narrowed over time, so that eventually elections in the liberal-democracies seemed only to produce an intra-elite rotation rather than fundamental policy changes. This was partly because the key ('centrist') parties were all committed to the same pragmatism and maintenance of the same managerialist hegemony. Further, all parliamentarians relied on the same bureaucratic managers for advice and carrying out the tasks of government. From a Marcusian perspective, managerial elites created one-dimensional hegemonies in which only pseudo-choice was offered. And so, in the liberal-democracies, managerialist rulers increasingly lost legitimacy as the twentieth century progressed, leading to declining voter turnouts, growing voter cynicism and a generalized distrust of politicians. A parallel East European crisis of legitimacy saw Soviet managerialists overthrown in 1989–90.

Significantly, the managerial era was also the era of mass communication, with the culture industry disseminating and legitimating 'mass' discourses that suited the needs of managerialist hegemonies. The Frankfurt School noted the interesting parallels between the 'mass' discourses of liberal (and social democratic) managerialism, Soviet managerialism and Nazi managerialism. In the 1950s managerialist discourses generally resonated with mass audiences, and managerialists gained widespread legitimacy in societies like those of the USA, Canada and Australia as they delivered new material prosperity (in the form of mass suburban housing, freezers, washing-machines, television, automobiles and rock-and-roll records). Product-delivery also helped to make 'science' into something of a new 'secular religion' (helped along by the excitement of rocket launches and 'the Space Age'). Among Anglo intellectuals, managerialist-serving discourses, like functionalist behaviourism, structural functionalism and systems theory, gained widespread currency. But this legitimacy progressively unravelled as managerialists and scientists were blamed for creating the threat of nuclear warfare and were criticized for their failure to find solutions to the Vietnam ordeal, and the problems of crime, inflation and unemployment.

Creating a hegemony requires both inwardly-directed discourses (to hold the hegemonic team together) and externally-directed discourses. The latter involve (media-ized) impression management (image-making) for the consumption of the ruled and are geared to legitimating the rulers. Legitimation problems arose once the managerialists began to lose touch with the external audiences and created discourses which resonated with fellow managerialists (i.e. the socially dominant) but which sounded 'elitist' to the ruled. Managerialists responded to the growing social problems of unemployment and crime by building bigger bureaucracies to administer 'top-down' policy and planning. These managerial 'solutions' made 'ordinary people' feel manipulated by 'experts' who appeared unable to solve social problems. One outcome was the emergence of conservative populism in societies like the USA, the UK and Australia that riled against 'elite' and managerialist interventions associated with welfare targeting sectional interests. By the time global networkers emerged (and began challenging the discourses and practices of managerialism), the managerialists already found themselves hegemonically vulnerable.

The 1980s and 1990s brought a series of socio-economic restructurings associated with the emergence of global network capitalism. Social relationships were altered in three ways so as to impact on the mechanics and processes of hegemony building. First, the new communication technologies which emerged in the 1970s evolved into a series of global communication channels. A new breed of entrepreneurial networkers learned to exploit these to accumulate wealth. These entrepreneurs found ways to generate wealth from exploiting rapid data-sharing (i.e. digital electronic information flows). Effectively, a new capitalist elite was born from learning (in an ad hoc way) to exploit new communication technologies. Some of these new entrepreneurs have built new business empires, creating long-term wealth-generating enterprises (e.g. News Corporation, Microsoft and America On Line), whereas others have only rejigged older discourses and practices (e.g. Michael Milken's 'junk bond' revolution). But there have also been corporations that reinvented themselves by learning to exploit the new communication technologies and, in the process, reworked Fordism into post-Fordist practices. An example would be Toyota's 'just-in-time' system of inventory management. Entrepreneurs driving this emerging global network capitalism necessarily shook up the old managerial hegemony by introducing new practices and new (rival) sets of players. As these entrepreneurs emerged, they pragmatically allied themselves to whichever ruling hegemonic faction (or individual) would promote their interests. For example, Murdoch worked with both Keating's Australian Labour Party and Thatcher's Conservative Party since both were prepared to create policy frameworks which aided his global information interests.

As the twenty-first century dawned, the struggle between managerialists and global networkers was far from resolved. But, in general, the networkers appeared to be gaining the upper hand in the struggle for dominance in OECD countries and OECD-dominated transnational fora with deregulatory, laissez-faire and 'globalization' discourses sounding confident and ascendant, while managerial, interventionist and 'national-protectionist' discourses sounded increasingly defensive and rear-guardist. Even setbacks, such as the rise of anti-globalization political parties like Australia's One Nation, and the 1999 anti-WTO demonstrations in Seattle, did not substantively undercut the overall international success of those promoting the merits of 'globalization' and an 'information economy' (i.e. global network capitalism's promotional discourses). Global networkers have, in fact, shown themselves to be highly proficient in the legitimating arts of (externally-directed) image and discourse management. Their promotion of the 'information superhighway' and e-commerce are excellent examples of successful rhetoric.

Secondly, new communication channels actually undermined some of the requirements for hierarchical-bureaucratic practices in both private and state corporation sectors and within the state bureaucracies (government departments). New communication technologies made it possible to by-pass old hierarchical chains of command. Because it was possible to share information instantaneously with anyone linked to the communications network, old, managerialist pecking-orders were undermined and hierarchical chains of command (relying on middle managers) became too slow and cumbersome when competing with fluid, 'networked' teams. Consequently, managerialist organizational structures faced increasingly deconstructive pressures during the 1990s. Hence, both business and government sectors experienced changes to their organizational practices and staffing structures – a process associated with the rise of neo-liberal discourses advocating the 'winding back of the nanny state', 'deregulation', 'flexible organization', 'outsourcing' and 'downscaling'. These organizational shifts necessarily impacted upon the construction of hegemonic alliances as the players learned to use the new communication channels and manipulate the data-flows. New information strategies and tactics were developed by 'spin doctors' who could go 'direct-to-source', lobby, 'end-game', 'side-channel', 'back-channel' and/or plant, disguise or manipulate information (both when building or maintaining one's own hegemony or when undercutting counter-hegemonic groups). Spin doctors, therefore, were no longer limited to using mass media for delivering their messages (although the mass media were still used).

Thirdly, global network capitalism and post-Fordist organization facilitated the creation of a plethora of new market niches, which led to the emergence of new 'lifestyle' identities). The new communication networks made disaggregating the 'mass market' possible because micro consumer demands could not only be rapidly communicated to producers, but the productive process could also be relatively easily re-jigged or re-tooled thanks to computer-integrated manufacturing. The result was a shift from economies of scale (Fordist mass production) to economies of scope (post-Fordist production of the widest possible range of commodities) (Crook et al., 1992: 179). This generated new social groupings and identities based on niche, consumption-based lifestyles. The new identities supplemented older identities (e.g. ethnic and religious) which were also re-invigorated by the de-massification and de-managerialization of society. The result was the emergence of 'identity politics' which are served by growing niche-based media. The 'new politics' leaned towards socio-cultural issues (related to lifestyle and consumption) rather than socio-economic (production) issues (Crook et al., 1992: 146). This made the task of building hegemonies infinitely more difficult as 'mass publics' fragmented into a plethora of grouplets based upon localism, ethnicity, new and revivalist 'belief formations' (e.g. religious, ecological) and lifestyles (e.g. homosexuality) because aspiring hegemony-builders now need to communicate to a plethora of new groups. Becoming hegemonic has become extremely complex given the need to master multiple discourses and develop strategies for building coalitions out of diversity. It also involves learning to use both niche media formats and remnant 'mass media' forms (the latter generally employed to target non-elite groups). Building dominance now requires developing a highly complex patchwork of (neo-feudal) media strategies.

Hegemony and the art of managing discourses

Becoming hegemonic is not enough. Hegemonic groups, as Gramsci noted, have to work at staying dominant. In part, this involves operating a discourse that keeps the ruling alliance together. However, another hegemonic task is maintaining a 'leading position' in society relative to all other groups so that the dominated accept the position of dominance held by the 'leading' group. This involves generating consent among the ruled, that is ensuring that the discourses, practices and 'authority' ('coercive capacity') of the ruling group are seen as legitimate (and ideally as 'natural') by the ruled. For hegemonic groups, the more 'naturalized' and obfuscated such discourses and practices are, the better because a naturalized set of hegemonic discourses or practices effectively positions the dominated into a set of 'hidden' power relationships. The discourses that are embedded in, and 'govern', institutions (as described by Foucault) produce an especially obfuscated and opaque form of power. Marx saw money as such a discourse. For Marx, money regulated social relationships within capitalism and disguised how the dominant (capitalist) group derived benefit from capitalist social relationships. This discursive process Marx called fetishism, that is where social decisions (regulating human relationships) are made to appear natural. Such discourses/ practices become extremely stable (from a Frankfurt School perspective, 'frozen' and virtually unchallengeable) because once naturalized, they become opaque 'givens' which do not seem to be the temporal creation of any hegemonic group. Hegemonic groups successfully building discourse closure achieve great stability. Twentieth-century Australia witnessed such hegemonic stability (Louw, 1997: 90–2).

But a fully naturalized hegemony is unlikely. Rather, hegemonies continually have to be re-made as dominant groups struggle to maintain their leadership through a process of negotiating with subordinate groups and a (related) process of discursive management. Those in power will have three discursive goals. First, they will produce discourses which advance and confirm their interests. Secondly, they will try to create as much discourse closure as possible by using the power they already possess to influence ('nudge') discourse-making processes in the direction of closures favouring the 'perspectives' and 'practices' that benefit themselves and their allies. Thirdly, they will try to regulate discourse shifts so that discursive change favours the interests of the already dominant. A good example of this was the Keynesian shift in the wake of the 1929 capitalist crisis, a shift which stabilized the basic outlines of the capitalist hegemony by constructing a social democratic reformism. Similarly, the 1990s saw the basic outlines of South Africa's socio-economic order retained within a reform package negotiated by the former apartheid rulers.

Groups that are already hegemonic have an advantage over newcomers because they have the resources to employ and/or offer patronage to intellectuals, and even to offer some intellectuals derivative power (in the form of positions on boards, commissions, advisory committees, etc.). During the era of social welfare, many social democratic intellectuals acquired real power, effectively becoming part of the managerialist-capitalist hegemonic alliances. By helping to create appropriately obfuscated discourses/practices and managing the welfare state, these intellectuals made themselves valuable within the capitalist hegemonic order. Those who are already hegemonic are also in a position to direct (or at least strongly influence) the discourses promoted within schooling systems. This is significant because it offers the prospect of implanting (ruling) discourses into the heads of children, which means that (most?) citizens will thereafter police themselves as they will have internalized discourses that suit the needs of the ruling hegemony. This was the basic conceptualization underpinning Althusser's (1971) notion of an ideological state apparatus (ISA). (Although Althusser somewhat overstated the 'closed' nature of language-systems, his ideas on ISAs do have some explanatory power with regard to how hegemonic closures can be built.)

In addition, those groups that are already hegemonic have an advantage over newcomers with regard to their ability for developing symbiotic relationships with the media. This is useful for facilitating discourse closures. However, relationships between various sections of the media and different factions of ruling hegemonies are subject to ongoing flux (and negotiation), which means symbiotic relationships are contextually-bound rather than ongoing and 'automatic'. Further, media-related discourse closure is complicated by the fact that intra-hegemonic factional struggles are often fought out in the media and this generates the impression of discursive turmoil and non-closure. However, the Frankfurt School would argue that such discursive battles in the media do not mean that truly antithetical ideas are allowed to surface. Rather, they would argue that such 'oppositional' ideas merely constitute superficial 'huffery and puffery', that is the 'freedom to choose that which is the same'. This can be seen in the way the USA's Democrats and Republicans, the UK's Labour and Conservatives and Australia's Labor and Liberal parties have struggled over the same 'middle ground' to the point where there is not much to differentiate between them. But, media battles (even when not involving substantive issues) help to legitimate liberal-democratic managerialism as a 'tolerant' system. This is helpful for constructing liberal hegemonies as long as no danger exists of ideas surfacing that fundamentally challenge the system's core underpinnings. Habermas (1976) argued that this was the real weak point of managerialist systems because if democracy was ever actually practised, it would constitute a threat to administrative rationality and lead to the disintegration of the system. The Frankfurt School's argument is that those ideas which are fundamentally contradictory to ruling hegemonic interests will be marginalized, repressed and/or belittled. Although this notion may exaggerate the capacity of ruling hegemonies to achieve closure, this notion should not be dismissed out of hand. Clearly, all ruling hegemonies would like to achieve closures if they can. The question is to what extent are they able to achieve such closures? Ultimately the success each ruling group has in this regard will depend upon its skills at managing discourses, that is making discourses/practices that are advantageous to both the dominant and taken-for granted (obfuscated and opaque) ruling group(s).

Ruling hegemonic groups necessarily intervene to try to influence the production and circulation (and even the reception) of communication. No ruling group(s) can afford to adopt a laissez-faire approach to communication given the centrality of communication in building and maintaining hegemonic influence. At the very least, discourse management requires ruling groups to pay some attention to five communicative mutables (discussed on pages 100–2). In the era of early capitalism many communicative functions would have been carried out by middle-class leaders themselves. But, progressively, the number of communicative functions has increased, and during the managerialist era, hegemonic communication emerged as a set of specialist functions. By the start of the twenty-first century, 'communication' was not only a set of specialist functions, but also a set of institutionalized practises with hegemonic groups employing a range of professional communicators ('spin doctors', PRs, journalists, educators, etc.) to practice the arts of hegemonic communication. These communication professionals concerned themselves with the following sorts of communicative-hegemonic issues.

First, ruling groups (and some aspiring ruling groups) will employ communication professionals who possess an understanding of the structures of meaning-making. These professionals develop strategies and tactics for using whatever discursive possibilities such structures may offer. The twentieth century saw discourse-making become progressively institutionalized (largely in accordance with industrial-managerialist logic) within schools, universities, research institutions, the media, and even in charismatic churches. These institutionalized sites provide platforms for the production and dissemination of discourses. Groups that are already hegemonic are in a position to influence the discourses in circulation within their area of jurisdiction by intervening to either facilitate or undermine the functioning of such discursive spaces. The extreme end of hegemonic action against such sites would involve censorship or disallowing such discourse-making machinery. For example, the late twentieth century has seen a number of hegemonies (e.g. the USA, China and Japan) take action to crush institutionalized religious cults. The Waco siege in Texas even involved the use of violence. More commonly, however, ruling groups 'regulate' the structures for meaning-making through intervening in ways that impact on the resources flowing into such structures. Institutions producing discourses of which the hegemonic bloc approves may receive direct funding from factions of the ruling alliance (or the state) or receive tax-breaks. They can also be favoured by regulatory decisions (e.g. spectrum allocation). Institutions receiving such funding, tax-breaks or regulatory 'favours' will often provide hegemonic groups with 'discursive space' in return. Alternatively, structures producing discourses not approved of by ruling hegemonies can be actively 'discouraged' through taxation and regulatory obstacles. Such hegemonic interventions, which are often so low key as to go unnoticed, are responsible for steering social discursive flows in one or other direction, by allowing some structures to grow, while 'encouraging' others to decline or die. Much discursive steering (i.e. hegemonic discourse management) is subtle and 'hidden', and only becomes 'transparent' at moments of hegemonic shift. So, for example, the end of the Cold War saw clearly-discernable interventions to steer meaning-making machineries into new directions in a number of 1990s' contexts, including in South Africa and the old Soviet bloc. These (non-opaque) interventions included a mix of funding shifts, regulatory shifts and direct political pressure for 'transformation'. Of the plethora of meaning-making structures in existence, the media probably now receive the most attention (from both hegemonic and counter-hegemonic groups) because from the mid-twentieth century onwards they became the key instruments for circulating discourses.

Secondly, communication professionals employed by ruling groups will need to pay attention to the personnel involved in meaning-making. Structures may provide the fulcra for discourse manufacture and circulation, but ultimately it is those staffing these structures who are the creative heart of the machinery. So, discourse management must involve a concern with meaning-makers, that is intellectuals. Managing discourse-making involves attracting 'the right' sort of person. Hence, discourse managers need to establish what an 'appropriate' candidate would be. This sets the parameters for what meanings are likely to be produced. Deciding what is 'appropriate' need not necessarily involve conscious decisions about 'worldviews' and ideological positions. Instead, decisions may (in the educational sector, for example) be made according to knowledge of certain methodologies. This can constitute a 'disguised' (unconscious?) form of discourse-steering. Similarly, setting salary levels and adopting recruitment procedures can be a decision about the sorts of people who will be recruited. Clearly, recruitment is a central function of discourse management. Hence, from a hegemonic point of view, only 'the right' people should be empowered to take recruitment decisions, that is those taking such decisions (e.g. editors) should hold 'appropriate' views themselves. So, discourses can be managed by promoting 'appropriate' people into those positions selecting the next generation of meaning-makers. Effectively, a process of 'cloning' by recruitment can be established. Naturally, recruitment mistakes can be made, and people can be appointed who produce inappropriate meanings. Such people will not be promoted. Some will be 'tolerated' but marginalized; while others will be driven out. In long-standing hegemonies such personnel management can be so naturalized that it becomes an 'unconscious' form of discourse management (and censorship). Only in rare circumstances will such personnel management cease being opaque and become a set of conscious acts designed to change a society's dominant discourse by removing intellectuals (e.g. journalists) from their jobs. Such deliberate interventions were implemented in post-Second World War (militarily-occupied) Germany and Japan, in East Germany (following reunification) and in post-apartheid South Africa.

Thirdly, communication professionals employed by ruling groups will pay attention to meaning-making practices. Such practices are learned both through education and training programmes and on-the-job socialization. (In the case of university-based intellectuals, these are one and the same.) Detaching training from meaning-making sites is not a problem in some sectors. For example, training teachers in colleges and universities (mostly away from schools) is a long-accepted practice which does not appear to have caused undue tension between practitioners and trainers (in part because teachers appear to feel some 'ownership' of the training processes and school 'placements' create a space for socialization to occur). However, the same cannot be said of media training, where tensions have emerged between practitioners and some media/journalism schools. This tension emerged when practitioners felt themselves losing control of media training processes (when in-house journalism apprenticeships were replaced by university programmes). Also, practitioners became concerned that university programmes involved too much 'critical media theory' and not enough practical skills. These programmes were seen to teach a set of inappropriate practices and values. On-the-job training and apprenticeships created the ideal conditions for cloning, that is ensuring that journalists were socialized into (existing) 'appropriate' sets of meanings and practices. Tensions will presumably continue until media practitioners feel they have regained some degree of control over media training. The question of who controls training is a significant issue for hegemonic managers.

Fourthly, communication professionals employed by ruling groups will pay attention to the issue of appropriating, recycling and reworking discourses from the past and from other contexts. Discourses and practices from the past are omnipresent in the form of residues underlying, intermeshing and interpenetrating contemporary discourses and practices. The British Empire left such residues in South Asia and East and Southern Africa, as did the Ottoman Empire in the Balkans and the Middle East. Further, discourses are continually migrating from their original context, and mutating and hybridizing with other discourses in new contexts. The spread of Christianity, Islam and Marxism are examples of this. Globalization processes are likely to intensify discourse migration and hybridization. Discursive migration, mutation/ hybridization and residues can have unrecognized influences. Discursive management therefore requires sensitivity to the contextual roots of any discourse/ practice, and its migrations and mutations. Such knowledge enhances opportunities for appropriating or reworking discourses for use in new contexts, and offers both hegemonic and counter-hegemonic players a set of tools for discursive intervention and manipulation. For those who are the targets of such manipulation, knowledge of how discourses are created, travel and mutate can provide at least some inoculation.

Fifthly, communication professionals employed by ruling groups need to monitor actual flows of meaning. The way meanings flow through social networks is a good indication of the arrangement of power relationships between individuals and groups. Constructing hegemony involves, in part, cobbling together sets of relationships between people – between sectors of the dominant, the dominated, and the relationships between these. Constructing hegemonic relationships therefore requires communicative interventions to regulate information exchanges and power relationships, so that the dominant 'orchestrate' (as much as possible) what is communicated to whom. There will be occasions when hegemonic players wish to retain and stabilize existing communicative patterns. On other occasions they may wish to alter communication flows to create new groupings or alliances, or to undermine existing groupings that are no longer deemed hegemonically useful.

During the managerial era, hegemonies became consciously managed. The move towards global network capitalism is generating shifts from hierarchical and bureaucratic managerialism to control through 'networking'. However, these shifts are not resulting in a diminishment of the wide array of institutionalized communicative functions established under managerial hegemony. What is changing is the style of control. Building hegemony in the global networking era appears to involve developing new communicative practices by rejigging (and mutating) existing communicative infrastructures and routines, rather than building a completely new infrastructure. At its core, the art of building hegemony remains unaltered. It involves becoming (and staying) dominant and powerful by using communications. Hegemony is built and organized by managing discourses, institutions and practices. Intellectuals (as specialists in setting communicative parameters) are necessarily implicated in all three functions. Becoming dominant simply requires being successful in getting one's 'definition(s) of reality' accepted as correct, and thereafter closing (or at least narrowing) discursive flow in favour of the then-dominant perspective. At the dawn of the twenty-first century, managerialists had seemingly lost the battle to maintain discourse closure although managerialist discourses and the intelligentsia serving the old managerialist hegemony were still far from dislodged. Effectively, a global networkers' hegemony is still emergent and new hegemonic discourses and practices are still being invented. The discursive battles between the managerialists and networkers are far from over. It is not even clear that the global networkers are assured of hegemonic dominance. Although some managerialist forms appear to have been completely defeated (e.g. Soviet managerialism), resistance from other managerialists (especially Keynesian managerialists in Western welfare sectors) is not yet exhausted. In addition, the role of 'luck' should not be underestimated in establishing hegemony. At the end of the twentieth century global networkers had a run of good luck. It may not continue.

Discursive resistances and weakening hegemonies

All hegemonic groups wish to remain dominant; hence they will necessarily attempt to stabilize those discourses and practices through which they secured hegemonic dominance. 'Stabilization' strategies can range from attempts to 'freeze' discourses/practices through to permitting 'reform', but on terms set by the hegemony. The 'freezing' approach is unlikely to be a successful strategy because there are always going to be contextual shifts which demand mutability. Also, there will always be those resisting the dominant hegemony. Oppositional individuals and groups will be constantly looking for (and finding) communicative 'gaps'. The bourgeoisie/burgers found their 'gaps' in the public sphere, in the 'spaces' the feudal elites could no longer police. The managerialists colonized the 'gaps' flowing from capitalism's socio-economic 'steering crises' – the First World War, the Great Depression and the Second World War. For the managerialists, the 1970s and 1980s brought a series of steering problems. Problems within civil society became especially intense during the 1980s. The 1989 Leipzig uprising against East German Soviet managerialists illustrates how an activated civil society can represent a crisis for managerialists. Effectively, 'the demands' and 'resistances' simply could not be 'managed away'. The problems got too big. A similar pattern was seen in South Africa where apartheid managerialists lost the capacity to manage multiple steering problems arising in the 1980s. In the face of massive problems and resistances, both the Soviet and apartheid managerialists engaged in attempts at reform, mixed with repression. But they were minimalist reforms, framed within the same sort of managerialist logic that gave rise to the systemic crises in the first place. Hence, the steering problems simply got more intense. As a result, the Soviet and apartheid hegemonic elites simply gave up. The Soviet decision to allow the Berlin Wall to come down (November 1989) and the announcement that apartheid was over (February 1990) were both deeply symbolic of the fate of managerialist elites who reformed too little and too late. Effectively, both systems became 'ungovernable' (unmanageable) and the old managerialist frameworks simply collapsed under the weight of multiple problems. The anarchy ensuing from these collapses was still in evidence as post-apartheid and post-Soviet societies entered the twenty-first century.

The responses of capitalist managerialism to its steering problems and discursive resistance have been quite different. The Western managerialists appear to have retreated and reformed more successfully than Soviet or apartheid managerialists. Liberal-capitalism allowed alternative sets of practices/discourses to emerge, and out of this emerged the global networkers whose practices appear to constitute a 'successfully reformed' capitalism. In addition, when it became clear that social welfare managerialism was no longer sustainable, liberal-capitalism began winding back the managed welfare system. This wind-back reform began when managerial solutions were found to be no longer working (e.g. when managerialist interventions created bigger systemic problems) and sustainability became an issue. In addition, the costs of this managerialist system were blowing out – demands were outstripping the capacity of managerialists to deliver. Similarly, national economic management and managed protectionisms were wound back when steering problems began to outstrip managerial solutions. Naturally, in the process of reforming the system, there were intra-elite conflicts between managerialists who opted for reform (and began attaching themselves to the emergent new networker elite) and conservative managerialists who put up resistance to change.

As the managerialists retreated in the face of the steering problems, the global networkers stepped into the 'spaces' and 'gaps' created by their retreat, and began aggressively promoting their alternative discourses and practices. But, in addition, a range of other alternative ('resistance') discourses have emerged as managerialism weakened. Among these are a number of ecological, conservationist and green discourses. Many of the green discourses are conservative and Ludditist and seek a return to some romantic idealist-utopian past. Another set of 'resistant' discourses involves a range of ethnic localisms and new tribalisms which seek 'autonomy', 'independence' and non-inclusion in emergent globalism. A third response to the turbulence of managerialism's retreat has been the rise of religions, including new cults, charismatic churches and a range of fundamentalisms (Muslim, Christian, Hindu and Judaic). These appear to offer 'psychological spaces' into which people can escape from the messiness of rapid change that has been brought about by managerialism's steering problems and wind-backs.

So hegemonies are never permanent fixtures. Dominance is always subject to being challenged. However, resistance in some contexts is pointless. When hegemonies are very strong, 'alternative' discourses and practices can at best cling to life in marginal spaces. But all hegemonies have life-cycles. They grow old and weak, and at those moments, those advocating 'alternatives' are presented with momentary opportunities for asserting their hegemonic dominance. Hegemonies are at their most fragile just after being born (before they have 'naturalized' their discourses and practices, and before they have consolidated their grip on the steering mechanisms of society), and then again when they grow old and weak. When dominant groups lose the capacity to set the intellectual agenda, negotiate new deals and alliances and police all the 'spaces' in society, opposition groups sense the weakness (because the old hegemony 'communicates' weakness). Alternative visions are empowered by the growing availability of communicative 'spaces' and 'gaps' as dominance slips away. And the more 'alternative visions' are able to colonize communicative spaces, and thereby become empowered, the greater become the crises facing the existing hegemonic group. Holding a hegemony together, once the crises born of weakness begin, becomes a little like trying to plug an already-leaking dyke. So weak hegemonies ultimately crumble, and one of (or an alliance of) the formerly resistant groups learns to become the new hegemonic group. These processes of hegemonic weakening, death and new birth have occurred again and again in history, with the end of the British Empire and the Soviet collapse being among the most spectacular of recent hegemonic upheavals. Not surprisingly, hegemonic crumbling is usually associated with the outbreak of war as aspiring hegemonic groups try to grab space from a retreating hegemonic order. Hence, the decline of the British Empire produced the two World Wars (as Germany tried to fill the power vacuum created by Britain's decline) and a series of smaller wars (e.g. Israeli–Arab and Indian–Pakistani), while the end of Soviet hegemony has already produced wars in the Balkans and Caucasia.

Trying to remain hegemonically dominant always involves dealing with those attempting to challenge one's hegemony. There will always be resistance. However, resistance (and alternative discourses and practices) is usually only a problem – that is can only seriously challenge a hegemonic group – during vulnerable moments. Hegemonies tend to be vulnerable when they are still new and working to entrench and 'naturalize' themselves, and when they are no longer able to renew themselves (when they become old and tired). The only other way hegemonies are overthrow is when more powerful external groups choose to intervene to overthrown hegemonies using warfare or economic sanctions, etc. (Of course, counter-hegemonic groups will always be on the look out for external players willing to intervene on their behalf when resistance groups are too weak to challenge seriously their own hegemonic rulers.)

So ruling hegemonies will always strive to keep themselves informed of all potential challengers, by keeping abreast of emerging (and declining) oppositional discourses and alliances and their growth and strength is a central function of maintaining a position of dominance. Challengers can emerge from a number of different sources: from break-away former members of one's own hegemonic alliance; from new players inside one's society; from foreign players seeking to intervene; or from alliances between these. Essentially, maintaining hegemonic dominance involves more than maintaining and promoting one's own discourses and practices. It also involves meeting constant challenges from counter-hegemonic challengers. The management of discourse consequently involves constantly renewing one's own discourses (to keep one's own ruling alliance and dominant profile intact), plus working to prevent potential counter-hegemonic discourses from ever becoming serious challengers. Communicative struggle lies at the heart of being hegemonic.

CHAPTER 6

Moving to an Informational Economy: The New Rules of the Power Game in Global Network Capitalism

There is now widespread agreement that a new form of economic organization began emerging in the last part of the twentieth century – a phenomenon explored by, among others, Harvey (1989), Lash (1990), Hall and Jacques (1990), Crook et al. (1992), Lash and Urry (1994) and Castells (1996). Castells contends that this new economy is informational and global, and makes the important point that 'informational' means more than 'information based' (Castells, 1996: 91) and 'global economy' means more than 'a world economy' (Castells, 1996: 92). He also notes that

> while the information/global economy is distinct from the industrial economy, it does not oppose its logic. It subsumes it through a technological deepening; embodying knowledge and information in all processes of material production and distribution on the basis of a giant leap forward in the reach and scope of the circulation sphere. In other words: the industrial economy had to become informational and global or collapse. (Castells, 1996: 91–2)

Capitalism has once again demonstrated a resilience unforeseen by Marx when he predicted that capitalism would collapse due to internal contradictions (such as a falling rate of profit). Marx correctly foretold of many of capitalism's contradictions and crises, but underestimated the capacity for capitalist elites to renew and reinvent themselves by modifying their discourses and practices, and even changing the 'staffing' of their hegemonic alliances. Ultimately, the shift from managerial capitalism to global network capitalism is as profound as the Keynesian-inspired shift from 'early capitalism' to 'managerial capitalism'. Capitalism appears to possess a great capacity for mutation, which means it will probably mutate again, if and when global network capitalism confronts a 'falling rate of profit' and/or other form of crisis.

The latest capitalist mutation raises three questions. First, what is the nature of this new form of capitalism – global network capitalism? Secondly, what changes does the mutation bring about in terms of power relationships? And finally, what is the significance of these changes for meaning-making?

Global network capitalism took shape over the last two decades of the twentieth century, and although this new variety of capitalism was still young (and rapidly evolving) in 2000, the basic outlines of the new global wealth-making system had become visible. Essentially a 'new' way of organizing wealth-making and people congealed during the 1990s when conditions emerged that created the 'space' for a new capitalist elite to invent itself. This new elite 'reformed' and 'mutated' the practices and discourses of industrial capitalism by learning (in an ad hoc way) to take advantage of two sets of opportunities that presented themselves. First, the information revolution of the 1970s and 1980s (satellites, fibre optic and co-axial cables, microwave telecommunications, networked computers and digitization) created the means for building global communication networks and/or the rapid collection, transmission and sharing of data and ideas. For capitalism this information revolution presented an opportunity for re-birth and re-invention of capitalist wealth-generation by providing new spaces for investment. These opportunities for re-invention were fortuitous because managerial capitalism was, along with the other managerialisms, encountering major systemic crises by the 1970s. (One reason for capitalism's crisis was that new areas for investment had become difficult to find. This generated problems by restricting capitalist growth.) The second opportunity presenting itself was the collapse of the Soviet empire. This collapse created conditions for the New World Order in which the USA became globally hegemonic. Not only did the Soviet collapse open up Eastern Europe for capitalist colonization and investment, but it fully opened up the former third world for such economic colonization because the third world countries could no longer protect themselves by 'playing' a bi-polar system.

These two opportunities – new areas to 'invest in' plus the communication technology to coordinate global colonization and investment – coincided during the 1990s. The result was the birth of a new set of players (the global networker elite) who built a new way of doing business globally. The global networkers' style of building overseas hegemony does not involve the British imperial approach of annexing new lands, dispatching occupation armies (and police forces) and planting new settlements. Rather, it borrows from the US comprador approach for overseas domination, in which local allies (compradors) are assisted to set up new 'independent' countries. These comprador hegemonies administer 'their' spaces in accordance with the needs of their allies in the global centre. This is a much cheaper way of organizing foreign populations than the British occupation model. Actual 'occupations' are now reserved only for those populations that are difficult to organize (e.g. Bosnia and Kosovo). The emergent global network capitalist model only dispatches small numbers of the networker elite to the peripheries for 'tours of duty': to help set up branch offices and production facilities; to assist the comprador allies strengthen their local hegemonies; and to teach appropriate discourses and practices to foreign allies. However, increasingly, such relocations and/or long-term tours of duty are not required because air travel means members of the networker elite no longer have to relocate their homes away from the core global cities. They can now pay short-term visits to the margins. Inspection, education and familiarization can now be done from a distance.

Significantly, Anglos (or those comfortable using English and/or Anglo discourses and practices) visibly dominate the emerging global networker elite, and the USA's global hegemony is beginning to take on the characteristics of an 'Anglo alliance'. This hegemonic alliance, which was made manifest in the 1990 Gulf War against Iraq, is seemingly based on a set of 'special affinities' between the USA and its junior partners of Britain, Canada and Australia. (Significantly, two other key players in global network capitalism are Germany and Japan – societies where Anglo practices and discourses were forcibly implanted during Anglo-American military occupations after the Second World War.) Hence, to a considerable extent, 'globalization' seems to be a phenomenon primarily involving the coordination/networking of an Anglo elite that has been scattered around the globe as a result of the British Empire and American hegemony. By extension, 'globalization' now increasingly involves implanting Anglo discourses into non-Anglo contexts, and implanting the practices of global network capitalism. It is still unclear if this will involve Anglofying the world, or whether Anglo discourses will operate alongside non-Anglo ones. What is apparent is that US hegemonic dominance now makes it possible to transpose unproblematically 'Anglo values and morality' into 'universal human rights'. Anglos are able simply to ignore or dismiss non-Anglo (e.g. Chinese) complaints about 'Western arrogance' because their own discourses are naturalized and opaque for Anglos.

One of the key features of global network capitalism is that post-Fordist production is now scattered across the globe (with capital being increasingly mobile). Products are no longer manufactured in one location. Instead, components are produced wherever it is cheapest to do so (often in Asia or Latin America), then transported to 'central' assembly sites, then marketed, and often warehoused, in multiple distribution sites. This requires a significant process of coordination and planning. Data has to be collected (e.g. about gaps in the market and the most cost-efficient labour resources) and analysed; financing, production and marketing decisions have to be made, often by teams who are themselves scattered across the globe; and productive processes have to be negotiated, established and coordinated. This sometimes involves alliances and/or cooperative partnerships, which can sometimes be short-term project-based arrangements. This system has become, as Castells says, an informational economy. In addition, computer-integrated manufacture (CIM) (Crook et al., 1992: 181–4) means 'flexible' short production runs are now possible. As a result, consumers can now be offered choice as long as the communication system exists to collect their demands, channel them to appropriate CIM facilities (for customized production), and deliver the product back to the consumer.

So communication has become central to global network capitalism. The system has become reliant upon the telecommunications/computer network and the conceptual, communication and coordination skills of the people driving the system. In short, the practices of this new form of capitalism are centrally dependent upon discursive creativity and communication networking or, as Lash and Urry (1994: 61) argue, the economy has become 'reflexive', that is reflection and information/symbol processing are now crucial to success. Cultural capital, knowledge and 'the network' itself have become as important as financial capital because 'good ideas' (e.g. good computer programs, well-conceptualized processes that save time, space or energy and biotech research) appropriately adopted, are fundamental in wealth-making. Consequently, building communication networks, and regulating flows of meaning through these, have become central components of global network capitalism's wealth-making machinery. Communication and media networks are now elements of the productive process. Consequently, the infrastructure and processes of communication/media have become central to developing and maintaining power relationships.

Naturally, as global network capitalism emerged and managerialism diminished, power relationships were altered. Shifts have consequently occurred in the processes of governance and hegemony, and the flows of meaning.

Re-organizing capitalism

Building global network capitalism effectively constituted a massive reformation of the capitalist system. In the initial stages of this process, managerial capitalism became disorganized and 'de-managed' (see Urry, 1990). From the 1980s onwards, the 'discursive formations' (discourses, practices and institutions) of managerial capitalism were deconstructed and deregulated as the old managerial elite lost the capacity to manage away growing systemic crises. The unravelling of the old managerialist discursive formations generated a growing sense of unease in the first world – the core countries of managerial capitalism. This gave rise to various 'postie' discourses. The notions of postmodernity (and all the other 'posts') and deconstruction were attempts to comprehend a disconcerting set of socio-economic and socio-cultural shifts (disorganizations) at a time when possible patterns of re-organization/reconstitution were still opaque. The era of 'postie' unease was an interregnum period, when the old discursive formations and practices of managerialism were visibly dissolving, but a new set of discourses and practices had not yet emerged to replace them.

However, during the1990s, deregulation (deconstruction) was replaced by re-regulation as a new networker elite shaped up and set about generating a discernable set of (global networking) discourses and practices and developing the hegemonic skills required to begin making these discourses dominant. By the beginning of the twenty-first century, the still emergent networker elite had made significant progress towards building its hegemonic order. The discourses/practices of a 're-organizing' capitalism had become virtually 'naturalized' in the key global cities (where the informational economy elite resided), particularly in the heartlands of global network capitalism – North America, the European

Union, Japan and Australia. As important, however, the new elite appeared to have moved a long way down the road of de-legitimizing many managerialist discourses like social welfarism, monetarism, Soviet planning and (third world) developmentalism. Large constituencies of people (and intellectuals) were still supportive of these managerialist discourses. However, their growing defensiveness, and in some cases even a reticence to advocate such discourses openly, revealed their weakness in the face of the confident, expansionist 'global networking' discourses.

In the struggle for hegemony, the emerging networker elite possessed an important advantage, namely its highly developed informational/ discursive skills. After all, the growing informational economy was precisely built by those who first learned to exploit the possibilities inherent in the new communication technologies, which they then used to restructure socio-economic and socio-cultural relationships. The emerging elite built new (global) communication networks and colonized (and modified) old communication infrastructures. Hence, by the turn of the century, they appeared largely able to dominate the communication infrastructures operating in the heartlands of global network capitalism. So, although 'resistances' were apparent among some pro-managerialist operatives of the media infrastructures, the global networkers were increasingly able to use global communication infrastructures to circulate their own preferred discourses and to limit the flow of 'oppositional' discourses (and/or belittle and attack them).

From the point of view of hegemony-building, the global networkers are communication players *par excellence*. They, and the intellectuals they employ, are highly skilled manipulators of symbols and communicative infrastructures. The global networkers have also been successful in politicking (global and local) alliances among themselves, in inventing a common vision, in promoting 'their' particularistic discursive formation as a 'universal good', and in making the development of a globalized informational economy appear to be inevitable. The rhetoric of the 'information age', 'e-commerce', 'e-service delivery', 'networking', etc. has now been 'naturalized' and has become inevitable. When this aspiring elite first began promoting its discourses/practices and its infrastructural needs (as seen in the early hype surrounding the proposal to build an 'information superhighway'), their hegemonic dominance was far from inevitable. But as the 1990s progressed, success bred success, and the aspiring elite of the 1980s began to look ever more capable of building a twenty-first century global hegemony.

A key feature of global network capitalism is that large transnational firms are the organizing hearts of the networkers' hegemony. The organizational principle of these transnational firms is the pepperoni pizza model (as described by Lipnack & Stamps, 1994). Power flows from being located at the nodal 'hub' of such firms (Lash & Urry, 1994: 23). The nodal hubs coordinate highly complex organizational entities by deploying a variety of organizational practices across the globe. Effectively, global network capitalism involves an 'untidy' set of practices/discourses. Re-organizing capitalism has involved moving away from a neatly structured world of uniformly hierarchical organizations and of populations organized into neat blocks of 'mass audiences', 'mass markets' and 'nations'. Instead, global networking capitalists are learning the art(s) of controlling multiple, overlapping 'territories' and jurisdictions in ways that replicate many of the practices of pre-capitalist feudal lords.

This shift in capitalist organization has also filtered into other sectors, including the political realm. For example, the very nature of state organization has shifted away from the Westphalian idea of clearcut separate states towards a global political system in which clear-cut sovereignty is no longer assumed. Westphalian sovereignty (established at the Peace of Westphalia in 1648) replaced the medieval idea of overlapping jurisdictions (Watson, 1992). Global network capitalism has effectively rendered such sovereignty obsolete. So although powerful states still exist (and remain valuable for global network capitalism), even the most powerful states no longer have clear-cut sovereignty, and those operating the political machinery have had to adjust to a network approach of organizing power, which, in some ways, involves a neo-feudal turn, that is a return to a pre-Westphalian model of the state. This is also why the term 'global' has assumed such widespread currency and has replaced the word 'international': because 'global' captures the essence of the networkers' web of transactions and the way in which these transactions simply ignore the old Westphalian 'national' borders. The global networking era does not render national hegemony-building and/or the national state irrelevant, but it does change the nature of 'national hegemonies' by making such national hegemonies simply one more 'layer' within a complex networked web of power brokers.

The networker elites are also having to develop ways of negotiating and/or coordinating the overlaps between themselves. Hence, the emerging hegemony is intensely communicative – dominance derives from being skilled at arranging communicative variables and communication flows. So global network capitalism advantages those possessing certain personalities and skills. Those with the personalities and skills previously advantaged by managerial capitalism are either having to adjust and re-tool or face being marginalized by the new rules of the game. Those emerging as the most successful appear to be those who are especially skilled at rapidly finding and processing information ('processors'), those who can set up effective communication networks ('coordinators') and those skilled at manipulating communication variables ('spin doctors' and 'data manipulators'). This requires using both existing communication channels and building new communication networks to facilitate rapid intelligence-gathering, manipulation and coordination of information. Those building the best databases, or knowing how to access these quickly, and those who are discursively flexible, appear more likely to emerge as winners. This necessarily advantages people rich in 'appropriate' cultural capital. (Apparently the most useful cultural capital for playing global network capitalism is West European – especially Anglo-American – and the discourses/practices of the Chinese trading diaspora.)

Ultimately the re-organization of capitalism is producing a new set of winners and losers. The new winners – the emerging elite of global network capitalism – were those quickest at acquiring (through both skill and luck) the cultural capital required to make the best use of the new communications technologies, and deploying these skills and technologies to solve the problems of coordinating global wealth-making. What Lash and Urry call the skills of 'reflexive production' (1994: 122). To some extent, becoming a member of the informational economy elite appears to have derived from precisely eschewing of the practices of bureaucratized managerialism and top-down planning, because these were too rigid, and hence too slow to cope with rapid global data-flows. The newly successful were those who were quick and flexible. Today they are found in the ranks of the new-rich who have built the knowledge-rich information and biotech sectors. In part, their success involved letting most of the decision making flow downwards to self-monitoring teams (Lash & Urry, 1994: 71 and 86) instead of trying to manage everything from the top (which necessarily involved wasting energy on trying to monitor huge volumes of rapidly flowing information). Success also seemed to involve eschewing 'mass'-thinking and tolerating instead 'difference' and 'fragmentation' (in the way feudal lords had done). Global network capitalism generates wealth out of serving consumer niches across the globe. Informational capitalism encourages niches to proliferate. The niches and differences are then networked and serviced.

communication-rich sites because they are densely wired and possess large airports, both of which are required to facilitate rapid global communication. These cities are also the places where the information rich and/or the highly skilled reside (because they are exciting locations, have good career opportunities and the best services and facilities for cultural consumption). All these factors have tended to turn certain cities into the controlling hubs of the global economy. Locations that are communications-poor and/or have poorly educated populations will necessarily be at the receiving end of the New World Order's power relationships. So the electronic communications revolution and air travel are shifting the style and location of decision making; shifting consumption patterns; shifting the style and location of production centres; and therefore shifting global trade routes. This is necessarily producing a new set of geographical winners and losers.

Considerable power is also accruing to the information-rich living in the urban areas of eastern Japan, northwest Europe, northern Italy and southeast England. Essentially, a new power triad is shaping up around three core political entities – the USA, Japan and the European Union (EU), with Germany seemingly emerging as the key EU player, although Britain's 'special relationships' with the rest of the Anglo-American world is enhancing its influence within the EU. Second-tier (regional) coordination centres are emerging where good communications infrastructures and skilled populations exist (e.g. in Singapore, Hong Kong and Sydney). The networker elite coordinates global network capitalism from these global cities which are increasingly 'clean' cities specializing in 'electronic informational production', service-sector labour and 'high-end' industrial production. These cities are the communication hubs from which global network capitalism's hegemonic dominance is coordinated – it is a hegemonic dominance that is preeminently an exercise in networking and hubbing. Power derives from coordinating communicative complexity on a global scale.

Increasingly, industrial production involving 'dirty', 'monotonous' labour practices is being relocated to places where cheap labour, possessing a well-developed work ethic, exists, regulatory requirements concerning pollution and work practices are lax, but an effective legal/policing system exists to create stable/predictable operating environments. This has resulted in the de-industrialization of many cities in the USA, Europe and Australia, as production has been shipped 'offshore' to Southeast Asia, coastal China and parts of Latin America. The global elite now coordinates these production facilities from their city 'hubs' via the information technology Internet, which keeps them in touch with their comprador allies. Alternatively, they conduct short-term inspection, education, marketing or familiarization tours of the 'margins', as and when required.

The de-industrialization process has been traumatic for many populations, as cities and regions reshuffled their economic bases. Whole populations have relocated to newly-'wired' growth points such as Denver, Houston, Seattle and Phoenix in the USA; Munich and Grenoble in Europe; and Sydney and Brisbane in Australia. Some cities 'de-industrialized' successfully, such as London, New York, Sydney, Pittsburgh and Dusseldorf. These cities made a successful transformation and have developed a mix of high-end industry, and service and information-economy sectors. But other cities and regions failed to transform successfully, such as Detroit, Newcastle (UK) and Adelaide (Australia). They either became high unemployment ghettos or lost their populations through migration. Other areas are still in the midst of traumatic transformation, including most of de-industrializing Eastern Europe.

Significant migration pressures have emerged as people try to relocate away from 'losing areas' of socio-economic decline towards the 'winning' areas. In consequence, 'migration policing' has become something of a growth industry in places like the USA, the EU, Australia and Hong Kong. Other areas have experienced outflows of their most skilled people during the 1990s (e.g. the old Soviet empire, former Yugoslavia, South Africa and inland China).

But some new losing areas are located within the very heart of global network capitalism, namely, the inner-city ghettos of the USA and those de-industrialized 'rust-belt' cities that have not successfully made the transition to 'informational capitalism'. (The USA's African-American and Chicano underclass is heavily concentrated in these ghetto areas.) Even the 'winning' triad-power areas have their losing sectors; it being suggested that they have become two-third/one-third societies (Lash & Urry, 1994: 146). Approximately two-thirds of the population of the OECD countries have been integrated into the 'informational economy', albeit that only a small percentage of these are members of the global elite. The bulk of the winning two-thirds work in information-processing, retailing, education, tourism or in other services sectors, and are themselves fully immersed in the flows of consumerist-discourse and niche identities that have come to characterize OECD social re-organization. However, one-third of the OECD populations have not been successfully integrated. This group comprises unemployed industrial workers, who lost their jobs when industrial plants moved offshore. They appear to have drifted into the status of a permanent unemployed underclass, living in high-unemployment, rust-belt cities (e.g. Buffalo in the USA, Roubaix in France and Wollongong in Australia).

As Lash and Urry (1994: 111) have noted, these problematic de-industrializing areas share something in common with Eastern Europe: from the point of view of an 'informational economy' they are 'dead spaces'. Those inhabiting these 'dead areas' do not have access to the information infrastructure and/or do not have the cultural capital required to utilize such networks. Most of Africa is also such a 'dead area'. Except for pockets in South Africa, the continent is not plugged into the infrastructure of global information capitalism, and few Africans have the cultural capital required to plug in. In fact, Africa currently looks set to be the main loser of globalization because Africans simply cannot compete in the global market. Many of the 'dead areas' are in real danger of socio-economic collapse because global network capitalists avoid investing in those areas which are perceived to be 'unruly' and 'ungoverned' (e.g. sub-Saharan Africa, most of the old Soviet Union and Columbia), whose legal systems are unhelpful to global network capitalists (e.g. Russia and Iran), or whose populations are unproductive (e.g. Africa).

However, it seems likely that the networker elite will respond differently to these 'dead areas', adopting one of three approaches. On the one hand, efforts will be made to integrate those areas that are perceived to be important for the expanding hegemony of global network capitalism because of strategic location, resources or potential markets (e.g. Russia). This will involve expanding the communications network to such areas, encouraging the emergence of network hubs (and local networker elites) in these areas and tying these elites/hubs into the wider network of global informational capitalism. Other areas, which are perceived to be 'problematic' but strategically important to global network capitalism's existing hubs (e.g. Bosnia and underclass areas of the OECD), will be policed (i.e. 'contained'). A third approach will be to 'cordon off' and 'abandon' those 'dead areas' where the costs of integration and/or policing are not seen as warranted. It is not clear yet which areas will actually be integrated, cordoned off, or abandoned as the New World Order hegemonic alliance establishes itself (i.e. 'enemies' and 'allies' will grow out of future conflicts spawned by the collapse of the Cold War balance of power, and the efforts of a networkers' hegemony to assert its dominance globally). Presumably, huge efforts (and resources) will be expended to try to move Russia towards integration into global network capitalism because the turmoil and migrationary pressures ensuing from a Russian socio-economic collapse would threaten the very survival of the EU (and probably the other triad-powers) because of Russia's nuclear arsenal. At the other extreme, it appears that little will be done to integrate sub-Saharan Africa into global network capitalism. The end of the Cold War saw Africa's Westernizing ('development'/ managerialist) elites stripped of their overseas (US or Soviet) allies and support. The effect was the widespread collapse of many African 'development' states (see Reno, 1995). But sub-Saharan Africa's subsequent slide into warlordism, banditry and warfare does not pose similar threats to a Russian collapse. Unlike the problems posed by the other 'dead areas', Africa's disintegration can be easily contained because any relocation of its relatively small, skilled population (mostly from South Africa) poses no threat of swamping other populations. In addition, by the turn of the century, Africa was largely economically irrelevant to global network capitalism.

Cultural imperialism: a useful concept?

Because global network capitalism has transformed power relationships locally, regionally and internationally, concepts involved in the distribution of power need to be revisited. One such concept is 'cultural imperialism'. Are the theories about cultural imperialism of any value when trying to understand emergent global network capitalism?

The notion of 'cultural imperialism' – dating back to the 1960s – essentially divided the world into villains and victims. One version saw the USA as the villain because it imposed its culture on to the rest of the world. The second version saw the whole first world as the villain because it imposed 'Eurocentric'/'Americocentric' culture on the third world. The first version blamed the dominance of American media (especially Hollywood); the second blamed the global dominance of the first world media (the 'media imperialism' thesis, formulated by NWIO theorists).

Two conceptualizations of cultural imperialism were developed. The first, associated with Schiller (1969), argued that cultural imposition resulted from a deliberate elite conspiracy. Schiller (borrowing from Mills, 1959) argued that during the 1950s and 1960s the USA, as a military-industrial complex, had fallen under the control of the federal government in Washington, DC. Schiller believed that the 1960s' expansion of American television around the world resulted from a planned effort by an American military-industrial elite to subject the world to US military control, multinational capitalism and American values. An American elite was seen to be deliberately conspiring to make other nations dependent on the USA, and the world's mass media were being enlisted to promote appropriate 'capitalist ideology' as part of this broader US military-capitalist plan. Schiller's approach requires us to assume that the US elite was extraordinarily coherent, effective and goal-directed – an elite possessing high levels of competence and the capacity to impose internationally its 'ideological machinery'. Schiller's notion was to influence the 'cultural dependency' thesis developed by Nordenstreng and Varis (1973), Mattelart (1980) and Hamelink (1983). Nordenstreng, Mattelart and Hamelink were all concerned about the loss of cultural diversity caused by the spread of 'Americanization' across the world.

A second conceptualization viewed cultural imperialism as a mediaized process, involving 'cultural loss' rather than 'cultural imposition' (Tomlinson, 1991: 173). Tunstall (1978) and Boyd-Barrett (1977) developed non-conspiratorial understandings of cultural imperialism by focusing on media processes that caused 'authentic local cultures' to be displaced. This displacement produced 'cultural loss' not because Anglo-American elites conspired to eliminate smaller, 'marginal' cultures, but because of an unequal ranking (and/or unequal power relationships) between countries. Smaller cultures were simply unable to compete with the economies of scale available to the larger, Anglo cultures because of the size of the Anglo market and the efficiencies of the global cultural machine. Tunstall specifically saw cultural imperialism as the outgrowth of the British Empire because the British had built an international media infrastructure through which Anglo-American cultural products subsequently flowed. As Tunstall said: 'in my view a non-American way out of the media box is difficult to discover because it is an American, or Anglo-American, built box. The only way out is to construct a new box, and this, with the possible exception of the Chinese, no nation seems keen to do' (Tunstall, 1978: 63). Tunstall's argument became marginally less valid during the 1980s when a number of instances emerged of smaller cultures deliberately attempting to counter the pressures of 'Americanization' by subsidizing the production of local cultural products. France clearly led the way. However, other examples were Australian films (facilitated by government subsidies) and quality television dramas facilitated by state subsidies to PSB sectors in the UK, Australia, Canada and South Africa. In Canada and South Africa, there was a deliberate focus on producing non-Anglo television drama – French-Canadian and Afrikaans – as part of local hegemony-building processes (enmeshed with long-standing anti-Anglo imperial sentiments). However, during the 1990s, Tunstall's arguments became progressively more valid as state subsidies for cultural production declined and American-dominated global media expanded its reach as the 'Anglo-led' New World Order entrenched itself.

The conceptual framework developed by the cultural imperialism/media imperialism theorists has mixed value when analysing global network capitalism. Some notions are unhelpful, while other insights are useful. Four themes are unhelpful. First, the villain/victim dichotomy is analytically unhelpful and has more to do with the discourses of post-imperial 'guilt' that emerged as European empires collapsed. Promoting 'guilt' and/or drawing attention to the brutalities and impositions of the European empires served the interests of those seeking to build new hegemonies in the 'spaces' vacated by the collapsing empires. The 'guilt discourses' have been promoted by at least four (sometimes competing) interest groups fighting over the empires' corpses. First was the USA, which largely 'inherited' the British and French empires after the Second World War, as it had 'inherited' the Spanish empire after the 1898 Spanish-American War. US imperial hegemony involved replacing direct imperial rule with indirect 'comprador self-government'. Hence, the US intelligentsia developed a vested interest in promoting a binary oppositional discourse of 'European brutality' versus 'American-promoted democracy'. This discourse helped speed up the transfer of hegemonic dominance from Britain and France to the USA. The US version of the 'brutality' discourse assumed widespread currency in the Anglo world. The Afro-Asian-Caribbean, anti-colonial aspiring elites were a second group promoting a 'guilt discourse' as a way of speeding up the withdrawal of their European rulers. Mahatma Gandhi was undoubtedly the most skilled anti-colonial campaigner in this regard. The Soviet Union was the third player promoting a guilt discourse. The Soviets were in competition with the USA and so modified a 'guilt discourse' to draw attention to US imperial guilt, while naturally deflecting attention from their own extensive empire. Lastly, there was an amalgam of ethnic minorities within the USA, Europe, Australia, Canada and New Zealand, including remnant groups of defeated native peoples, the descendants of African slaves and migrants living in the imperial heartlands. These various minorities discovered that mobilizing a 'villain/victim' discourse could be useful when politicking and bargaining with their ruling hegemonic groups. At different moments, various alliances have emerged between the above four interest groups, although the only issue that ever fully unified all four was a shared anti-apartheid discourse. The problem with the villain/victim dichotomy is that it is about 'taking sides' in hegemonic struggles rather than analysis.

A second (and related) unhelpful theme of the cultural imperialism thesis is that it (implicitly) offers simplistic solutions. The assumption is that destroying 'the villain' will necessarily fix 'the problem'. Hence, cultural imperial theory became entangled with 'solutions'/'alternatives', such as the NWIO proposal. NWIO claimed to offer a means for overcoming cultural imperialism. In reality, it generally served the interests of corrupt and repressive ruling elites. The villain/victim model is a good example of a modernist-managerialist discourse built on the assumption that 'truth' can both be 'discovered' and 'managed' into existence. It is built on two assumptions: that blame can be definitively allocated (clear 'villains' can be identified because no grey areas exist); and that a criterion can be discovered for differentiating between good and bad power relationships or forms of domination. (This criterion can presumably somehow be detached from the corrupting influence of hegemonic power relationships.)

A third problem is that many cultural imperialism theorists lived in first world contexts and had limited understandings of the third world and its internal hegemonic struggles. The 'third world' could conveniently serve as a romanticized (victimized) 'other'. Having constructed a mythological idealized 'other', the 'imperialism theorists', as Tomlinson (1991) notes, then claimed the right to speak on the behalf of the 'victims'. Speaking for 'victims' was empowering for the intelligentsia constructing these discourses.

A fourth unhelpful theme of the cultural imperialism thesis is the notion of conspiratorial elites. Hegemonic elites involve large, complex and shifting alliances rather than small, conspiratorial cabals. It is more helpful to understand power as the outcome of processes, rather than conspiracy. Elites certainly emerge out of, and drive, hegemonic processes, but these processes, and the elites themselves, are too complex and multidimensional to be reduced to the work of shrewd cabals. Ultimately, the media-ized ('media imperialism') approach to cultural imperialism, as developed by Tunstall, Boyd-Barrett and Tomlinson, has greater explanatory power than the Schiller-type approach because it involves exploring the impacts of media processes and practices, rather than searching for conspiratorial elites (be these American, first world, or capitalist) which are deliberately planning to impose their culture on to others. It is more useful to focus on communication infrastructures, industrial arrangements, technology, processes and practices than conspiracies as the source of the 'problem'. These media infrastructures and processes have been developed in the first world and then exported to the third world both deliberately and unintentionally during the colonial period. The problem, according to Boyd-Barrett, is that these media are now embedded in the third world and have created 'dependency' on first world media technology, discourses and practices. These infrastructures are seen as Trojan horses through which first world culture can penetrate and supplant third world culture, not because of an elite conspiracy but because the hegemonic alliances that replaced the European empires have retained these infrastructures.

However, the cultural imperialism theorists also developed some useful themes. In particular, they focused attention on the role media (and cultural products) can play in building and maintaining intercontinental hegemonic dominance. Skewed international power relationships and the struggle for political domination have existed for as long as humans have built neighbouring political formations. However, what was new in the twentieth century was the development of media technologies, which became important instruments for hegemonic conflict. By the start of the twenty-first century the emergence of a global informational economy, and ever-proliferating (globalizing) information Net, made a concern with the role of media/culture in global relations even more important. Hence, despite problems with aspects of cultural and media imperialist theorizing, it is work that deserves some consideration when exploring the emergence of global network capitalism.

The notions of 'media imperialism' and 'cultural loss' are also potentially helpful when conceptualizing the possible cultural impacts that global network capitalism may have. The hegemony being built by the networker elite has a number of interesting characteristics. First, global electronic communication channels are central to both the economy and the politics of the New World Order. The practices, discourses and power relationships of global network capitalism are unimaginable outside these communication infrastructures. Secondly, the networker elites now build and politick their hegemonic alliances globally and/or regionally. Thirdly, autonomous spheres (involving local cultures, niche interest groups, social movements, lifestyle groups and local-level hegemonies) are proliferating. These autonomous spheres are, in turn being networked into regional or global alliances. Effectively, the hegemonic elite of global network capitalism is emerging from those with the skills to build and coordinate complex communicative networks and alliances (which link a multiplicity of spheres and niches). Building hegemonic dominance has become a highly complex business because it has become a two-step (or even multi-step) process. Multiple overlapping sub-hegemonies are now networked into ever-larger and more complex hegemonic alliances.

The global media network is consequently being used for a number of hegemonic purposes. First, an emerging hegemonic elite (plus a wider group of second-tier 'information rich' functionaries and compradors) now use the global media/information network to intermesh with each other. This group is developing similar practices and living environments. Their global cities (from New York to Munich, and Sydney to Singapore) and lifestyles are becoming increasingly interchangeable. Although they are not all Anglo-Americans, the global information rich appear to be almost universally familiar with Anglo discourses and are able to use the new global lingua franca of English. English, for example, dominates the Internet, and this group widely consumes Anglo culture products. The rapid diffusion of Anglo culture is not happening because an American elite is conspiring culturally to dominate others. Rather, it is happening because the global media network is Anglo-American built, and a globally-dispersed Anglophile group, which wants to immerse itself in Anglo discourse and cultural products, exists. Under these circumstances, English as a coding system, Anglo discourse and Anglo cultural products necessarily acquire a prestige, status and usefulness which is derived from an already existing dominance. This encourages usage by (both elite and non-elite) non-Anglos from Taiwan to Russia. Effectively, the growth of Anglo cultural domination now seems globally unstoppable, not because it is being 'manipulated' or 'conspired' into existence, but because of the perceived centrality of Anglo players within the 'hubs' of global network capitalism. In a sense, Anglo economic and cultural power is so overwhelming at the turn of the century that Anglos do not have to conspire to be dominant.

This is not to say the global media network is not used for the purposes of manipulation and domination. Using communication for creating dominance over the ruled is a natural part of hegemony-building. Manipulating communication variables (selecting/de-selecting, emphasizing/de-emphasizing, lying, spin-doctoring, building narratives and discourses, etc.) has always been a part of building and maintaining hegemonies. If anything, future hegemonic labour will seemingly require greater volumes of manipulative communication given the new centrality of 'information' to the very functioning of global network capitalism. Hence, in the first instance, it seems that future hegemonic struggles may be increasingly 'informational' and 'communicative'. Struggles will be over control of information data-bases, deciding what information is stored (and discarded), for what purposes it is stored, who is empowered to decide what is stored or discarded, who can access what information, the mechanics of accessing information (e.g. 'search engines'), the configuration and geography of information networks, the ownership and regulation of networks, and attempts to construct discourses and narratives around which 'cultural identities' can coalesce. Under global network capitalism the outcomes of such informational and discursive struggles will ultimately decide which individuals/factions/alliances hold power. The outcomes of informational battles will become hegemonically decisive.

But within the New World Order many of the battles will have global consequences – even local and regional battles will tend to produce results that ripple through the entire global system (because of its networked character). This is where the cultural imperialism thesis fails to help explain the functioning of the New World Order. Certainly the hub areas dominate the margins. However, within the emergent global network communication flows are no longer uni-directional; between the global cities are multi-directional exchanges (see Sinclair et al., 1996). Those manipulating communication variables within the global system are as likely to live in Tokyo or Sydney as New York. Certainly, within this network, Anglo cultural practices tend to be dominant. However, one of the features of global network capitalism is that it precisely allows spaces for niche identities (and even encourages such niches if they are profitable). Anglo dominance within the network certainly means the Tunstall-type analysis of cultural domination flowing from media configuration deserves attention. However, under global network capitalism, the very nature of cultural dominance needs to be re-thought. After all, Hollywood cultural products are perhaps more likely to be experienced as LA-centric 'cultural imperialism' (i.e. a set of 'foreign' manipulative discourses) in the rural American South, than they are in Sydney. The point is, inside the scattered 'hubs', which now include formerly marginal places like Sydney and Singapore, the dominant discourses of global network capitalism will (if the hegemonic elites are successful) come to seem 'natural' and 'unproblematic'. Outside these hubs, the manipulative nature of the dominant discourses will be more obvious. It is no longer possible to allocate 'inside-outside' status on the basis of the old geographical dichotomies as conceptualized by the cultural imperialist theorists. A more complex geography of networked dominance (and exclusion) is emerging.

Another feature of the new hegemonic struggles is that they will take place globally because the networkers (emerging as the drivers of global network capitalism) are now dispersed globally, and their alliance-building is taking on a global dimension. And the processes of hegemonic struggle look set to occur at enormous speed because of the now instantaneous nature of global information-flow. The instantaneousness of information-flow within the global network has already transformed decision-making in business, diplomacy and warfare. In a system built around the organizing principle of 'informationalism', influence flows to those possessing the communicative machinery and cultural capital most rapidly to capture, transmit, receive, filter, process, interpret, respond to (sometimes 'adjust' or manipulate) and/or generally participate in global communication flows. This undermines the old cultural imperial idea, which is built upon the conceptual dichotomy of first and third worlds. This dichotomy is being dissolved by the new global hegemonic dispensation. Essentially, within the emerging networkers' hegemony, there are now winners (members of the global elite and their partners) within the old third world, and losers in the old first world. The emerging hegemonic elite is now dispersed globally and is in the process of building a networked (global) alliance to coordinate its dominance. Certainly, those global networkers living in key US cities currently have a disproportionate influence with global network capitalism. However, networkers in other locations are now effectively part of a 'global alliance' and appear to be full participants in a global communicative exchange. So, although the New York–Washington nexus may look like the key coordinative centre of global network capitalism, decision-making in this nexus necessarily involves inputs (via the Internet) of networkers across the globe. Hence hegemonic struggle and politicking in Washington–New York increasingly becomes enmeshed with inputs from Brussels, Tokyo, Hong Kong, London and the other global cities.

Essentially, within the networkers' model, the nature of becoming hegemonically dominant alters as global processing and manipulation of electronic communicative variables becomes central to politicking alliances, promoting 'favourable' discourses and undermining and/or blocking 'oppositional' discourses. Hence, just as the most successful global network capitalists are beginning to look like feudal lords, located at the centre of pepperoni pizza empires (of multiple, overlapping 'territories' and jurisdictions), so hegemony building is being similarly transformed within the ambit of global network capitalism. To join the ranks of the hegemonically dominant seems increasingly to involve being a networker and to be skilled at orchestrating 'difference' and 'niche identity'. It also involves an ability to work with enormous complexity because building hegemonies involves working with multi-layered, overlapping jurisdictions (as the era of neat and tidy 'national' administrative blocks fades). Essentially, within the ambit of the networked global cities (and their hinterlands), two levels of hegemony-building seem to be emerging: one involves mobilizing 'identity', 'local' constituencies and economic interest; the other involves networking these into alliances.

'Identity' constituencies have emerged from global network capitalism's facilitation of lifestyle groups, 'identities' and diasporas. Essentially, a variety of 'identity', local-issue and economic-interest groups are proliferating within the same geographical spaces. Mobilizing these groups, and/or building 'identity' or 'local' hegemonies, involves a mix of face-to-face and media-ized communication. Building local and/or 'identity' hegemonic dominance requires people with knowledge of the grassroots issues and an ability to mobilize local discourses, practices and styles. However, the extensive electronic communications web now makes it possible for 'identity', 'economic' and 'local' hegemonic sub-elites to be networked into wider alliances that can be local, regional or global. The same, of course, holds true for counter-hegemonies. In fact, the greens' call to 'think locally, act globally' clearly articulates the emerging pattern of hegemony- and counter-hegemony-building facilitated by the infrastructures of a global information economy. Hence, building hegemony seems increasingly to involve learning to network 'differences', with hegemonic elites coalescing out of those most skilled at orchestrating, juggling and coordinating multiple issues, identities and shifting alliances. And these alliances and networks can be overlapping. For example, an ecology group can simultaneously be part of a global pressure group and a 'local' rainbow coalition.

The media system growing up under global network capitalism differs from that under managerialist-capitalism in a number of respects. First, 'mass' communication is being fragmented by multiple 'niche' communications. Secondly, the convergences (facilitated by digitization) between all forms of communication modifies the nature of media production. The managerialists promoted their discourses via uni-directional mass media (especially radio, television and film) and 'communicative manipulation' was literally industrialized. Under managerialist-capitalism, 'appropriate' discourses were produced by a commercialized culture industry. Many first world discourses were then fed through media infrastructures built in the third world during the colonial era. Essentially, during the managerialist era there were three discernable sets of managers: first world (capitalist managerialism), second world (Soviet managerialism) and third world (development managerialism). Two managerialist discourses dominated (and competed), namely 'capitalism' and 'Soviet communism'. The third world managers were always in a subservient relationship and never really developed their own discursive formations – usually third world developmentalists were dominated by first world managers, but some third world countries became part of the second world hegemonic sphere. The first world–third world comprador pecking-order came to be called 'neo-colonialism' (Nkrumah, 1968) which was seen as a modified 'imperialism' (of the US comprador variety). The 'cultural imperialism' thesis was a sub-theme of this cosmology. During the managerial era, media practices were similar across all three systems – all three used uni-directional mass communication to promote discourses serving the interests of (various forms of) managerialism. The communication practices during the managerial era generally involved top-down planing targeting mass audiences (as seen in advertising, public relations, propaganda and mass education). The media system emerging under global network capitalism operates differently from this managerialist approach because proliferating 'niche' communication and (technologically-driven) media convergences have changed the nature of communication flows. So being a communication spin doctor under global network capitalism is infinitely more complex given that there are so many more variables to consider in an environment of multi-directional networked niche communication.

Anglocentric discourses tend to be dominant within global network capitalism's media networks because Anglos mostly built the network, and Anglos (or Anglophiles) dominate the emerging hegemonic elite of global network capitalism. The dominant (Anglocentric) discourses of the emerging networkers' hegemony now flow globally, not because of a Schiller-type conspiracy, but because the networkers are globally dispersed and the communication network they have built is, by definition, global. American communication products (especially southern Californian and New York products) are especially prevalent, in part because of commercial pressure (itself a capitalist discourse) to use the cheapest available product, and Americans learned to generate the most cost-effective communication and cultural products. However, even this is changing as Canada and Australia are increasingly the source of cultural material flowing through the global communications net. But, of course, this material remains Anglo and promotes discourses and practices that service the needs of Anglo-dominated global network capitalism. Hence, even though niche identities are now easier to maintain amid the plethora of available communication channels, it is probably not yet opportune to put aside all aspects of the 'cultural imperialism' debate because of the clear preponderance of Anglocentric material within the communication channels of global network capitalism.

But if cultural imperialist notions are to be deployed, they need to be used with great circumspection, keeping in mind Tomlinson's work on deconstructing and problematizing the underlying assumptions of the 'cultural imperialism' theorists. A number of preliminary questions suggest themselves. Is global network capitalism simply a re-badging of US comprador imperialism, or is it a 'post-imperial' phenomenon? If a particular cultural group holds power, does this necessarily mean, as the cultural imperialists suggest, that other cultures will be automatically subsumed and/or acculturated? Is such acculturation necessarily a bad thing? Why have some cultures consciously resisted being subsumed (e.g. the French and Afrikaners), whereas others put up little or no resistance? If cultural formations are subsumed, does this mean they are 'less resilient' formations, or is resilience only possible if contextual variables facilitate successful resistance? Are cultural changes brought about because external practices/discourses arrive at opportune moments, and so are adopted, or because of 'imposition'? Is the very notion of cultural imperialism simply based upon a deeply conservative (and patronizing?) idea of wanting to preserve exotic cultures? If cultures are seen naturally to absorb outside influences, grow and mutate – as witnessed by Anglo culture itself – why is there concern about 'preserving' cultural formations? Is it not simplistic to blame communication channels and/or dominant hegemonic groups for cultural shifts in dominated regions? Is it, for example, possible that the role played by indigenous comprador groups is more important than (or at least as important as) 'the media' in promoting the absorption of 'foreign' cultural practices/discourses? More controversially, is it better to be included as a dominated player within global network capitalism (e.g. be employed in Guangzhou) or to inhabit an excluded 'dead zone' (e.g. be unemployed in a Nairobi shanty-town)? Which is preferable – having to adapt to Anglo (?) cultural practices/discourses because of inclusion into global network capitalism, or preserving one's culture at the cost of non-inclusion? It seems at least likely that the New World Order offers no third option? Overall, what seems important is to avoid, as Tomlinson says, 'speaking for others' when such issues are addressed.

Ultimately, the cultural imperialism theorists help to focus attention on the possible effects that skewed power relationships may have on cultural production when the dominant are of a different culture from the dominated. But care should be exercised when deploying the cultural imperialism thesis.

Building domination

Ruling elites are the product of successful hegemony-building. Building hegemony involves making practices and discourses which serve the ruling group's interests. Dominance that is achieved by naturalizing 'appropriate' discourses and practices is the most effective because, once naturalized (and hence opaque), the ruled 'police' themselves and so less coercion needs to be employed by the rulers.

At the turn of the century a capitalist networker elite had visibly emerged, and the process of naturalizing the practices and discourses of networking capitalism was far-advanced in the global cities of the OECD countries. Few in these cities now question the 'inevitability' of an 'information age', capitalist future. And even the least popular of global network capitalism's labour practices, such as casualization and outsourcing, are increasingly treated as 'unchallengeable'. However, the emerging networker elite has encountered resistance to its discourses and practices from a range of old managerialists (including Keynesians, reformed communists and developmentalists), those seeking a return to the certainties of the labour practices negotiated between unions and managements during the managerial era, and those in high unemployment areas where industrial plants have been closed. In the areas of high unemployment in the OECD countries, opposition often assumes the form of new far-right discourses. Further, an influential set of OECD resistances have emerged from the ecological/green movement which challenge the very assumptions underpinning global network capitalism's discourses and practices, while another set of OECD resistance discourses are shaping up around opposition to globalized labour practices. In non-OECD countries, the discourses of global network capitalism are generally less securely embedded – their acceptance resides with smaller groups of the 'information rich' in these countries.

The discourses of global network capitalism are centrally concerned with individual consumption; not the consumption of 'mass' fashion, but 'niche' consumption. Consumption becomes the means for constructing the self. Identity emerges from the consumption of products and services as symbols. As Lash and Urry argue:

> We live in an increasingly individuated and symbol-saturated society, in which the advanced-services middle class plays an increasing role in the accumulation process. This class fraction assumes a critical mass in the present restructuration. As symbol-processing producers and as consumers of processed symbols they are crucially implicated in the contemporary accumulation process. (1994: 164)

Global network capitalism trades on symbol saturation. It sells 'difference', and each of these 'differences' bestows upon the purchaser an identity, such as that derived from purchasing foods produced in ecologically-sensitive ways, or crafting one's body-image through purchasing exercise regimes and/or diets. Ever-shifting, ever-mutating spectacle and fashion are the source of profit. To cut one's self off from purchasing the latest available symbols, whether these be mobile phones, clothing brands, fashionable tourist destinations, new trendy foods, or the latest children's games, is virtually tantamount to refusing a socially-acceptable identity. Global network capitalism has found a way to commodify identity and, in the process, to create self-policing populations because once one has adopted the discourses and practices of one's 'chosen identity', one acts in accordance with the 'requirements' of this identity. The result is the proliferation of new 'cultures' and new 'imagined communities' as well as the re-packaging and commodification of some old cultures and identities. An example of new 'cultural identity' formation would be the various new 'lifestyle' discourses and practices, such as those involving 'going to the gym' or eating the latest health foods. An example of an old cultural identity that has been re-imagined and commodified into a valuable tourist package for Australia would be 'aboriginality'. In the process, the discourses and practices of 'being' Aboriginal are actually being re-invented. Some new imagined communities are local, but others become truly global. And these global identities are sometimes transformed into 'virtual groups' where those holding this identity communicate with each other via the global communications Net (e.g. pokemon clubs).

Constructing the self through consuming the multitude of identities now available via the global communications network effectively involves becoming 'a construct' of the symbolic frameworks manufactured by global network capitalism. By subsuming oneself within identities supplied by the informational economy one simultaneously folds oneself into society's dominant discourses and becomes an self-policing agent. Consequently, one becomes complicit in constructing an 'affirmative culture'. In a sense, the processes of 'identity formation' via the consumption of commodified cultural forms within global network capitalism overlaps with the commodified cultural production/consumption of managerial-capitalism as described by Adorno and Horkheimer (1979). The only difference is that under managerial-capitalism, 'mass' media generated a 'mass' affirmative culture (i.e. a 'mass' identity), whereas under global network capitalism, niche media generate a mosaic of mini 'niche' affirmative cultures (i.e. 'niche' identities). By succumbing to the rituals, discourses and practices of the new niche identities, individuals participating in the resulting 'imagined communities' become complicit in creating the very discursive closures that confirm the existing hegemonic order. The Frankfurt School may have described an earlier era, when mass media/mass culture was more homogeneous than that seen today. However, it appears that the processes of 'commodified closure' of discourse may actually have been carried over from managerial-capitalism to global network capitalism. The Frankfurt School's work may consequently still have value when exploring the socio-cultural effects of a global network capitalist hegemony. It is even possible that 'creating dominance' via symbolic manipulation may even be more intense under the hegemony of the global network capitalists than under the managerial-capitalists because communication is so much more central to the functioning of the contemporary informational economy.

The proliferation of a mosaic of (ever-shifting) identities has meant the fracturing of the old political constituencies and allegiances of managerial-capitalism. With status being increasingly linked to symbolic consumption, new patterns of social hierarchy are emerging. Hence, those trying to organize political constituencies have needed to re-think completely their appeals and strategies. Constructing, and holding together, hegemonic alliances has become much more complex, and communicating with increasingly fragmented constituencies now involves mastering a multiplicity of niche media discourses. It has also involved mastering new communication practices. Under managerialism, top-down rhetorical communication was deemed sufficient for professional communicators. This is no longer the case. A wider repertoire of practices is now required to communicate with a multiplicity of niche identities. So, in addition to top-down methods, professional communicators now also need to mobilize a range of dialogical approaches, including participatory and consultative communication. They also need to know how to manipulate information in data-bases as an intervention strategy. Further, hegemony-builders in information-rich environments have the problem of keeping track of the emergence of a shifting mosaic of new niche groups which constitute potential threats to the ruling hegemony. (Many of these potentially-oppositional groups will themselves network globally.) This has generated new dilemmas for intelligence agents. Both intelligence and policing agencies have had to develop new skills for monitoring and sifting through the now huge volumes of communication coursing through the global information network, for hacking into data-bases of those deemed 'hostile', and for preventing others hacking into their own data-bases. Essentially, hegemonic labour has become intensely symbolic.

The network capitalists appear to be stabilizing their hegemonic dominance in the OECD countries. The networker elite exudes confidence as its discourses and practices become increasingly naturalized and opaque. By 2000 informational capitalism's global dominance had acquired the mantel of inevitability. As global network capitalism's hegemonic dominance was established in the OECD heartlands, a number of previously influential discourses began to wane. Anyone seen to be associated with the discourses of Soviet managerialism and development managerialism acquired an almost pariah status. The ways in which these two discourses were marginalized did much to confirm Kuhn's (1974) hypothesis about the death of paradigms. Keynesian managerialism was increasingly marginalized and undermined, but did not acquire the pariah status of the other two managerialisms. An interesting fate befell a number of discourses that had grown up during the discursive anarchy of the 1980s and early 1990s. During this interregnum, when managerial hegemonies were in decline, but before a new networker capitalist hegemony had shaped up, a number of 'minority discourses' were developed by feminists, gays and various ethnic-brokers in the OECD countries. During the interregnum shake up, Keynesian managerialists tried to stabilize their weakening hegemonies by developing alliances with these minority groups. These alliances saw the development of managed 'political correctness' when Keynesian (social democratic) managerialists helped these minority groups to create a series of institutionalized and managed discursive closures. Towards the end of the 1990s these mini-bureaucracies and the discursive closures ('political correctnesses') began to experience pressure from an emerging network capitalist hegemony, which developed the capacity to assert its own (network-capitalist) discourses and to wind back managerialist structures, including the mini-bureaucracy of the Keynesian allies. At the turn of the century, network capitalism had not yet succeeded in imposing a discourse closure (or perhaps a series of mini-'niche' closures) of its own, but the tide had turned in favour of the networkers' hegemony within the OECD area.

In the non-OECD areas, the collapse of the Soviet Union meant the demise of opportunities for playing contending powers off against each other (as had been possible under a bi-polar international system). From 1990, the USA was the only state able to project its power globally, and by the late 1990s global network capitalists and their allies had become hegemonically dominant within the USA. Hence, by the dawn of the twenty-first century, global network capitalists possessed the capacity to project their influence globally, both coercively (via the USA's military machinery) and discursively (via the global information networks which revolved around the hubs of OEDC global cities). Consequently, even societies controlled by those nominally espousing Soviet managerialism, such as China and Vietnam, effectively began 'reforming', that is implementing the practices of global network capitalism. The two Soviet elites initially refusing such 'reforms', namely North Korea and Cuba, came under sustained pressure. Some developmental elites adjusted to the New World Order and adopted the discourses and practices of 'market-based reform' and 'de-managerialization' advocated by global network capitalism. The global network capitalists 'rewarded' these 'reformed developmentalists', and 'reforming Asian-Soviet managerialists' by relocating industrial plants out of the OECD countries and into their spheres (e.g. Guangdong). Second-tier network hubs emerged to administer these relocated industrial zones, such as Singapore, Mexico City and Shanghai. Other developmentalist elites simply collapsed and/or saw their spheres decline into 'dead spaces' as they were by-passed by the new global economic flows (e.g. sub-Saharan Africa).

What is not yet clear is whether a 'core' and 'marginal' set of networking hubs will emerge. Will second-tier centres, occupied by comprador elites, emerge as a permanent feature of global network capitalism? Alternatively, will the networkers in the second-tier cities grow into full partners within a single global network capitalist elite? Will a distinction solidify between a relatively 'information rich' labour aristocracy in the OECD countries and a more exploited labour force in Southeast Asia and Latin America? Alternatively, will the eventual distribution of (global network capitalist) social hierarchies eventually look similar in the USA and China? Global network capitalism is still too new a phenomenon to answer such questions.

What is clear is that a new hegemony is shaping up. Global network capitalists and their allies are already far-advanced in building dominance in the OECD countries. They are able to exert considerable influence over the rest of the world. The New World Order is unique in two respects. First, network capitalists hav formed what appears to be the first hegemonic alliance with the capacity to build truly global dominance. They are doing so within a system that is assuming the outlines of a loose networked (neo-feudalistic?) federalism. Secondly, the hegemonic dominance of this emerging networker elite is dependent upon a global electronic communications network. If the network goes down, their hegemony is terminated.

CHAPTER 7

Circulating Meaning I: Making News

Building hegemonic dominance involves, among other things, circulating appropriate discourses. Hegemonic labour requires making, distributing and naturalizing meanings that serve the interests of the dominant group(s). School and university curricula, news, other (non-news) television narratives, radio narratives, films and advertising have emerged at the key discursive fields for building dominance. At the end of the twentieth century, manipulating data-bases began to emerge as a seventh discursive field for building dominance. The question as to which of these discursive fields is most important for planting and nurturing hegemonic discourses is a moot point. By the end of the twentieth century television was certainly regarded as very powerful (most powerful?), but was it television news or other television narratives (dramas, soaps, films, etc.) that most influenced viewers?

Each of the above discursive fields has its own sites and practices. Discussing any of these sites and practices serves to illustrate the way in which intellectuals develop symbiotic relationships with hegemony-builders. This chapter will focus on just one site, namely news production, and upon the intellectuals who make news, namely journalists.

Are journalists merely agents of the hegemonically powerful, or are they autonomous? This chapter will seek to answer this question by exploring news as it emerges from the intersection of three variables: the sites where production takes place; the dominant practices within these sites; and the discourses privileged by those working in these sites. It will be suggested that it is possible for journalists to be simultaneously agents of the powerful and autonomous beings, that is they are not simply the play-things of the powerful, but are ensnared in webs of discourse and practice which set parameters on autonomy. Essentially, each news-making site has its own set of preferred practices and discourses which 'guide' the work of the journalists working at that site.

The sites of news-making

Newsrooms are the productive fulcra for news-making. But newsrooms (whether in newspaper offices or radio or television studios) are part of larger organizations. Hence, newsrooms are locked into a wider chain of organizational influence. Newsrooms, as sub-structures within larger organizations, necessarily conform to the practices of their host bodies. This includes being influenced by pressures emanating from owners (whether private or the state), although this influence is often indirect and opaque. Such sites also conform to the organizational practices of the wider society hosting them. Further, news-making sites are not autonomous of wider organizational and hegemonic pressures, but such pressures are usually not the result of commanderism (i.e. an owner or manager issuing directives) or conspiracy (i.e. small groups conspiring to take control of key social sites). Rather, news-making is 'constrained' in a more indirect manner. Hegemonic dominance is created through the staffing practices (recruitment, promotion and dismissals) employed within these sites and by decision-making concerning rules, procedures and the configuration of technology within these sites. The hegemonically dominant are at their most successful when meaning-making decision-makers police themselves and their staff in ways which confirm the needs of the ruling hegemony, when day-to-day operational decision-making plus longer-term policy setting in newsrooms operates within a conceptual framework that complements hegemonic needs (or at least does not cut across core assumptions of the ruling hegemony).

A fundamental parameter-setter in newsrooms involves decision-making over staffing – who is hired and fired, and who is promoted to key decision-making positions. A key hegemony-steering decision in meaning-making sites is choosing who gets promoted to those positions where staffing decisions are made. Ultimately, decision-making over staffing is perhaps the core mechanism for moving meaning-making in a preferred direction because newsroom staffing profiles necessarily determine which discourses are promoted and which are shunned. Owners (private or state) exercise control over staffing profiles indirectly

– they appoint the boards overseeing the organizations. Owners and/or board members will overwhelmingly be members of ruling hegemonic elites. Boards, in turn, appoint chief executive officers (CEO). It is unlikely that a CEO would be appointed whose worldview was incompatible with that of the owner and/or board. The CEO, in turn, appoints and promotes staff into key decision-making roles and they, in turn, hire and fire and train and socialize the rest of the staff. In the case of a newsroom these staff are the gatekeepers of news-flows. So staffing decisions are indirectly gatekeeping decisions. Importantly, influence over staffing can be exercised by 'commonsense' rather than 'commanderism', that is CEOs can generally work out the preferred discourses of their boards/owners, as will the senior staff. Consequently, there is no need for directives concerning which discourses should be favoured because good staffing decisions (from CEOs downwards) can be relied on to create self-policing mechanisms (through staff 'cloning'). Discourses serving the hegemonically dominant will be adhered to because staff cloning will ensure 'appropriate' gatekeepers are in position. This also means that the mechanism of steering discourse via staffing decisions is opaque during those periods when hegemonies have normalized themselves. Only when hegemonies undergo fundamental ruptures do staffing mechanisms as discursive control-measures become visible. For example, from 1995 to 1997 the South African Broadcasting Corporation purged the bulk of its white staff, who were associated with the previous regime, and replaced them with staff holding views 'appropriate' to the gatekeeping needs of the new regime. By 1998 the new hegemony could rely on a normalized (and hence opaque) staff cloning process at the SABC to deliver appropriate discursive closures.

At first sight it might appear that the emergence of a new communication environment (which includes the proliferation of multi-channel niche media and the information-laden Internet) will make discourse closures through staffing processes less likely. However, under global network capitalism, positioning 'appropriate' gatekeepers is still an operative hegemonic mechanism. Many more (niche) media production sites are now involved, but these sites are networked into large global corporations so that hegemonically-appropriate 'commonsense' staffing decisions (working from the global CEOs downwards) can still be relied upon to deliver gatekeepers with apposite worldviews. The Internet does not substantively undermine this gatekeeper role because sheer information overload has made people turn to professional information-sorters (e.g. journalists, data-base packagers, search-engine and hyperlink designers) to guide them through (and or sift) the growing volumes of available information. New 'information-processing' occupations simply become new gatekeeping roles within proliferating media (information) corporations. This means employment practices can still play a role in building hegemonic dominance and, although newsroom practices have been modified by online technology, the issue of creating gatekeepers through staffing practices has not been altered.

Another parameter-setter within meaning-making sites is decision-making over funding. Funding and staffing issues are often related – for example, deciding who gets to expand their team ('empire building'). Those viewed favourably by boards and CEOs are granted funding to employ staff, deploy new technologies and establish pet projects – that is, they are granted the organizational capacity to influence meaning-making. Being viewed favourably within media organizations (and so being granted funding) implies being seen as someone who can be relied upon to organize the production of discourses valuable to the dominant hegemony. So, within media organizations, funding decisions (like staffing decisions) impact upon the direction of discursive production.

News-making is also 'constrained' by work practices (news game rules). Some practices are the result of conscious local-level decision-making; others are 'inherited' from wider organizational practices (e.g. company policies) or even from more generic practices (e.g. 'Fleet Street' traditions). Related to these practices are questions of how technology is employed. Decisions over deploying technology (i.e. whether to fund new technology use, and how, when and where to deploy it) necessarily influence the fulcrum within which meaning is made. This, in turn, impacts on the sorts of meanings that can be made.

It is not only newsroom practices that impact on meanings made. The practices of the wider organization are just as important when it comes to setting parameters. For example, within newspaper organizations, the print deadlines set by circulation departments and printers necessarily influence journalistic work routines. More importantly, within commercial news organizations, newsroom practices are necessarily entangled with the needs of the advertising department, not because of direct advertiser pressure upon editors and journalists (although such pressure may occur), but because commercial media have to collect, package and deliver audiences to advertisers (Smythe, 1981: 8). The task of any editor in a commercial medium is to generate and package the sort of material that will appeal to the audience that advertisers are interested in. One of the easiest ways to achieve this is to appoint staff whose worldviews correspond to those of the intended audience, but editorial intervention is also sometimes required. Effectively, what transpires is a form of 'market censorship' so that discourses that may alienate the desirable target audience(s) are avoided. Golding and Murdock (1978) suggested that this disadvantaged 'working-class' opinions in the British press, and Louw (1984) suggested that it disadvantaged black opinions in apartheid South Africa because in both cases these sectors were not attractive to the commercial media (because they were deemed to have insufficient disposable income to be attractive to advertisers). Over time, newsroom practices will naturalize the collection of certain genres of information (i.e. those 'appropriate' for the target audiences) as well as the cloning of appropriate practices and staff recruitment. Once naturalized, the 'constraints' on news-making will no longer be noticed. Within that production site a certain set of discourses and practices will simply be routinized as 'the way things are done'.

Routinizing news-making

News is the product of a set of institutionalized work practices – practices that are enmeshed with discourses about the 'profession' of journalism (i.e. self-images) and discourses about audience. Journalists learn to work, and to understand themselves and their work, in a certain way. It is possible to identify a 'generic' Anglo pattern of news-making practices and newsroom structures, a pattern that has been carried across the globe during the periods of British and American domination. This Anglo pattern ultimately has its roots in the 'New Journalism' of the nineteenth-century commercial newspapers developed by Pulitzer, Stead and Northcliffe. This pattern subsequently spread to radio and television newsrooms.

Journalists are confronted by huge volumes of information and an enormous array of phenomena that could qualify as news. Creating news therefore involves sorting through these and selecting which will actually be allowed to reach audiences. So news-making is a process of selection, emphasis and de-emphasis. Journalists refer to this process as knowing what is 'newsworthy'. Effectively, journalists are gatekeepers (White, 1950), allowing some information through the gate, but blocking other information. For anyone concerned with creating hegemonic dominance, the latter (blocking process) is of vital concern. Creating discursive dominance has as much (and possibly more) to do with what information is left out, as what is disseminated. As Cohen said, the media 'may not be successful much of the time in telling people what to think, but it is stunningly successful in telling its readers what to think about' (1963: 13). As gatekeepers, journalists decide what information is left out, and therefore determine 'what is thought about'. So journalists become agenda-setters, creating 'the agenda' and setting the 'parameters' for what is discussed within a society. And, as Noelle-Neumann (1991) has pointed out, these gatekeeping and agenda-setting roles have the capacity to set in motion a 'spiral of silence'. This means that social discourse is progressively closed because people fall silent if their views do not coincide with what the media portray as 'majority opinion'. So the role of 'gatekeeper' or 'agenda-setter' holds great social significance.

Gatekeeping has been institutionalized in sites called newsrooms, where the process of selection, emphasis and de-emphasis has been turned into a set of systematized routines. Significantly, it is the very routinization of the process that has tended to render it opaque to journalists themselves. Anglo journalists, in particular, who work within an essentially empiricist worldview, believe news is 'out there' and that they simply 'find it'. They apparently find it because they 'know' what is 'newsworthy'. Constructivists, such as Tuchman (1978), however, argue that journalists 'construct reality' rather than 'find it'.

News, as Tuchman (1978) says, is a 'window on the world'. Journalists, through their work practices, effectively break a window-opening through the wall, and so create a partial view of the overall panorama – that is only one portion of 'reality' is available through the window-opening. The rest, outside the frame, is hidden behind the wall. News is consequently always skewed by the size, shape and position of the window-frame. But this skewing is not usually the outcome of conscious decision-making aimed at deliberately creating partiality. Rather, the window's position is the outcome of whatever set of practices, work routines and discourses journalists have been socialized into accepting as 'the way things are done'. The partiality (and hence distortion) of news derives from the news-frame – a frame built by journalists applying their particular conception of newsworthiness. It is possible to identify a broad Anglo conception of 'newsworthiness', a conception with its roots in what can loosely be termed the 'Fleet Street' tradition. This Anglo conception of newsworthiness has been reproduced in journalism training programmes throughout the Anglo world. These training programmes, plus on-the-job socialization, have effectively cloned the Fleet Street model from Los Angeles to New Delhi, and Sydney to Johannesburg. And so, despite minor regional mutations, a remarkably similar news-frame exists across the Anglo world. Training has been fundamental in spreading this 'Anglo window'. The British Empire approach favoured sending Fleet Street and BBC staff to the colonies, either as colonial migrants or on secondments to train locals, while the Americans have preferred routing overseas students through US journalism schools. Once a journalist has internalized the appropriate vision of 'newsworthiness' and the work routines to accompany this vision, the model becomes 'naturalized' (and 'self-policing'). Thereafter, journalists need not confront the fact that they are constructing a partial, skewed 'window on the world'.

So making news is about newsworthiness. But to become a useful analytical tool, the obfuscated and mythologized notion of 'newsworthiness', as used by journalists, needs to be given substance. Essentially, newsworthiness is a learned, perceptual mechanism for routinely guiding journalistic decision-making when journalists are engaged in the reporting process – that is how journalists do their job (practices) and what they believe themselves to be doing (discourses). Effectively, a process of selection, emphasis and de-emphasis has been routinized in the following way. First, journalists are trained to work according to a set of formulas. Consequently, they repeatedly look for the same things and routinely ask the same questions. The formulas effectively narrow the options for what can emerge as news by 'guiding' the information-gathering process. There are two key formulas: WWWWWH-questions ('who' does 'what' and 'when', 'where', 'why' and 'how' do they do it) and the inverted pyramid (see page 139). Journalistic training privileges the writing of 'hard factual news' that this WWWWWH-formula delivers. These questions are an excellent short-hand method for getting to the essence of 'immediate' events-based stories (such as motor accidents or fires) but the formula becomes a great hindrance when trying to report on complex issues embedded in convoluted contexts (such as the reasons for the outbreak of warfare). The hard factual news or WWWWWH-formula does not equip journalists to report on complex situations, but it does serve to confirm the professional discourse of 'objectivity'. The idea that one is 'objective' because only 'the facts' (WWWWWH) are reported is a powerful professional-discourse and 'value-system' and is central to Anglo journalistic practice. In essence, because hard, concrete facts are privileged, the stories acquire a 'tangibility' and so appear 'factual' rather than 'constructed'. Tuchman describes this as 'facticity' (1978: 82). It allows journalists to hide from themselves the 'constructed' and 'partial' nature of their stories. Further, just as the WWWWWH-formula directs journalists to look at the world in a certain way, so too has television journalism developed a standardized matrix of 'action' images that are sought out. Effectively, television news has developed a visual formula that drives journalists to produce a certain genre of news that seeks out 'action' and/or the visually spectacular. Because of this visual formula, the WWWWWH-formula and the inverted pyramid formula, television news produces radically simplified news constructs that eschew complexity.

The inverted pyramid directs journalists to grab audience attention at the start of the story, in the introduction. The heart of the story is packed into the first or the first two paragraphs. One does not construct an argument by building towards a conclusion (i.e. a pyramid formula); rather, one puts the 'conclusion' at the beginning of the story (the inverted pyramid formula). In part, this inverted pyramid formula emerged in response to the practice of newspaper 'stone-subs' (in the era of 'hot-metal' printing), who cut stories from the bottom to make them fit the page. Journalists learned that important material at the end of a story stood a good chance of being edited out, whereas material placed in the first few paragraphs was generally the least likely to be cut. The inverted pyramid is now an entrenched and immovable practice not only in newspapers, but also in radio and television journalism. This focus on 'the intro' mutated within television news into the 'sound bite'. Effectively, television journalists seek out spokespersons who are able to provide 'snappy one-liners'. This makes television news even less able to report on complex situations than newspapers. Public relations personnel use their knowledge of journalistic formulas and the demand for 'sound bites' to maximize their chances of placing news stories that promote their employers' interests.

A second feature of the routinization of journalistic practice is the importance of contacts in the news-gathering process. Contacts are the people journalists regularly consult when wanting information or 'quotes'. Each newsroom tends to develop a pool of contacts who are constantly consulted. News is effectively made through the symbiotic relationship that develops between journalists and this pool of contacts – journalists need contacts to provide quotes and information, while the contacts need journalists to develop their 'profile' or to promote a particular idea, product or organization. For many people, becoming a regularly consulted contact is vital for their career. For example, politicians need 'profile' and ultimately the media are the 'dispensers' of profile and/or fame. So any aspiring politician has to develop relationships with journalists, both directly and through the ever-expanding teams of public relations officers, spin doctors and media consultants. The need to 'cultivate journalists' saw the growth, throughout the second half of the twentieth century, of the phenomenon of 'professionalized contacts', that is, a public relations (PR) industry. By the turn of the century no large organization (commercial or state) was without its publicity machinery, staffed by communication spin doctors and professionalized contacts (often ex-journalists).

The pool of contacts used by any newsroom constitutes a very small minority of the overall population. Ultimately, the choice of contacts reflects how that newsroom sees the community it reports on, the choice of contacts being fundamental in defining the shape and position of the 'window' or news-frame discussed by Tuchman. A key mechanism for creating this window is on-the-job socialization of journalists which involves news editors or senior staff passing on 'appropriate' contacts to junior journalists as they are inducted into the newsroom. Learning who news editors and editors consider to be 'appropriate' contacts constitutes an important part of the staff-cloning process in any newsroom. This will be learned by having contacts 'passed-on' and by encountering disapproval when 'inappropriate' contacts are used. Using contacts narrows the 'window-frame' in two ways. There is a tendency to favour quoting the hegemonic elite in part because members of the hegemonic elite are already deemed to be 'important' people and hence 'newsworthy', and secondly because members of the already existent social, political and economic elites tend to have the resources to staff publicity machines. The ability to run PR machines has become an increasingly important skill if people want to become 'reliable' contacts. Reliability involves always being 'contactable' and delivering 'appropriate' quotes in a timely fashion, that is understanding journalistic deadlines and their need for quotes to fit their organization's 'in-house style' and editorial policies. This is the second way in which using contacts narrows the window-frame: journalists stop telephoning their contacts when the first one tells them what they want to hear.

When constructing a story, journalists will work through their contact list, starting with the person who is considered the most 'appropriate' contact. Consequently, news construction has come to favour (and hence promote) certain kinds of people – those with the resources to maintain publicity machines or who are able to deliver 'quotes' and an 'image' concurrent with media requirements. To some extent these requirements have altered the nature of hegemony-building as television becomes ever more central to circulating discourses. Building dominance now drives hegemonic groups to recruit so-called 'video politicians' (like Ronald Reagan or Tony Blair), who have appropriate televisual images and demeanours that suit the electronic media. Secondly, there is now a need to gain access to enormous financial resources in order to pay for the professionalized publicity machines required for promoting hegemonic discourses. In the USA this led to the emergence of political action committees (PACs) to raise money to pay for these PR machines. Contributors to PACs effectively 'buy influence' in Washington. This has introduced a new dimension into hegemonic alliance-building. So, developing a 'professionalized contacts' machinery for television has had the effect of modifying power relationships and the nature of hegemony-building (Smith, 1989: Chapter 2).

Will the importance of contacts decline as ever-greater volumes of online information become available to journalists? There is no doubt that journalists will increasingly use online data-bases as resources to construct their stories (Brooks, 1997). However, data is not going to replace the need for persons with 'televisual images' and PR specialists delivering contacts and quotes. In addition, the emerging online environment will increase the cost of maintaining a professionalized publicity machine because an additional set of staff will now be required to maintain web sites and answer e-mails.

A third feature of routinizing the work of journalists is the importance time plays in imposing certain practices. Time necessarily plays a significant role in news selection processes because news-making takes place within the parameters of deadlines. Newspaper deadlines were traditionally set by the requirements of circulation departments, that is their need to deliver newspapers to the furthest point of the distribution zone. The emergence of multiple editions (updated every few hours) and online newspapers has taken some of the pressure of deadlines off newspaper journalists, but not to the point of removing deadlines *per se*. Television news has to be produced in accordance with television scheduling, and so deadlines remain a powerful feature of television news practices. News has to be produced regardless of what is actually happening outside the newsroom because newspapers are printed at fixed times and radio and television news bulletins go on air at fixed points in time. Hence, news practices have to build in the requirements of deadlines. In addition the 'window-frame', as described by Tuchman, is largely built during office hours. So newsworthiness is implicitly tied up with production routines – the development of regular working hours for journalistic staff and the meeting of production deadlines. PR personnel use their knowledge of such time constraints to maximize their chances of placing news stories.

A fourth aspect of the routinization of journalistic practice is inducting new staff into newsroom procedures. Each newsroom will have a set of procedures and a related organizational culture. Some of the routinized procedures for collecting, writing and submitting stories will only be found in a particular newsroom (and perhaps tied to a senior staff's idiosyncrasies). Other procedures will be found across whole media groups, when all the newsrooms in the group share a set of procedures and an organizational culture. All procedures set parameters on news production, and so socializing journalists into an organization's procedures helps to steer their production into conformity with the genre associated with that organization. Similarly, journalists are socialized into an acceptance of the newsroom bureaucracy, hierarchical pecking-orders and the particular style of office politics operative in their newsroom. There is a relationship between the hierarchical chains of command and the bureaucratized procedures that are operative. It has been suggested that this is a defining characteristic of news production, namely that news is the ultimate bureaucratized meaning-making – that news is simply the outcome of a highly routinized process of collecting and processing information, where the process is guided by formal rules. Hence news takes on the characteristics of an 'eternal recurrence' (Rock, 1981) – it is meaning that looks repetitive, precisely because it is meaning that is emerging from a repetitive set of bureaucratized procedures. For those building hegemonies this is the useful thing about news: it is a form of meaning-making that is highly susceptible to manipulation for two reasons. First, the existence of hierarchical bureaucracies in media organizations means that it is possible for hegemonic elites to 'diffuse' their discursive needs downward (from the CEOs), although owners and CEOs need not employ commanderism to achieve compliance. Secondly, the existence of predictable journalistic routines and procedures mean that ex-journalists (as PR people and communication spin doctors) can employ their knowledge of these procedures to 'plant' stories at the right time and with the right person, so as to maximize the chances of these stories being used.

Another aspect of journalistic practice to be routinized is the presentation of the news. Procedures have been developed for designing newspapers and giving some stories prominence. Newspaper sub-editors have a whole range of techniques at their disposal to emphasize some news and de-emphasize other stories in accordance with editorial policy. This includes decisions about which page a story is placed on, where on the page it is placed, the size of the headline, whether a photograph will accompany the story and what sort of photograph will be used (see Hall, 1981). Similar mechanisms for emphasizing some news stories, and de-emphasizing others, exist within television and radio production practices. Hence, radio news directors decide on the running-order of stories, and in television production, news directors, producers and tape editors decide running-orders and which graphics and images to use. Such 'presentation' decisions crucially influence the overall narrative being constructed and so impact on the interpretation of the news. These 'design' and 'presentation' decisions have also been routinized, with those taking these decisions having internalized a whole series of professional discourses which 'guide' their work practices.

As the twentieth century drew to a close, a new medium – the Internet – began to emerge out of the conjunction of new communications technologies. And so, new communications professionals emerged to staff the Internet production sites, such as multimedia designers and data workers (specialists in buying and creating data-bases and transferring meanings from old-technology formats into digital formats, copyright specialists, etc.). Not surprisingly, the old news production sites developed an interest in this new form of communication and in the 1990s many newspapers and broadcasters built their own web sites and online newsrooms to feed these sites.

As might be expected, many routines and practices associated with print and television newsrooms were transplanted to the new Internet production sites. Journalists have simply become 'data-inputers' into Internet sites. The tyranny of print deadlines and television and radio schedules have been dispensed with, only to be replaced by 'procedural deadlines' when web sites are routinely updated. But essentially online news is still made within set bureaucratized routines, and online news still frames reality in the way described by Tuchman; only now, multimedia designers have at their disposal a new set of tools for potentially manipulating audiences that were not available to the older media formats – namely, Internet users can literally be 'guided' by hyperlinks and search engines. No doubt future hegemonic struggles over the creation of dominant meanings will need to pay attention to such 'guidance' techniques.

Symbiotic relationships in news-making

News-making revolves around journalists, their practices and the organizational sites into which they are embedded (newsrooms). However, journalists and news editors are also enmeshed in sets of symbiotic relationships with other professional communicators who are complicit in making the news.

The routinization of news-making effectively directs journalists to privilege certain news-making sites over others. Some news is random and accidental, such as aircraft crashes and motor accidents. But even the reporting of this 'random' news has been considerably 'de-randomized' by the journalistic practice of using police, ambulance and hospital spokespersons as sources for 'locating' and reporting such events. But, in general, it is non-random news that has become the staple fare of contemporary news production. Most news now comes from four 'institutionalized' sets of news-making sites: the politico-legal system; the sports industry; the entertainment industry; and the business sector. In addition, 'news-shapers' (Soley, 1992) could be considered a fifth news site, that is those who are promoted as 'experts' by the news media and who are consequently called on to 'comment' upon and/or discuss events with journalists. The development of 'sound-bite' television reporting greatly enhanced the use such news-shapers. These news-shapers are people whom researchers at broadcast organizations have deemed to be 'appropriate' experts, and who can be relied on to deliver comment that is both editorially 'suitable' and which conforms to the 'sound-bite' needs of the broadcast media. The news-shapers are seen as 'specialists' in one of the four news fields mentioned above and so will be routinely called upon to comment upon and 'frame' the news. On-air discussions between these news-shapers and journalists often become a form of editorializing, serving to set agendas in accordance with the editorial policy of the news organization concerned.

Each of the four news-making sites have professionalized their relationships with the news media. All major organizations in society have developed publicity machines. Some of these publicity machines are now heavily accented towards marketing communicators (e.g. the sports sector); others are geared towards 'spin doctoring' (e.g. the PR and 'damage-control' machines of politicians); while others are concerned with 'image-building' or 'public lobbying' (e.g. many business sector PR departments). These publicity machines are now integral to the making of news. News has been substantively 'public relations-ized' as journalists have developed a symbiotic relationship with those staffing publicity machines. For news organizations it is simply much cheaper to use professionally-produced material made available by these publicity machines than to produce it themselves. Publicity/PR machines have effectively evolved into a form of journalistic 'out-sourcing'. In the process, co-dependence has emerged between journalists and publicity machine personnel, as both have developed routines that intermesh with each other. Contemporary journalistic routines for news-gathering would simply collapse without the publicity machines with which journalists now connect. And the professional hegemony-builders (politicians) and sports personalities (plus the sports marketing machines underpinning their activities) would have no one to perform to if journalists did not provide the media conduits through which they reach their publics.

A neatly harmonized (and professionalized) set of team practices has emerged which symbiotically meshes journalists with a whole range of people whose careers revolve around professional 'image-making' (e.g. PR people, spin doctors, marketers, politicians, sportsmen and women and entertainers). Journalists need image-makers and image-makers need journalists, and so each has necessarily developed routines and practices for 'using' the other. Out of their routinized co-dependence emerges 'news'. Essentially, the second half of the twentieth century saw meaning-making (including news-making) become progressively more public relation-ized, with the culture industry producing a particular form of intellectual practice involving professional communicators working to skew meaning-production in favour of their employer's interests. These professional 'skewers' are at their most successful when journalists become dependent upon them to supply information. As newsrooms have become leaner (because of cost-cutting measures), the pressure on smaller news staffs to fill the 'news holes' has necessarily grown. This has tended to shift news-making practices into even greater dependency on PRs hence the growing public relations-izing of news. Consequently, for those who can afford to employ PRs and spin doctors, it has become easier to manipulate news. In general, those who can afford such publicity machines are members of hegemonic elites.

Clearly news production is a complex process involving many communication professionals. The relationship between these professionals and hegemonic elites does not look like a simple, one-way transmission of messages, with professional communicators simply and uncritically producing messages at the bidding of hegemonic elites. However, a complex set of (sometimes obfuscated) relationships exists between ruling elites and professional communicators which generally ensures that these professionals overwhelmingly produce and circulate messages that service the needs of hegemonically dominant groups. These relationships seem to fall into three broad categories.

First, those who succeed in establishing their discourses as the dominant measures precisely win the struggle for hegemony. This necessarily involves finding ways to exercise influence over the institutions of the culture industry. Such influence may entail direct ownership and/or membership of media boards. But 'influence' need not be that direct. Hegemonic elites, by definition, constitute the membership of influential social networks. These networks, which include media owners, board members and editors, have been called the 'cocktail party circuit', the 'old boys' network', 'new boys' network' or 'new girls' network'. Hegemonic elites transact a lot of their business informally within these networks, business that ranges from brokering 'deals' to swopping favours at the race meeting or the golf club. Membership of these networks is restricted, but it is not static. As hegemonic elites mutate, so too does the membership of these influential, informal networks. Very few members of these networks will have any form of direct control over news-making processes, but their capacity to mobilize such networks to influence news production should not be underestimated.

Secondly, those with command over resources, which does not have to be one's own property, are necessarily in a position to 'buy influence', including influence over meaning-making processes. This may entail 'buying favours' or even outright bribery. But usually it simply involves being in a position to employ 'appropriate' people. For example, those who can afford to employ skilled PRs and spin doctors are more likely to influence news production in ways beneficial to their interests. PRs and spin doctors are hired for their knowledge of journalistic gatekeeping. Their job is to use their knowledge of newsroom routines and practices to find ways of setting the agenda for the agenda-setters. If successful, the stakes are high for those involved in the struggle for hegemony. The endgame for the builders of hegemony is to set in motion a 'spiral of silence' which closes discourse and so secures hegemonic dominance.

Finally, ruling elites are necessarily at their most secure (and so can use less coercion) when they succeed in naturalizing their preferred discourses and practices with three key groups of people: the gatekeepers of the culture industry; those who manage, hire and fire these gatekeepers; and those who train and educate these gatekeepers. Ultimately, when journalists see existing economic relationships as 'natural', the mechanics of existing political decision-making as legitimate and existing coercive arrangements (i.e. justice, policing and military systems) as legitimate, they can be relied upon to 'ask the right questions', and produce reports and images that confirm the existing hegemonic arrangements. Successful hegemonic dominance involves achieving a naturalized and routinized system for staffing the culture industries (perhaps especially newsrooms) with intellectuals who broadly accept the discourses and practices of the ruling hegemony. Hegemonic closure of discourse will be most effective when those involved in media training programmes, media staffing decisions and establishing media work practices routinely take decisions that confirm the discursive needs of the existing hegemonic order, and set up mechanisms to clone themselves. When hegemonically 'appropriate' decision-making is routinized, ruling elites need not intervene to secure their discursive needs, and discourse closure becomes naturalized and opaque.

CHAPTER 8

Circulating Meaning II: The Public Relations-izing of War

Global network capitalists are still engaged in the process of building a global hegemony, which has come to be called the New World Order (NWO). NWO is based upon the USA possessing overwhelming military dominance. Following the collapse of the Soviet Union, the USA was left as the only country with the capacity to project its power globally. US power has placed US-Anglos at the centre of the emerging global networker elite. However, the US core appears to be deliberately networking itself with non-US Anglos, especially those in Britain. Globalization entails a new form of hegemony-building. This is generating a new genre of warfare – one conducted by a 'dispersed' elite that has networked itself globally, an elite which is building a global economy, culture and hegemony that is highly information-ized and media-ized.

The collapse of the Soviet Union produced global instability. Such massive dislocations in balances of power always lead to eras of warfare as new power blocs re-align. If past experience is anything to go by (as witnessed by the wars set in motion by the imperial decline of Spain, Austria, the Ottomans and Britain), the world will now experience some decades of conflict until a new global balance of power is established. But the new batch of wars that are likely to emerge from the Soviet collapse look set to be of a new genre. And these new wars will become enmeshed with the work of building a new hegemony – i.e. the hegemonic-labour required to tie together a global networkers' alliance. So the new wars will, in part, be bound up with the processes of constructing a new (globally dispersed) ruling elite. The emerging global networkers' hegemony is not only inventing a new socio-economic dispensation, the new ruling bloc is simultaneously inventing a new global, coercive machinery to enforce the NWO.

Shifts in the making of hegemonies and wars

A key feature of the hegemony being built by global network capitalists is that, at its core, are Anglos who are now dispersed globally as a result of five hundred years of British and then American colonial settlement and assimilation. At heart, today's Anglo hegemonic style remains derivative of the original Anglo-Saxon pattern of conquest and assimilation (developed when subduing England). The Anglo pattern of assimilation, as refined in the USA, proved particularly valuable for expanding Anglo hegemony into a global phenomenon. The upshot of this success is that today's emerging NWO elite shares a common adherence to discourses and practices that are essentially Anglo or at least derived from Anglo sources. The particularistic nature of these discourses and practices is obscured from those working inside these discourses and practices – they now appear 'universal' to Anglos because of their globally-dispersed nature. Non-Anglos recognize the 'particularism' of these discourses and practices but, under a NWO hegemonic regime, have simply had to learn to adapt to them. This can be seen in the way non-Anglo journalists have adapted to the Anglo 'model of communication' and 'political marketing' as used by NATO during the Kosovo conflict (Brivio, 1999: 515).

Because the network capitalists are globally dispersed, they rely on media, communication and information for the very functioning of both their informationalized economy and their hegemony-building efforts. Not surprisingly, global networker hegemony-building appears to be strongly informational and media-centric, involving high levels of input from professional communicators such as PR specialists and spin doctors (PRs). The communication genre underpinning this global network is the Anglo 'culture industry' model with its roots in the commercialized meaning-making of Stead, Pulitzer and Northcliffe. The materials coursing through this communication network are often enmeshed with the networkers' hegemonic needs for both naturalizing and universalizing their (Anglo) practices and discourses and with promoting cultural cooption on Anglo terms (as seen in the discourse of multiculturalism).

As one might expect, the coercive dimensions of hegemony-building now also involve high levels of media-ized, public relation-ized (PR-ized) activity. Given that the emerging networker elite is composed of highly media-centric people, both 'media' and 'discourse' have emerged as increasingly central to the new genre of warfare being developed. The new digital communications technologies have changed the nature of warfare, the reporting of wars and the propaganda techniques for selling war. The first war of this new genre was the 1990 Gulf War. But it was a genre that had actually been shaping up throughout the 1980s, beginning with the Falklands War in 1982. By 1990 the US military were ready to launch their first fully public relation-ized war. Global network capitalism had found a genre of warfare that perfectly matched its hegemonic needs.

The hegemony being built by global network capitalists necessarily has three (overlapping) concerns. The first is negotiating a set of transglobal alliances to hold the emergent elite together. The second is developing a set of legitimate discourses and practices and circulating these among the populations of global network capitalism's OECD heartland. Some of these discourses and practices are quite localized (e.g. only applicable in Australia), but others are diffused throughout global network capitalism's entire sphere of influence. The third is developing coercive mechanisms to either pacify or contain those who are seen to pose a disruptive threat to the global networkers' hegemony. This coercive dimension includes 'policing functions', ranging from pacifying the ghettos of the global cities, 'peace-keeping' in Bosnia and 'weapons inspections' in Iraq, through to 'containing' alternative power centres (e.g. China).

For those organizing global network capitalism's hegemonic wars this has created problems. To date, the NWO wars (e.g. various 'peace-keeping' actions and 'pacifying' the Gulf region) have been fought against enemies who pose no real threat to the OECD populations financing and fighting the wars, that is the USA and its allies. However, because of the nature of the political processes within the OECD countries, these populations have to be persuaded to support the coercion being used. As Young and Jesser (1997: 2) point out, 'public support' has become a prerequisite for successfully pursuing these wars. Essentially, because global network capitalism is precisely built upon 'informationalism' and infrastructures facilitating massive flows of meaning, the OECD populations are highly media-ized. This means that although these wars are 'far away', 'non-threatening' and not about 'survival' (for the OECD populations), they will become media events significantly impacting upon the consciousness of both the networker elite and the wider populations of OECD countries. Hence, under global network capitalism, 'selling' these wars becomes enmeshed with both (intra-elite) alliance-building and (extra-elite) legitimacy-building. Consequently, NWO warfare becomes highly PR-ized because it is seen to be imperative to keep media images positive; or at least prevent them from becoming negative.

The PR-izing of war means that, before the war begins, the enemy needs to be demonized. And given the strong 'individualist strand' in Anglo thinking, this demonization has tended to involve creating an identifiable villain, for example, Saddam Hussein (Iraq), Slobodan Milosevic (Yugoslavia/Bosnia/Kosovo) and General Wiranto (Indonesia/Timor). This vilification process has often involved associating the person with Hitler as folk-devil, a trend initiated in the 1989 Panama operation to remove General Noriega from power. But in addition to vilifying the enemy, the logic of binary opposition necessitates also creating the 'victims' who are to be saved from the villain. Finding 'victims' to 'save' has become an important device for justifying the use of NWO violence against foreigners. Military PRs have found it useful to 'piggy-back' upon discourses that already have widespread currency among key OECD intellectual gatekeepers (e.g. journalists, teachers and the university intelligentsia). There already exists a whole pool of idealistic discourses born of OECD affluence, and these are usually associated with the 'conscience-mobilizing' campaigns of 'social justice' NGOs like Amnesty International or Oxfam (Ignatieff, 1998: 21). Military PRs and psychological operations (psy-ops) personnel have found these 'idealisms' to be a great resource when mobilizing OECD populations for war, demonizing enemies and justifying NWO warfare. Essentially, mobilizing 'victimhood' discourses that are already 'trendy' in journalistic circles, means that psy-ops stories, promoted by military PRs, tend to receive no critical scrutiny from journalists. Propaganda is easily 'placed' in the media if it confirms existing journalistic bias and/or fits their news frame.

There is no doubt that warfare has always been accompanied by propaganda, as Knightley's (1982) work has demonstrated. Even staged media events to whip up public support and demonize the enemy are not new. The first fake propaganda newsreel dates back to the 1899–1902 Boer War (Young & Jesser, 1997: 28). However, despite the long (dishonourable) track record of media involvement in covering warfare, there is no doubt that from the Vietnam War onwards the military grew increasingly concerned with television's impact on waging war. This resulted in warfare being substantively media-ized and PR-ized. Every war involving Anglo-Americans since Vietnam – the Falklands (1982), Grenada (1983), Panama (1989), the Persian Gulf (1990), Somalia (1992–93), Haiti (1994), Bosnia (1992–95), Kosovo (1999) and Timor

(1999) – has seen the military become increasingly sophisticated as agents of hegemonic coercion. The military has become skilled at not only killing people, but at using the media (especially television) as a powerful tool of warfare.

The catalyst for developing the new media-ized genre of war was Vietnam (Young & Jesser, 1997: 275). The US military believed it learned two lessons from the Vietnam War. First, that if an anti-war consciousness develops among one's own civilians, the war will be lost because political pressure will grow to end the war. Secondly, television images have the capacity to promote an anti-war consciousness and to disrupt the legitimacy of using coercion. Further, if a war was not carefully PR-ized, television images of the war have the capacity to seriously destabilize the legitimacy of hegemonic orders. The military went as far as blaming television for losing the Vietnam War because television was unable to deal with the complexity of warfare. Instead, the immediacy of television left viewers with negative 'impressions' and 'emotions' (MacArthur, 1992: 82). Hallin (1986: 213) has pointed out that blaming television for losing the war is simplistic because the television coverage was only one element in the process leading to the collapse of America's 'will to fight'. Hallin's (1986) examination of media content also demonstrated that US media coverage of the Vietnam War was far from uniformly negative. Nonetheless, the new PR-ized genre of warfare did effectively grow as a strategic response to General Westmoreland's perception that television coverage of the war produced an inherently distorted perspective because it emphasized the visually dramatic, violent and miserable (Westmoreland, 1980: 555).

The US military's perception that television caused their defeat is an exaggeration. However, there is no doubt that television is a problem for those employed by ruling hegemonies to deploy coercion (i.e. the military and police). The key problem is that the immediacy of television images makes such images appear unmanipulated. Television viewers get the impression that they are actually privy to what is going on because television images seem so real. But television images are manufactured. Viewers only get to see what the camera was pointed at, not what was behind the cameraman or what happened when the camera was turned off. They do not see what was edited out, or the countless other gate-keeping decisions. So as Knightley (1982: 381–3) notes, television images of warfare (or other news for that matter) do not portray 'reality' or a 'fair', unbiased perspective on the war, they just seem to convey such a 'reality'. And when conflict and violence is involved, television is almost guaranteed to skew the portrayal of such news. So although television may not have been to blame for America losing the Vietnam War, it was a significant contributing factor. Media coverage of the Tet offensive and My Lai massacre were public relations disasters for the US military, which massively undermined civilian support for the Vietnam War and undercut the credibility of military briefings. But, in part, they were disasters because of bad timing. These stories emerged when the ruling hegemony was already in trouble over its handling of the war. Tet added to the de-legitimation of the ruling hegemony, it did not cause it. Had these stories broken earlier, they may not have had the same impact. Nonetheless the US military took the lessons of Tet and My Lai to heart and set about ensuring that such PR disasters would not happen again. They learned to public relations-ize warfare, and to pay serious attention to curtailing negative television images from reaching the public.

The first step in learning to PR-ize warfare happened by accident in 1982. The British campaign to recapture the Falklands from Argentina involved dispatching a task force to a remote location substantively isolated from the rest of the world. To cover this war the British media sailed as part of the expeditionary force. They effectively became part of the British military's PR machine because they were within a 'closed' deployment, 'trapped' on naval ships and utterly dependent upon the military for getting information, dispatching their stories and indeed even for their survival. Although the resulting stories clearly lacked credibility, the military saw how the media could be corralled, and therefore controlled. Also during the 1980s, military PRs witnessed South Africa's highly media-ized civil war, and the consequences of not containing negative images of conflict. The outcome was that highly emotive images of South African violence became a widespread feature of Western television news, leading to public pressure on Western governments to 'stop apartheid'. No similar pressure was mounted against other (often more) repressive third world governments because repression in these other societies was not televised. These lessons were not lost on the US military.

The Falklands became, by default, a testing ground for media control (Young & Jesser, 1997: 277). When the USA invaded Grenada to overthrow its government in 1983, the military applied a media management policy derived from the Falklands lesson. They simply excluded the media from the island to be invaded, creating, in effect, a news blackout. When four Western journalists managed to get on to Grenada they were arrested and removed (Young & Jesser, 1997: 129). US military PRs released televisual images of the Grenada war which, in the absence of other material, were used. The South African government tried to copy this technique in 1985 and halt the production of television images of black township violence because these were generating hostile US public opinion (and pressure for sanctions). However, banning camera crews from townships was badly handled and became a bigger PR disaster since it confirmed the image of the South African government as authoritarian. It also did not stop the screening of negative images because US television networks had large stocks of such material which were simply endlessly recycled.

South Africa's handling of journalists may have become a model of what not to do, but for the US military Grenada was a major PR coup, demonstrating that they could block negative television images. But Grenada was a small, insignificant island that could be sealed off from the world. The question was could such a media management strategy (for depriving the media of 'negative' images) be successfully applied to a larger and less isolated theatre of war? The campaign to change the Panamanian government in 1989 demonstrated that the US military could successfully manage the media in non-island contexts. During this war the 'news was not actively censored, but passively censored by ensuring lack of access and delay' (Young & Jesser, 1997: 148). Towards the end of the conflict this management of the media unravelled because ex-President Noriega was not captured as quickly as had been planned. However, an important feature of the Panamanian campaign was that the US successfully demonized Noriega (a difficult task given that Noriega had previously been a US ally). This moved the public relations-izing of war another step forward.

By 1990 the US military had developed a new model of media-ized warfare in which public relations and psy-ops were central features of the planning and execution of the war. As Engelhardt says of the 1990 Gulf War, it was 'the war to reestablish war' (1994: 92). War was once more going to be made to 'appear' acceptable, even in highly media-ized societies. Essentially, all the lessons learned since Vietnam were brought to bear on the Gulf War. The war was to be organized differently now with a view to deliberately excluding negative television images and carefully legitimating one's own coercive actions. As Young and Jesser (1997: 280) say, the Gulf War was constructed in accordance with the 'primacy of politics', that is alliance and legitimacy considerations were as important as military issues.

So the Gulf War was meticulously planned and organized as a media (and psy-ops) operation. Young and Jesser (1997: 292–4) describe the planning of these new media-ized wars as involving the following. Long-term forward planning now includes significant media and political/hegemonic strategizing. Warfare planning now builds into its core a media policy. Opposition leaderships is demonized in preparation for the war. In fact such demonization are usually a good indication that war is coming. Demonizations is often accompanied by identifying refugees and exile groups and promoting them as future alternative governments. Demonization also involves the selective portrayal of history, especially where intervention is being made on one side of a civil conflict (as occurred in Kosovo). The target regime will be destabilized, embarrassed and made to look unreasonable and irrational through political, economic and diplomatic manoeuvres. Much energy is expended on creating public approval and declarations of support for action against the target. For example, 'flag nation' allies are enlisted and legitimacy is sought from the United Nations (UN) and regional political groupings. These ends are achieved through diplomatic lobbying and economic inducements. The media is targeted with a view to creating public approval for action. The deployment of troops involves building up an overwhelming superiority in numbers and firepower so as to ensure quick victory. This deployment will include media exclusion from the deployment zone. The media will be corralled and managed throughout the actual war. Media manipulation and deception will be practised, with military PRs providing good televisual images. As soon as possible after the war, the military withdraws and hands over to the UN, a regional grouping or a new government created from former opposition groups or exiles, etc.

The Gulf War set the pattern for this new public relation-ized genre of warfare. To begin with, Saddam Hussein (a former US ally) was demonized, the media being coopted into this demonizing process. 'Flag nation' allies were brought on board to legitimate US deployment; in particular, Arab allies were sought and induced to join the alliance through having their US debts written off. Once military deployment began, the media were corralled and managed. Journalists were formed into 'pools' far removed from the battlefront, where military PRs could feed them information. Pool journalists were only granted access to events that were strictly controlled. Censorship was achieved through denial of access to military engagement and news blackouts at the start of the war. All interviews had to be conducted in the presence of military escorts, and all copy and images cleared by the military before transmission. Military PRs ensured a 'flow of favorable military sourced information to fill the vacuum created by media restrictions. Material ranged from information provided at carefully controlled briefings which bypassed journalists on the spot, all the way to carefully sanitized television coverage of high technology weaponry in action' (Young & Jesser, 1997: 280). Military spokesmen were auditioned and selected for their 'media presence'. The media was stage-managed, manipulated and lied to, and they believed the lies (Taylor, 1992: 220–1). But the media were also used as an avenue for diplomatic signals and intelligence-gathering. Extraordinarily, the media meekly went along with this. Effectively, the media became a vehicle through which 'the government and the military made direct approaches to the public through the immediacy of television' (Young & Jesser, 1997: 191). Television became a direct tool of hegemonic labour, a tool for legitimating the use of violence against Iraq. For the US military the Gulf War was a tremendous success. They asserted NWO hegemony over the Gulf region, thereby insuring oil supplies for global network capitalism. They developed new, networked ('coalition') command systems, and not only successfully turned the media into propaganda tools (through deploying PR/psy-ops), but seemingly got journalists to enjoy being coopted by the military (MacArthur, 1992: 227–9).

Implicit in this new approach to war is the recognition that media coverage of conflict now directly affects state responses. Shaw (1996: 7) notes that Western politics has been transformed by mass communication in so far as groups in conflict zones can now use the media to appeal to Western electorates. Further, images of conflict impact on public opinion, and hence affect the room for manoeuvre that Western politicians have. So wars are now played out on a media-ized global stage, the implications of which no military planner can ignore. Public relations-ized warfare is the military's response to this new theatre of conflict. Wars now have to be designed as media events which, if all goes according to plan, actually strengthen the dominance of the ruling hegemony by generating a 'feel good factor' and enhancing legitimacy for the ruling alliance.

A crucial dimension to the military's perception of waging media-ized warfare is the creation of media events that appear as bloodless as possible, so that war can again become 'acceptable'. This is based upon a belief that televised images of blood during the Vietnam War caused American public opinion to swing against warfare. Consequently, military PR now aims to sanitize war, 'portraying it as a low risk Nintendo game. [.] Military PR also reflects the American penchant for the upbeat, the happy endings, with a minimum of groans, blood, and deaths' (Pinsdorf, 1994: 49). At heart, creating an Nintendo war means working to exclude images of dead bodies, blood and brutality. This type of warfare has also seen the development of a new militaristic language that aims to mystify and obscure as much as possible. Taylor calls this the creation of a 'terminological fog' (1992: 45), such as using phrases like 'collateral damage' for civilian deaths and 'sorties' for bombing. Words like 'dead', 'enemy' and 'war' are avoided. Brivio notes that a technical military language is deployed which 'uses acronyms and euphemisms to sterilize the horrors of war' (1999: 516). On the other hand, reports will be circulated of how the (now demonized) opposition uses brutality against its 'victims' (who are, of course, to be saved through the intervention).

But the PR-izing of war goes beyond military PR units. Outside PR consultants are also hired by belligerents. In fact, the most spectacular PR success of the Gulf War was the work of a PR firm, CFK/H&K hired by the Kuwaiti government. This firm arranged for a 15-year-old Kuwaiti girl to lie to a US Congressional Committee that she had witnessed Iraqi troops throwing babies out of incubators (MacArthur, 1992: 58–9). The story was calculated to promote the 'Saddam as Hitler' notion and to feed the need for 'victims' to rescue. This incubator story had an enormous impact on Anglo public opinion. And once planted, it spread throughout the global media network. This served to legitimate NWO aggression against Iraq. As important, the incubator story, as well as the 'oil-covered sea birds' story, whose plight was untruthfully blamed on Saddam's 'ecological terrorism', had the effect of coopting mainstream Anglo journalists into the anti-Iraq camp since both stories were designed to generate outrage by violating those discourses with widespread currency among journalists. Once coopted, the journalists could be relied on to play the part as functionaries of the PR-ized war effort.

The PR-ized genre of warfare, perfected by the USA in the Gulf War, was subsequently deployed in all US-led interventions during the 1990s – in Somalia, Haiti, Bosnia and Kosovo. The Australians also deployed this genre with almost textbook precision in their 1999 Timor war. They demonized the Indonesian military and pro-Indonesian militia, eulogized Timorese exiles and resistance groups, successfully mobilized NGO 'victimhood' discourses, enlisted both UN and 'flag nation' support, prevented the media from gaining direct access to the war, successfully managed and manipulated the media, turned military commanders into television stars, succeeded in getting the media to rely on sanitized military PR televisual images and used the war to strengthen the legitimacy of Australia's ruling hegemony.

Nintendo warfare

The new genre of warfare has got much to do with technological developments. New media technologies have not only changed socio-economic dispensations, they have also impacted on how wars can be fought. During the 1980s the USA led the world in deploying networked computers as coercive tools. The USA also led the way in developing 'smart' killing machines. Enormous firepower can now be delivered to any part of the globe in ways that radically reduce the need for US ground combat. From the Second World War onwards, the USA has perfected the art of bombing – aerial technologies (bombers and missiles) are used to pulverize enemy forces, socio-economic infrastructure and morale from a safe distance before ground troops are actually committed. Adding digital communication technology to weaponry was a natural extension of this US style of warfare. This digitization of warfare played a role in the collapse of the Soviet Union because it is an enormously expensive form of warfare. Partly as a response to trying to keep up with US military spending, the Soviets spent themselves into bankruptcy. By the mid-1980s Gorbachev recognized that the Soviets were economically unable to sustain this form of warfare, and so effectively called an end to the Cold War. From this was born the NWO, a network capitalist hegemony founded upon a (highly digitized) US military machine.

The beauty of this digitized 'smart weapons' warfare is that it can make wars look clean if PRs mobilize it correctly. During the Vietnam War, high altitude aerial bombing lost its 'cleanness' when it became visually enmeshed with images of bloody ground combat. So although US aircrews were portrayed as skilled professionals, with no vindictiveness towards those they bombed (Hallin, 1986: 137), the overall impression of the war was of a bloody, dirty and messy affair. During the Gulf War this was not allowed to happen. Instead, military PRs used the Gulf War's aerial warfare to 'create the impression of a 'clean' techno-war, almost devoid of human suffering and death, conducted with surgical precision by wondrous mechanisms' (Franklin, 1994: 42). In place of blood and dead bodies were 'weapons counts' and the blowing up of 'inanimate things' like buildings and bridges (Engelhardt, 1994: 88). As Franklin says of this PR-ized warfare:

> Why not project the war from the point of view of the weapons? And so the most thrilling images were transmitted directly by the laser-guidance systems of missiles and by those

brilliant creations, 'smart bombs'. Fascinated and excited, tens of millions of Americans stared at their screens, sharing the experience of these missiles and bombs unerringly guided to a target by the wonders of US technology, a target identified by a narrator as an important military installation. The generation raised in video arcades and on Nintendo could hardly be more satisfied. The target got closer and closer, larger and larger. And then everything ended with the explosion. There were no bloated human bodies, as in the photographs of Vietnam and Gettysburg. There was none of the agony of the burned and wounded that had been glimpsed on television relays from Vietnam. There was just nothing at all. In this magnificent triumph of techno-war, America's images of its wars had reached perfection. (1994: 42)

In this media-ized 'hyperwar' what got lost was the physical effects of modern weapons on human beings (Taylor, 1992: 29). For those at the receiving end of the bombing the effects are brutal, but when the PRs do their jobs well, these new digitized techno-wars can be made to look like video-games for all the multiple audiences that military PRs are targeting: the folks back home who must not be allowed to become negative or pessimistic about the war; the various publics in allied or friendly states who need to be kept on-side; and those publics inclined to support the enemy. The latter groups must be denied images of war's brutality which they can mobilize in oppositional PR campaigns. However, media-ized wars need to be quick wars if the discourse closures are to kept intact. Hence, NWO wars have involved troop and high-tech deployments that ensure absolute superiority over enemy forces. If PR closure is to be effective there must be no time for public protests to emerge, and no trickle of body bags back home (Taylor, 1992: 3). If the war cannot be brought to a speedy closure, controlling information flow becomes a problem, as was seen in Somalia when withdrawal followed quickly on the heels of 'messy' war images reaching US television screens.

New information technology has facilitated the informationalization of war in four ways. First, new digital technologies have produced 'smart' killing machines which can be deployed to deliver quick wars. This 'smart' technology is, at heart, informational, and converges seamlessly with the needs of PRs trying to make war look like the deployment of 'clean' technology. It makes it possible to construct images of warfare as a video-game. Secondly, just as economies have been informationalized, so too have wars. One of the reasons digitized warfare can deliver speedy victory for those possessing the new technologies is the capacity it generates for gathering and processing huge volumes of information (intelligence), which improves decision-making over (physical and psychological) targets. Thirdly, the global information network has necessarily become an effective conduit for disinformation and psy-ops campaigns aimed at destabilizing 'the enemy', or even for delivering real-time 'diplomatic' signals. Fourthly, OECD populations are now effectively media-ized. They are heavily influenced by media images. Military planners cannot ignore this because images of conflict can be especially 'emotional' and hence produce backlashes against their activities.

Fortunately for these military planners, OECD television news has an insatiable appetite for quality 'action' images delivered more or less instantaneously. If military PRs can supply appropriate images and information, it will tend to be used, particularly if alternative sources are denied to them. This has become the basis for the PR-izing war – the managing of information flows has become central to the conduct of warfare. The very immediateness of these media-ized wars is the most powerful weapon of the military PRs. Because viewers appear to have instantaneous access to real-time images, they are made to seem more real and unmanipulated. The Gulf War, for example, generated the illusion that satellite-age television gave audiences real-time, direct access to the action of wars. Because CNN covered the bombing of Baghdad, 'the illusion was created that war was being fought out in full view of a global audience' (Taylor, 1992: 278), but this merely served to disguise the processes of selection, omission and propaganda actually taking place as well as disguise the fact that no real information was being provided by the spectacular 'lights show'. It also hid the fact that the real action on the Iraqi front and in Kuwait was not being shown. The Gulf War showed that, when used well, television can be a military PRs dream medium.

As societies have been informationalized and digitized, so OECD military strategists have had to adjust and PR-ize their thinking in accordance with the emerging global media-ized context. Hence, military PR and psy-ops machines have become a growth industry. The PR machines created for events like the Gulf War are impressive. As Engelhardt (1994: 85) notes, these machines have to be able to do several things: organize around the clock on on-location support ('minders'/ 'handlers') for journalists who are allowed into the area of operations; to manage thousands of journalists (allowed into the 'pools' and briefings); to coordinate messages released at different sites around the world; to schedule information releases to suit the routinized schedules of newsrooms (in a range of time zones); and to provide high-quality images to feed television's need for ongoing action. Military PRs have had to become highly skilled users of all the possibilities opened up by the latest media technologies. During the Gulf War the military created a global PR machinery of scriptwriters, make-up artists, graphic designers and film editors to back up the performances of their generals-as-actors (Engelhardt, 1994: 86). The Pentagon in Washington was at the heart of orchestrating the script for the Nintendo war. The coordination and instantaneous sharing of the script and images was made possible by the global communication net. During the Kosovo War a similar globally-networked PR machine was developed, operating out of three centres – Washington, London and Brussels. This machinery had to develop spokespeople who could be credible digital performers, that is who could project the right televisual image, speak in appropriate sound bites, and look the part of professional digital-warfare warriors. In this regard, Generals Schwarzkopf and Powell certainly performed as skilled actors during the Gulf War. But nine years later during the Kosovo War, NATO opted instead for a 'civilian' spokesman, Jamie Shea. Shea was also a skilled television performer (with a PhD in First World War propaganda).

The new technologies of news-making

Newsrooms have also been changing under the impact of technology shifts, and journalistic practices have shifted as a result of the new technologies. First, instantaneous global communication has dramatically increased the pressure on journalists to deliver information speedily. Secondly, audiences have been 'visualized' by television and PC screens – they now expect good-quality 'action' images as a matter of course. Thirdly, the new technologies have produced a convergence of words, images sound and data into a single 'informational' stream. This means that there is now literally a flood of 'informational bits' that the media can use and this makes the sifting/gatekeeping process (of selection, emphasis and de-emphasis) much more complex. The gatekeeping problem is exacerbated by the speed at which decisions have to be made.

By the time of the Gulf War the media had responded to, and adopted, many of the new technologies. These make it possible to cover wars in new ways. From the point of view of reporting war, the key shift was that it was now possible to construct 'virtual newsrooms' that spanned the globe – a reporter on the other side of the world can be integrated into newsroom communication and decision-making as if actually physically present in that newsroom space. Journalists can connect their laptop computers to home-base computers via the global Net. This makes it possible to file stories in real time, communicate by e-mails with the newsroom hierarchy and access data-bases anywhere in the world. Portable satellite telephones and faxes also provide journalists with instantaneous contact with their newsrooms, and with other sources of information. Importantly, digital technology now makes it possible to send written copy, photographs and voice through the system. In addition, television cameras are now small, light and easily to handle. The portability of equipment makes the capture of televisual images much easier, even in conflict situations. And these images too can be easily fed into the global Net and delivered instantaneously to newsrooms on the other side of the world.

But to facilitate this flow of digitized information, large news organizations have permanently to rent satellite transponders to guarantee the functioning of their globalized virtual newsrooms. And for large stories (like the Gulf War and South Africa's 1994 elections) flyaway satellite uplinks are actually transported to the distant news sites. The costs of transponders and flyaways are very high, which has forced news organizations to cooperate and share, and has led to news becoming even more driven by business considerations. As a result, attracting audiences through sensationalized news is increasingly important as a means for paying for the new technologies. These technological issues also push news organizations into working closely with PRs. For example, PRs helped to arrange the transportation of CNN's flyaway uplink by military helicopter during the Gulf War. The South African government was equally cooperative during the 1994 elections.

The new communication technologies mean that huge quantities of digitized information now flow into newsrooms in the form of e-mails, written copy, video images, sound bites and computer-generated graphics. During the Gulf War even spy-satellite images flowed to newsrooms. These digital signals can be edited and changed, ranging from innocuous alterations such as the frame capture of video images (to make these images useable by the print media) to more problematic digital editing, when images and sounds are actually fundamentally altered.

Naturally, PRs also have all this technology at their disposal. They, too, capture images and sounds and generate computer graphics. And in some cases military PRs will have exclusive access to images, such as those from spy-satellites and the laser-guidance systems of missiles, which they can then feed to news media at appropriate moments. PRs also edit the images and sounds to improve their impact. Such digital editing is both easy to do and very difficult to detect, making digital media a propagandist's dream-tool. PRs feed their material (after suitably editing it) into the same global informational Net. Pinsdorf contends that at the time of the Gulf War military PRs were far ahead of news organizations in understanding the uses to which new communication technologies could be put. 'The military won big because it manipulated, knew what it was doing. The press [.] was caught lagging behind the new technology and the military's new sophistication in media relations' (Pinsdorf, 1994: 51). In essence, the psy-ops-ing of war news has taken place. Military PRs and psychological operations (psy-ops) personnel worked out how to use the new global communications Net far quicker than the news media did. These PRs understood how to use all the weak points of newsroom practice – newsroom routinization, the pressure of time and the need for good, action-oriented visuals. They also understood those discourses that tend to predominate in mainstream OECD newsrooms (such as 'social justice' and 'ecological sensitivity' discourses) and how to piggyback propaganda upon these discourses. Further, they understood the general tendency towards a 'PR-ization of news' driven by the need to cut costs – it is simply cheaper for news organizations to trim staff levels and use good quality PR material. This PR-izing of news is, in part, driven by the need to deploy expensive new communication technologies which necessitates cost-cutting in other areas (such as staffing).

In essence, the 1990s have shown that NATO PRs have at their disposal the communications technology, financial resources, and communication and psy-ops expertise to deliver the images and information that perfectly match the needs of the news organizations they seek to feed. Military PRs have become experts in using the global communication Net to deliver news that neatly meshes with the routinized needs of news organizations. Effectively, a symbiotic relationship has grown up between the media and PRs which has negatively impacted upon the quality of news. During the Gulf War, the negative outcome of this symbiosis was clear; it resulted in news that Naughton has called 'the journalistic equivalent of candyfloss: delicious to consume but devoid of substance' (Naughton, in Taylor, 1992: 34). So, ironically, the deployment of the new technologies to create virtual newsrooms does not appear necessarily to produce better news. As Massing noted, 'to get the real story in the

Gulf [War], reporters did not have to travel to Saudi Arabia. Most of the information they needed was available in Washington' (Massing, in MacArthur, 1992: 149). Effectively, those who went to Saudi Arabia were in any case simply fed information produced by Washington-based PRs. At least by the time the Kosovo War errupted the media had learned that they did not have to travel to exotic places to be fed military PR material – it was sufficient simply to attend the NATO briefings in Brussels, Washington and London.

If the coverage of NWO conflict is anything to go by, it seems that new communications technologies may have actually benefited military PRs more than journalists. These new technologies help generate the illusion of instantaneous access to events across the globe. In reality, well-funded military PRs can produce 'controlled illusions' that look like coverage, that is a skilled PR can use the very instantaneous nature of televisual coverage to enhance the illusion that audiences have access to what is happening, when in reality the real action is happening off-screen. It is an illusion that is excellent for PRs because one does not think about that which is not brought to one's attention. The PR-izing of warfare under the NWO has been built upon the principle of effective agenda-setting – getting the media to focus only on what one wants the audience to think about.

In summary, network capitalists appear to be achieving something close to global hegemonic dominance. This includes a global coercive capacity (mostly due to the overwhelming dominance of the US military machine). As significant, this hegemonic apparatus has developed a highly sophisticated public relations system, which is seemingly able to keep the media on-side while violence is being deployed. So currently, global network capitalism is militarily very secure, with the only coercive threats facing the NWO hegemonic bloc being the possibility of terrorism and some crime warlord activity. Most crime warlords pose no significant hegemonic threat and have already been demonized in the media. (One possible exception exists in southern Colombia where FARC guerillas, supported by the cocaine trade, pose a significant hegemonic threat to the NWO's local Colombian allies.) The terrorist threat is more problematic, although it is in no way fundamentally threatening to the NWO. Those groups who would be inclined to use terrorism against the NWO are weak. They use terrorism because they perceive themselves to have no other way of challenging the overwhelming dominance of the hegemonic order they oppose. Past experience would seem to indicate that the media's response to terrorism will be contradictory, a mix of reporting that both assists and undermines those using these tactics (Schlesinger et al., 1983). But overall, if the 1990s' successes of the military PRs is anything to go by, it seems likely that NWO PRs will have little problem in demonizing terrorists when and if they strike in future.

CHAPTER 9

Circulating Meaning III: Making Sense of Distant Places

Global network capitalism is a transglobal phenomenon driven by a networker elite from its base in global cities. The global networkers' hegemony is underwritten by the military might of the USA and a network of alliances radiating out of Washington, of which NATO is the most important. Under the New World Order, decisions made in the key global network centres (e.g. Washington, New York, London, Brussels, Berlin and Tokyo) now impact on every corner of the globe, and those charged with governance in these key centres now routinely concern themselves with the issues and events arising in the far-flung corners of network capitalism's 'neo-imperial' domains. Effectively, a new geography of decision-making has emerged within which even places distant from the centres of global power are routinely monitored and taken into account when political and economic decisions are made. And, thanks to global information technology, the monitoring of, and decision-making about, such distant places can now take place in real time.

In effect, a system of 'global governance' is emerging, a system built around instantaneous global flows of information. Some of this information flows *directly* to the financial and business elites and/or to the decision-making elites at the White House, the US State Department, the CIA, the Pentagon, the US Congress, the IMF, the World Bank, the European Commission, NATO headquarters, the Japanese MITI (Ministry of International Trade and Industry), etc. However, some information impacts upon key global decision-makers in a *multi-step* fashion. Global news-gathers disseminate news about distant places to

OECD populations. These populations (and members of the elite) form impressions of distant places, issues and events from such news, and these impressions often translate into electoral pressure upon political representatives to act in certain ways towards distant populations. In the case of the USA, this is especially important because US foreign policy (underpinned by the US military machine) lies at the heart of the New World Order. As a consequence, the nexus of the US media, the US voting public and the US political machine has become centrally implicated not only in the governance of the USA, but also in the governance of the larger system of global network capitalism. Hence, the processes whereby Americans, and to a lesser extent the USA's OECD allies, 'make sense of distant places' now has real consequences for the people living in those distant places.

Increasingly, then, journalist coverage of foreign places can impact on the governance of these 'distant places'. Governance based upon foreign news-driven 'mediated realities' is emerging. This form of governance has inherent problems because, as Gaye Tuchman (1978) argues, journalists construct a 'window on the world'. This window is always a partial view, a skewed picture. For consumers of local news some potential exists to moderate the in-built distortion produced by news practices. In the local context, consumers (including politicians) can, to some extent, carry out their own 'reality checks' by comparing their own 'lived experiences' and understandings with what is reported in the media. But when it comes to the reporting of distant places, such 'reality checks' are not possible. So news consumers become virtually entirely dependent on the news media to help them make sense of distant places to which they themselves have no direct access. The news windows constructed to view distant places have all the problems of partiality and bias discussed in Chapter 7. But foreign news windows tend to be even more distorted, both by accident and design. And when distortions occur, they are generally not redressed because there is no pressure to correct them – because distant audiences do not recognize distortions and, as Wallis and Baran (1990: 231) note, it is difficult for foreigners to redress reporting inaccuracies at a distance.

Distance and double misreadings

Relying on the news media to understand distant places produces a double misreading in the OECD heartlands because OECD journalists are generally ill-equipped to read distant contexts, and so, therefore, are their audiences. Not only do OECD audiences have already limited understandings of distant contexts, but they are forced to rely on partial/ skewed journalistic reports to build up any kind of picture of foreign places. These 'partial pictures' acquire a 'reality' in OECD countries which then serves to frame the way the next generation of foreign correspondents and their news editors look at, and hence report, the distant places. Once a prejudice (whether negative or positive) has rooted itself within a newsroom culture, that prejudice will unconsciously inform future news-making about that particular group of people.

For OECD audiences, if distant issues are not reported, they do not exist. What 'exists' is what enters one's consciousness. For OECD populations, television increasingly sets the agenda for what these highly 'media-ted' populations think about and discuss. When it comes to foreign contexts, this agenda-setting role is almost absolute. As regards the reporting of distant places, 'televisualized' agenda-setting generates a particular variety of partiality – one often governed by emotive images. Television is very good at presenting visually sensational and uni-dimensional material, but television is a poor medium for dealing with complicated issues and contexts which require non-sensational, analytic unpacking of their complexity. Watching television news tends not to leave audiences with a store of knowledge of the details and facts of what is happening, but rather with a blur of images. So watching television news generally leaves audiences with strong (yet ill-defined) feelings and emotions, but little understanding of the issues underpinning what they see. Neuman et al. discuss how television news creates 'common knowledge [which helps] people think . . . and structure their ideas, feelings and beliefs about political issues' (1992: 3). They argue that television is good at putting obscure and distant events on to the agenda, but are correct in that television is good at creating 'common knowledge' about distant places (Neuman et al., 1992: 86). However, it is 'common knowledge' that is likely to be highly skewed and partial due to the nature of the medium. As Wallis and Baran note: 'radio and television are *immediate* and emotional media. The emotional prerequisite for successful communication in the broadcast media means that news, ideally, should be both informative and dramatic if it is to grip' (Wallis & Baran, 1990: 246–7, original emphasis). Hence, foreign news selection tends to be geared to the highly visual, dramatic and emotional because such news is more appealing to audiences. This leaves television audiences with a highly 'visualized', reductionist 'knowledge' of foreign places that is extremely limited and often devoid of factual detail. This tends to leave audiences with very strong feelings about foreign issues that are ironically based on a highly limited repertoire of information. Neuman et al. (1992: 63–4) provide the example of intense antagonism towards white South Africans in the 1980s based on US television coverage of the anti-apartheid struggle. A similar antagonism developed towards Serbs in the 1990s as a result of Anglo media coverage of the Bosnian and Kosovo Wars.

At heart, the problem with television reporting of distant places is that television news seeks out the visually dramatic and the emotional. Television news compresses, simplifies and eschews complexity and ambiguity. Wherever possible television news production will reduce complexity to binary oppositions, mobilizing what Hartley (1982: 21) calls 'hooray' and 'boo' words because this makes good, emotive television that can attract and hold audiences. Foreign situations can be more easily simplified into facile 'good guy' versus 'bad guy' scenarios than local situations because audiences have no way of personally verifying reports on distant places. In this regard, Westmoreland's complaint that television news is simplistic is instructive:

> Television brought war into the American home, but in the process television's unique requirements contributed to a distorted view of the war. The news had to be compressed and visually dramatic. Thus the war that the Americans saw was almost exclusively violent, miserable, or controversial: guns firing, men falling, helicopters crashing, buildings toppling, huts burning, refugees fleeing, women wailing. A shot of a single building in ruins could give an impression of an entire town destroyed. . . . Only scant attention was paid to . . . the way life went on in a generally normal way for most of the people much of the time. (Westmoreland, 1980: 555)

Sadkovich notes a similar process at work in reporting the break-up of Yugoslavia. He says:

> Television seems able to portray only a limited range of emotions because it lacks linear development and nuance. It homogenizes and reduces complex situations, events and emotions to simple standard items that are almost mythic. . . . Television precludes careful exegesis in favor of simple

explanations of group conflict and reality in general. It invokes and evokes, it does not inform or explain.

If Television is a dream, it also decides what is real. . . . As the tube creates and idealizes some groups and ideas by focusing on them, it makes other disappear by ignoring them. Because it is the key source of news for most Americans it has seriously distorted our view of reality. (Sadkovich, 1998: 60)

Sadkovich also examined how US journalists mobilized 'name-calling' (1998: 82) and/or emotion and drama during the Yugoslav conflicts, such as the story of the Serbian boy and Muslim girl killed in each other's arms. 'As drama the show was wonderful. As news, it meant nothing' (Sadkovich, 1998: 68). Yet such visual dramatization has become the stock-in-trade of US televisual coverage of distant places – dramatization which then spills into non-US television. This often generates deep emotional responses among television audiences, which can, in turn, produce emotionally-driven foreign policy formulation. Having recognized the power of negative televisual images on foreign policy-making, the US military developed a strategy for limiting these (see Chapter 8).

But it is not only audiences who misunderstand distant places; journalists regularly misread and misunderstand the foreign contexts to which they are sent. When journalists (and news editors) cover foreign contexts, they engage in their task with already existing pictures and discourses in their minds. These images determine the questions they ask and the images they seek. Hence the partiality of news frames tends to be recycled and reproduced so that discourses about foreigners and foreign places are resistant to change.

Journalistic misreadings occur due to a number of factors. Journalists arriving in a new context are foreigners, not rooted in the history or codes of the society they are expected to report on. Journalists necessarily experience real difficulties when sent to cover societies grounded upon unfamiliar religions (such as Anglo journalists in the Muslim world), or to societies that are extremely complex (such as the Balkans, Russia or South Africa). Van Ginneken (1998: 125–6) notes how journalists often read the history and mores of their own societies into foreign contexts when trying to make sense of these places. In the process, they simply produce a distorted view of 'the other'. Karim, for example, notes how the Western media, when confronted with socio-political complexities they could not understand in the Caucasus and former

Yugoslavia, simply produced a reductionist explanation based upon 'religious differences' and 'irrationality' (Karim, 2000: 177). Further, when encountering 'difficult' and 'foreign' places, journalists often herd together into expatriate communities consisting of Western media people, businesspeople, embassy and intelligence staff, and NGO humanitarian and aid workers (Van Ginneken, 1998: 134). These expatriate communities tend to be cut off from the countries in which they live and so invent 'closed-shop' interpretations or 'scripts' to describe the 'difficult cultures' surrounding them (Van Dijk, in Karim, 2000: 179). It is these 'closed' interpretations that the 'folks back home' get to hear (via journalists and embassy dispatches). Van Ginneken notes that once created, these scripts or 'prime definitions tend to stick' and be recycled (1998: 113).

Misreadings also occur because journalists carry their cultural biases with them when reporting on foreign contexts. Further, they carry, by extension, the biases of their news editors since journalists necessarily respond to requests and pressures from their home base to deliver stories conforming to 'home needs' (see Cohen et al., 1995). In this regard, Karim (2000) and Said (1981) have discussed the anti-Muslim bias in Western media. Van Ginneken (1998: 110) argues that journalists effectively judge others in terms of their own cultural biases. So foreigners operating in ways that confirm the journalist's own cultural norms seem sensible and normal, while anyone operating outside these norms becomes 'incomprehensible' or even 'despicable'. Attention is drawn to such 'incomprehensible' and 'despicable' behaviour while 'dark issues' in one's own culture are forgotten and blotted out (Van Ginneken, 1998: 111).

Significantly, Anglo values have become something of a measure of 'normalness' (or even 'truth') in the global media system. This is due, in no small measure, to the growing centrality of the US media (such as CNN) within this system and because of the central position occupied by the USA within the New World Order. Consequently, Anglo journalists assume their values to be universally valid and uncontested 'truths', partly because the New World Order is a *de facto* Anglo hegemony. Measuring other cultures against Anglo values is thus taken for granted. So, for example, the American trajectory of socio-economic development is seen as a valid model for all to emulate and the Anglo-American model for organizing the state (as a 'unified majoritarian democracy') becomes a self-evident truth. When Americans came to believe in the 'melting pot', (i.e. cultural integration and assimilation) that became the measurement criteria for all. When 'multiculturalism' replaced the 'melting pot', the journalistic measurement criteria also shifted. Those not adhering to Anglo-American models of societal organization become 'despicable' and/or 'incomprehensible'. North Korea, Iran, Afghanistan and Libya have become such 'incomprehensible' societies, as have all Muslim fundamentalists. ('Muslim fundamentalism' has become a major 'boo word' in the Anglo global media.) Generally, black African conflicts – for example, in Somalia, Sierra Leone, Rwanda and Zaire/Congo – have also been presented as incomprehensible, although the opaqueness of these conflicts is often indirectly 'explained away' by alluding to Western 'common knowledge' of the 'inherently' despicable nature of 'darkest Africa'. Similarly, ethnic wars in the former Yugoslavia were seen as despicable by the Anglo global media, while the Balkan peoples become incomprehensible for failing to behave in a 'civilized' (Anglo) way. In an earlier era, Afrikaners were deemed despicable for violating the Anglo model of socio-political organization. However, Anglo journalists tried to make Afrikaner actions comprehensible by equating apartheid with American white supremacy and slavery (i.e. because the Dutch *verzuiling* model which underpinned apartheid was unknown to Anglos, they simply ignored it, and mistakenly substituted another explanation for the behaviour of Afrikaners). If the global media are to be believed, Anglos fight wars, engage in conflict and impose their will on others because they have 'good reasons' to do so, whereas other people do so because they are despicable or uncivilized, or just plain 'odd'. So Anglo hegemonies are routinely normalized while non-Anglo hegemonies are routinely measured against Anglo norms and/or in terms of their usefulness to Anglo hegemonies.

A third reason for the misreading of foreign contexts is the journalistic practice of deploying simplistic role labels. This takes place because journalists are often faced with the problem of making incredibly complex foreign contexts easily comprehensible for overseas audiences. Although the habit of shorthand labelling pragmatically achieves this, it can also simplify to the point of distortion. In this regard, Wallis and Baran (1990: 231) cite the BBC's use of race labels to describe 1980s' South Africa. Van Ginneken (1998: 105–8) looks at similar usages in the case of Libya, Iran and Eastern Europe. Ultimately, the journalistic practices of labelling and seeking the visually dramatic and sensational necessarily eschews complexity in favour of de-contextualized and de-historicized reductionisms. For example, the complexity of Kosovo was reduced to the label of 'ethnic cleansing' and the complexity of South

Africa was reduced to a struggle against 'white supremacy'. The problem is that such reductionisms, when applied to foreign contexts, can become 'reality' because the audiences have no direct knowledge of the context being described. Simplistic labels grow into 'truth' for the audiences (and the editors) back home. They also become reality for the next generation of journalists sent to cover these foreign contexts, who then frame their questions in terms of such learned, preconceived labels.

A fourth reason for journalistic misreading is that journalists routinely use binary oppositions when describing foreign contexts. Foreign places are peopled by 'good guys' and 'bad guys'. Some individuals and groups are idealized, while others are demonized and vilified. The process of demonization and idealization is frequently directly related to the foreign policy requirements of one's own hegemonic order. Hence, in an increasingly Anglofied global hegemony, it is the US media's binary oppositions that have generally acquired a universalized naturalism. Not surprisingly, those demonized become pariahs whom one is not just 'allowed' to dislike, but one is 'supposed' to dislike. Over the past decades pariah groups have included Libyans, Iranians, Afrikaners and Serbs. There is also an ill-defined unease about 'Arab-ness/Muslim-ness' in the Anglo global media, although this has not (as yet) grown into full pariah status.

The binary opposition model often slips into a victim–villain discourse, in which victims are portrayed as needing to be rescued from villains. This villain–victimhood discourse allows 'nature' to be the villain in the case of natural disasters and/or some ill-defined villains who are discursively portrayed as bringing about 'climate change', which then causes natural disasters. Since the 1980s, the villain–victimhood discourse has become influential, and has even produced a whole industry of NGOs, and aid and humanitarian agencies that specialize in helping 'the weak'. Those perpetrating the victimization are often equated with the Anglo folk-devil status of Hitler. Once such a folk-devil is successfully evoked, aggression against the villain can be easily justified since it involves saving the 'weak' from being victimized. Not surprisingly, New World Order military planners and political spin doctors have learned to mobilize both the villain–victim and folk-devil discourses.

For the global media machine the most valuable foreign stories are those that can be cast as binary oppositions, in which the weak/victims are helped and the villains are defeated. In a sense, such news provides a form of 'collective therapy' (Van Ginneken, 1998: 32). It is as if OECD audiences need 'good news stories' to make them feel better. This 'news as therapy' is even more appealing if the audiences can be made to believe that they have personally helped the victims by donations to aid agencies or sending 'their' troops to rescue victims. Mandela's inauguration as South Africa's president is a classic example of such a 'binary opposition', 'good news', 'collective therapy' portrayal, in which victims were 'miraculously' rescued from villains. Coverage of the Mozambique floods in 2000 fell into the same news genre. These floods received significant coverage in the global media (when other equally large human tragedies were being ignored) because this story neatly complemented the Western media's binary 'needs'. The floods provided victims to be helped, while those who did the helping were white South Africans. The story could thus simultaneously serve to recuperate white South Africans (now that apartheid was dead), demonstrate that the 'South African miracle' was working (and so confirm past 'collective therapy'), and provide the sort of images of weak and dependent black Africans so beloved by OECD 'media voyeurs' of third world poverty and misery. (This story originally got on to the global news agenda – unlike other African disasters – because of strong South African–Mozambican connections in the South African Broadcasting Corporation. For example, the then-head of SABC-News was Mozambican, Mandela's wife is Mozambican, and the flooded area was fortuitously easy to cover from well-serviced South African towns.)

But the binary opposition model also generates 'problem groups' for the global media, groups which cannot be unambiguously 'idealized' or 'villainized'. This can happen, for example, when former pariah groups need to be recuperated (e.g. Russians after the collapse of the Soviet Union), or when groups of former 'allies' become 'enemies' (e.g. the Iraqis in the Gulf War or the Indonesians during the Timor War). In such instances, the 'problem group' is often divided into 'bad guys' ('supporters of Saddam' and the 'Indonesian military') and 'good guys ('ordinary Iraqis' and 'civilian Indonesians'). Another 'problem group' comprises allies with 'dark secrets' (e.g. Iraq's and Turkey's repression of Kurds, or Indonesia's massacre of communists and its repression in Irian Jaya, Ache and the Moluccas). These problems produce 'silence' – no television cameras are pointed in this direction. Then there are 'problem groups' who have formerly been portrayed as victims, but who now begin behaving in ways that might call into question the old binary opposition model (e.g. the repression, corruption and mismanagement seen in many African states). The 'discomfort' produced when the old binary oppositions unravel causes the media to fall silent. 'Uncomfortable' issues 'disappear' because they are taken off the television screens. The way in which Africa has generally fallen off the news agenda is an example of this. Similarly, journalists pay scant attention to the enormous post-Soviet social, religious and ethnic tensions in Russia, as well as the repression of Russians in some former Soviet states because these problems get in the way of the preferred 'post-communism' news agenda.

Then there are 'foreign groups' enmeshed in OECD issues which prevent their media portrayal in a binary opposition format. For example, despite some striking similarities between Israeli and white South African aggression/repression, the Israelis were never unambiguously caste into the role of villains because of the strength of the US Jewish lobby and Western guilt about the Holocaust. Further, binary oppositions that are routinely deployed by the media are sometimes shelved when using them would generate too much 'discomfort'. As Karim (2000) argues, attention is always drawn to a religious binary opposition when Muslims can be cast as repressing Christians, but it is dropped in favour of 'ethnicity' when the reverse is the case. Media coverage of the Zimbabwean conflict, when white farmers were driven from their homes in 2000, presented OECD journalists with the difficulty of negotiating their way out of the previously-constructed Southern African binary opposition of victims ('powerless blacks struggling against racism') and villains ('powerful white racists'). Interestingly, most OECD journalists could not bring themselves to reverse the binary opposition. Instead most OECD-journalists stepped beyond simplistic race labels (traditionally deployed to describe Southern Africans), and instead explored Zimbabwe's complex politics that went 'beyond race'. This ironically served to 'erase' the racism underpinning the farm seizures. Ultimately, however, the mainstream media's response was to fall silent about farm seizures because this was the easiest way to deal with a situation which destabilized old binary oppositions and journalistic prejudices.

A fifth reason for journalistic misreadings is that when sent to report on foreign contexts, journalists tend to subconsciously select contacts with whom they can work comfortably, that is contacts who are as culturally close to them as possible, or people who confirm their own worldviews (Van Ginneken, 1998: 91). For example, in non-Western societies, Western journalists generally cultivate contacts among Westernized elites because it is easier (and more culturally comfortable) to associate with, and understand, people who broadly mobilize the same discourses as oneself. Such contacts also tend to express views that confirm the cultural biases and prejudices of news editors back home, whom journalists have to please. Choosing foreign contacts who are culturally proximate to oneself necessarily skews the reports produced, and can even build in biases of which the journalist is unaware. An example of this can be found in the way Anglo journalists who have been sent to cover South Africa have done their job. They have favoured white Anglos leaning slightly to the left (e.g. opposition politician, Helen Suzman), or Anglofied/Westernized blacks (e.g. Anglican Archbishop Tutu) for contacts. Such people are culturally proximate to Anglo journalists and so confirm their worldviews. Significantly, foreign correspondents based in Johannesburg have generally lived in affluent suburbs, mostly inhabited by white Anglos and some Westernized blacks, have socialized with South African Anglos, sent their children to white Anglo schools, and have routinely lifted stories from the local English, liberal press. Consequently, the perspectives of one (minority) local interest group gained a disproportionate airing on the international stage. This has necessarily skewed foreign news coverage of South Africa by inadvertently incorporating 'local struggles' into the journalistic picture that has been presented (in an unconscious and unacknowledged way). Examples include the struggles associated with an Anglo dislike of Afrikaners for 'taking the country away from Anglos in 1948', and Anglo efforts to develop 'moderate' and 'Westernized blacks' who can be coopted into an alliance against 'radical blacks' and Afrikaner nationalists. Ironically, because of this Anglo bias, the voices of the majority of South Africans have seldom been heard in an unmediated and authentic way. The experiences and views of the non-Anglo majority (black and white) is effectively 'avoided' because it remains 'incomprehensible' to global (Anglo) media workers, and drawing contacts from the Westernized/ Anglofied black elite and white Anglos is so much easier and more comfortable. Similarly, in Russia, the global media have clearly felt more comfortable relying on 'liberal reformers' as contacts. This is partly because their interpretations confirm what editors back home want to hear and because the worldviews of liberal reformers tend to be more proximate to those of Western journalists than other Russian constituencies, whose perspectives tend to be rather incomprehensible from within a mainstream (Anglo) global media perspective. The news bias that results from over-dependence on one section of the population can have serious consequences for foreign policy-formers. For example, a reliance on Westernized Iranians as contacts necessarily skewed reporting on Iran, which was to leave the West unprepared for the Islamic uprising against the Shah's Westernization policies in the 1970s.

A sixth reason for journalistic misreading is that foreign issues are read in terms of 'home' understandings and agendas. For example, the US media has read South Africa's race relations as if they are the equivalent of US racial problems (Neuman et al., 1992: 112). As a result, white South Africans have been equated with white supremacists from US southern states, the anti-apartheid struggle has been equated with the civil liberties struggle of a US minority group, and the US history of race relations (tied up with slavery) has been read into the South African context. In addition, US political battles being fought by African-Americans became conflated with struggles in South Africa. Conflating these two radically different contexts have produced journalistic readings that border on the mythological. Anglo journalists have also tended to assume that the outcomes of Western struggles over secularization, multi-party democracy and gender equality have a teleological 'naturalness'. Once such struggles are not seen as 'Western', but as 'universal', journalists assume they have the right to read (impose) their contemporary measurement criteria – their 'home' battles and 'home' agendas – into foreign contexts. It also means that journalists are licensed to be lazy because they do not have to engage seriously with the difficulties confronting overseas decision-makers, but can simply 'judge' them in terms of their 'home-base' contexts. Much of the reporting of China's post-communist reforms, for example, eschew the complexities, contradictions and dangers confronting the reformers. Not only can this produce mis-readings of societies with different socio-economic trajectories from the Anglo world, but it also produces foreign 'resentments' about 'Western misunderstanding' and 'interference', as has manifested itself at various times in locations like China, Iran, Malaysia and Indonesia.

Spin doctoring 'tourist journalists'

Because US power underpins the New World Order, the processes by which Americans 'make sense of distant places' now has real consequences for non-Americans. In particular, the impact of television news on US policy-making means that non-US players who are interested in impacting on US foreign policy must now pay attention to how they can influence the journalists collecting information about their countries. Not surprisingly, in zones of crisis one now finds groups who explicitly use the media (such as CNN) to try to appeal *directly* to Western audiences (Shaw, 1996: 7). The notion of a passive 'periphery' merely receiving information from the 'core' and/or of the 'South' being manipulated by the 'North' cannot be seen as valid. In the emerging global communication system it is simply wrong to assume that the 'margins' are always passive victims because players on the 'peripheries' also now actively engage in spin doctoring and manipulation of communication variables in an attempt to impact on decisions being made in key OECD centres (especially the USA).

Essentially, as global networkers asserted their (network capitalist) hegemony over the world, a number of processes have been modified, including the conduct of international politics, information flows and the nature of news reporting. A new form of journalistic practice is shaping up, driven by new technologies and a growing professionalization (and public relations-izing) of news contacts. In the arena of foreign news, the relationships between newsrooms based in the global network capitalism's 'core' OECD sites and 'non-core' areas have also shifted. New technologies have opened up the possibility of building 'newsrooms without walls' in which journalists and camera operators are free to roam widely, collect material relatively easily from remote sites, maintain regular contact with distant home-bases and easily download audio, visual and written material into home-computers from these distant locations. Air travel also means that it is now relatively easy to deploy journalists and camera crews to distant locations to cover breaking stories. It is therefore becoming less important to base journalists in foreign locations. Instead, the phenomenon of 'tourist journalism' is emerging when camera crews and journalists fly in, cover stories and (thanks to satellite hook-ups) file these in real-time with home newsrooms, and then fly out to the next story. Tourist journalism overlaps to some extent with 'parachute journalism' from an earlier era. However, tourist journalists are in constant contact with their home-bases (i.e. they virtually take their newsrooms with them) and piggyback upon the comfortable infrastructure built for global tourism. So the new style is more voyeuristic than the old 'parachute journalists' because, increasingly, contemporary tourist journalists jet into foreign locations for very limited periods, spend much of their time in sanitized, air-conditioned hotels (where one can also watch CNN) and, except for working with an organized industry of local spin doctors and public relations people, they hardly interact at all with the local people or contexts.

On the one hand, tourism journalism means that news can (and does) now come from anywhere. It also provides even small governments with a potential communications vehicle with a global reach. Nonetheless, this global news machine has an Anglo heart and a centre that is very much geared to an American audience. After all, those who try to manipulate the global news machine understand where power resides in the new global hegemony, and so they use the global media machine to try to influence those who count, namely those who drive the New World Order. Hence, CNN may wish to claim that they are not 'American' and that their staff composition reflects an 'international focus', but the reality is that CNN has a US home-base, its practices and discourses are Anglo-American and CNN's influence and importance precisely derives from it being a communicative conduit to the decision-making heartland of the New Word Order, which is *de facto* a Pax Americana.

Tourist journalists can be more easily manipulated than local journalists because they spend short periods of time in unfamiliar places, and given the impact that news images can now have on foreign policy formulation in the OECD heartlands, the tourist journalists necessarily become key targets for spin doctors and PRs. So, for example, many CNN staff have reported an awareness of how governments around the world use CNN to distribute messages globally (Volkmer, 1999: 153–5). Manipulation of the global news agenda is in no way uni-directional, although the centre of the global news machine does set the broad parameters for what is considered newsworthy. Certainly, players all over the world (large and small) are able to influence this agenda, although to be successful at manipulating the global news agenda (i.e. selling a particular message and/or successfully capturing the attention of the power-brokers of the New World Order) requires playing in terms of the rules (discourses and practices) of the Western news machine (especially the Anglo-American machine). Ultimately, it is not only OECD communication players (like US military PRs) who are able to spin-doctor the global news system; the system can be spin-doctored by players on the margins as well.

A good example of spin doctoring from the margins was the creation of the South African 'miracle discourse' in 1994 (Louw & Chitty, 2000). A television spectacle was choreographed by South Africa's then ruling coalition – the African National Congress and National Party (the party responsible for apartheid) – to sell the idea of a 'miracle' transition to democracy in which the 'good guys' won', the 'bad guys' lost and 'justice' triumphed. A scripted, stage-managed show was organized (largely by Afrikaner bureaucrats) with tourist journalists in mind and was geared to producing the sort of 'festive' television event beloved by global television news (see Dayan & Katz, 1992: 5–12). Ultimately, the key target audience for this PR spectacular was African-Americans because it was hoped that South Africa could use this black constituency (much as Israel has used the US Jewish lobby) as a conduit to US policy-makers. Because most journalists jetted in for a short period (the elections and Mandela's inauguration), it was assumed that they would not be in the country long enough to get on top of the situation, and so they could be spin-doctored. The South Africans built an International Broadcast Centre to supply tourist journalists with quality images of the 'miracle transition', and to provide the facilities for each television crew to personalize these images with its own voice-over. The IBC actually made it technically possible for tourist journalists to cover the 1994 elections without even venturing out into the conflict-ridden South African community. The outcome was a tremendous spin-doctoring success, with almost the whole world watching the same pooled images and receiving the same PR message – the miracle which South Africans had found through negotiation and the creation of a social order worthy of foreign investment (Louw & Chitty, 2000: 292–3). Within this media spectacular Mandela provided wonderful PR material because he could be constructed as an icon of 'liberal reasonableness'. For the South African choreographers, attaching a 'saintly' aura to Mandela was invaluable PR, given the worth of 'icons and symbolism within global television news' (Volkmer, 1999: 106). At the end of the choreographed television spectacle the camera crews went home and South Africa's turmoil and transition to one-party dominance disappeared from the global news agenda.

Overall, it seems that tourist journalism has become a central fixture of the emerging global media machine and newsrooms without walls. For spin doctors on the margins this can be a good thing, as it provides them with at least some opportunities for influencing the images that reach the key global cities. However, if non-skewed coverage of distant places is the measurement criterion, then the emergence of tourist journalism, festive television events, the televisualizing of diplomacy (and warfare), the closure of discourse through normalizing one set of discourses and practices (those acceptable to Anglo-Americans), and the widespread public relation-izing of journalist contacts, must be seen as less welcome developments. But, for better or worse, this has become the nature of the new media environment and, by extension, now appears to be one of the given variables within foreign policy decision-making.

CHAPTER 10

The Limits of Power: Resisting Dominant Meanings

In the meaning-making process there are many pressures for closure, that is attempts to direct, narrow or close meaning in favour of one or other sectional interest. Hegemony-theorists propose that ruling groups have an advantage when it comes to closing meanings because they have the necessary power and influence to steer meaning-production towards their preferred understandings of the world. Some closures flow from unconscious beliefs and behaviours (such as journalistic practices), while other closures are deliberate and calculated interventions (such as the public relation-izing of war). It is clear there will be some people and interest groups *trying* to exercise control over meaning-production. However, communication involves a highly complex set of interactivities and so is *not* a process that *can* simply be controlled by those wishing to do so. At most, one might argue that 'distortions', 'restrictions' and 'closures' occur within the *production* processes, and that some possibilities exist to 'shift' and 'channel' meanings within the complexity and messiness of the communication process. But understanding what possibilities exist for 'control' also requires grappling with communicative messiness and unpredictability which necessarily limits the possibility for controlling the final outcome of any meaning-making process. Understanding what these 'limits' are is as important for those wanting to manipulate and restrict meaning-flows as it is for those interested in resisting discourse closure.

The key factor militating against discourse closure is the fact that meaning-making involves a process of sharing and engagement between a communicator and someone who has to receive, read and use the meaning being imparted. Active human subjectivity has to engage with any message before any meaning is actually made. Therefore, the receiver of a message is as much part of the meaning-making process as the person encoding the message. This leaves open the possibility that the meaning intended by the encoder may never actually be realized because the message can be interpreted, ignored, mis-read, deliberately reconstructed or even resisted.

Interpretation and meaning-making

Stuart Hall provides a useful perspective on the role interpretation plays within the overall process of constructing meaning. Hall (1980) says that encoding a message is merely the first step in the process of creating meaning, and the process is not completed until the message is decoded. Hall argues that all messages have encoded into them a 'preferred' meaning (i.e. the meaning the hegemonically-dominant would prefer the decoders of the message to accept), but preferred meanings will not always be successfully conveyed. Instead, Hall (1980) proposes three potential decodings. The first occurs when decoders simply and unproblematically accept and internalize the 'preferred' meaning(s) as intended by the encoder. A second possibility is that decoders, operating within 'an oppositional code', reject the message. A third possibility is a 'negotiated' meaning that results when decoders accept some elements of the 'preferred' meaning, but reject other aspects. Hall's encoding/decoding model effectively reads the notion of hegemonic struggle into the communicative process.

Hall's encoding/decoding article generated a new genre of 'audience' and 'reading' studies when it became fashionable within cultural studies to emphasize the role of the reader (as an active meaning-maker) and to devalue simultaneously the analysis of media *production*, or the idea that the media might have the power to manipulate audiences. In its extreme form, this new genre of cultural studies views the active reader as something of a 'resistance hero' – the simple act of watching television in one's own home could be romanticized into a act of 'resistance' against hegemonic meanings. Fiske, for example, saw 'disruptive reading' (1987: 72) as a form of resistance and equated the act of watching a particular television programme as representing housewives resisting patriarchy (Fiske, 1987: 72). Naturally, this idea of 'resistance' appealed to an

OECD-based, left-leaning intelligentsia with nothing to 'struggle against' in the comfort of their middle-class suburbs.

The first of the post-Hall encoding/decoding studies was Morley's (1980) *Nationwide* study. Morley examined how trade union officials, apprentices and black students read texts. He discovered that people decoded messages in ways that did not correlate to their social position; as active readers, Morley's subjects often decoded messages in unexpected ways. In part, this unexpectedness flowed from Morley's anticipation that audiences would read messages according to their class positions. Instead, *Nationwide* discovered that readers decode as individuals, not collectively as a 'class'. For cultural studies practitioners, because of their left-wing assumptions, this result was something of a trauma. The trauma precipitated a *de facto* shift away from studying 'audiences' as a collective towards studying 'readers' as individuals, as well as a devaluation of communication-production studies and the associated notion of 'ideology'. Hence, after Morley, reader-responses and ethnographic audience analyses became a more popular focus within cultural studies. The result was a series of studies of how readers encounter media texts (Hobson, 1982; Ang, 1985; Tulloch & Moran, 1986; and Buckingham, 1987). This genre of work strangely paralleled the sort of highly intellectualized text-based readings previously associated with literary practical criticism, except that these new ethnographic audience studies focused on media texts and leaned politically to the left. This genre of work also overlapped with aspects of uses-and-gratifications theory, an approach which has examined the 'uses' to which people put media products (Blumler & Katz, 1974).

Hall's encoding/decoding article and Morley's study had major impacts within Anglo communication studies, generating a recognition that if meaning-making was to be understood, it was necessary to look beyond the practices and discourses of professional communicators, beyond production, beyond the media and beyond notions like ideology and hegemony. Effectively, Hall and Morley generated a recognition that there was another element involved in the emergence of meaning, namely, *interpretation*, and interpretation grew from the subjectivity of individual recipients. In the (Anglo) cultural studies tradition, 'interpretation studies' came to focus on how audiences read and used media texts and, in the process, played a role in the emergence of popular cultural forms. Another equally important (European) tradition of interpretation studies is reception theory (Holub, 1984). However, strangely, the work of reception theorists like Jauss and Iser, which focus on the role of the 'perceiving subject' as the maker of meaning, has not been engaged by those in Anglo communication studies who are interested in the nature of 'interpretation' and 'active readership'.

Certainly, the focus on 'audiences', 'active readers' and 'interpretation' generates a new set of insights about communication. A key insight is that meaning is slippery – meanings cannot be 'fixed' by a communicator because the meanings that are produced (encoded) can be interpreted (decoded) in a multitude of different ways. Effectively all texts are necessarily 'unfinished' when they are encoded. As Fiske says, texts appear to contain many possible meanings at the point of encoding (1987: 85). Fiske's suggestion is that texts can be read in many different ways because they are polysemic and so are always open to readers 'negotiating' their own particularistic understanding out of the multiple meanings available within a text. This view of communication dovetails neatly with constructivist logic which contends that all human understanding is 'constructed'. But, whereas audience studies and reception theory emphasize the role of 'readers' in constructing understanding, this author views over-reliance on the reception-end of the communication process to be as flawed as an over-emphasis on the production dimension. Rather, a holistic understanding of meaning-making requires focusing on the co-role that both encoders and decoders play in co-constructing meaning. This process of co-construction involves multiple players, embedded in ever-shifting contextual arrangements within which there are simultaneous pressures for 'opening' and 'closing' reading (and coding) possibilities. Essentially, 'active reading' (decoding) is no more of a privileged site for 'open' meaning-making than are production (encoding) sites. Active reading is no guaranteed panacea against the pressures for closing or narrowing meaning possibilities. Readers are, after all, able to decode in ways that 'close' and 'narrow' meanings. Hence, just as lying and manipulation can be 'distorting' features of communicative coding, so misinterpretation and misunderstanding can be 'distorting' features of decoding.

'Closure' of the reading process

The idea that 'active reading' necessarily works against discourse closure is naïve. This highly romanticized view of audiences appears to have been premised upon a left-wing need to find 'sources of resistance'. As commendable as it may be to seek out mechanisms for resisting hegemonic closures and power-elite manipulations, it is simply overly optimistic to assume that decoders (audiences/readers) are necessarily able to 'see through' communicative partiality and manipulation. The reading process itself can suffer from 'closures'.

Decoding/reading can be just as biased, partial and skewed as encoding/media production. Readers, after all, engage in any decoding process with preconceived pictures in their heads. The process of reading/decoding never starts from 'ground zero' because readers and audiences bring to the task of interpretation their existing beliefs, frames of reference, biases and prejudices. Except for young babies, humans have acquired language, which means they have internalized a particular set of signs and codes. As Whorf (1971) has noted, once we have internalized the signs and codes of our language community, our perception of the world will thereafter be 'guided' by the linguistic 'possibilities' (and 'limitations') of that language community. Therefore we 'see' (and 'think about') that which we have 'words' to express, and fail to see that for which we have no coding apparatus. For example, because Eskimos have numerous words to describe 'snow', they will instantly see multiple varieties, while those with a more limited repertoire of words for 'snow' will not actually see the differences. So our language communities (coding systems) set parameters on what we 'look for' and hence 'see'. This in turn influences the repertoire of pictures already stored in our heads when we encounter the next text that we need to decode. So, from a Whorfian perspective, our perception is always 'guided' by our coding system and so is always 'partial'. There will be phenomena that we 'fail to grasp' because we are unable to 'perceive' the coding possibilities. On the other hand, there will be phenomena we are inclined to 'foreground' in our perceptions because the language system to which we belong has socialized us to pay particular attention to some signs and codes. For example, Englishmen foreground 'class' and Southern Africans foreground 'race' in their coding systems.

This Whorfian view can be read in connection with the idea of intertextuality which proposes that any one text is necessarily read in relationship to other texts (Fiske, 1987: 108). When we encounter a text we necessarily see it in the light of images, ideas, agendas and biases which we have already acquired from previously processed texts. In a sense, intertextuality means that readers are, to some extent, always 'pre-coded'. For example, when an intellectual encounters a new book, s/he reads it in the light of prejudices acquired from previously read books and other texts. Similarly, new television images of Mandela will be read in the light of prejudices acquired from previously encountered televisual images of (and other texts concerning) Mandela and South Africa. Effectively, we are always 'primed' and 'guided' by previously internalized texts. As we internalize texts, we effectively build up a repertoire of codes that provide the framework for navigating our way through future textual encounters. In the contemporary world, television has become an especially important source of 'priming texts' that influence how we (intertextually) encounter the world. To borrow from Tuchman (1978), television can be seen to act as a 'window on the world', giving us access to some images, but excluding others that the cameras do not focus on. Hence, television texts are 'windows' with enormous agenda-setting powers. Over time, the ideas, themes and images that are selectively placed on to our agenda by television become an important set of texts (or repertoire of images) that we presumably use for future intertextual reading acts.

It is also important to note that once an individual has internalized a text and accepted that text's particular interpretation, s/he develops a 'commitment' to that particular frame of reference. Thereafter, if new texts are encountered that contradict the perspective already internalized, tension and cognitive dissonance can result. Not surprisingly, many social psychologists argue people pay 'selective attention' to incoming information and engage in 'avoidance behaviours' to steer clear of information that will cause them cognitive dissonance because it contradicts what they already believe (see Abelson et al., 1968). Should people fail to avoid texts causing cognitive dissonance, they can engage in a process of 'rationalizing away' the new information in order to preserve the integrity of the originally internalized text. So it cannot be automatically assumed that 'active readers' are 'competent' decoders (although neither should it be assumed that competent reading is an impossibility).

Our competence as readers can (in certain circumstances and contexts) also be influenced by a tendency to conform to group pressures. Social pressures (perceived or real) can make readers/decoders as complicit as encoders/producers in generating discourse closures. Sherif's (1936, 1937) work on the phenomenon of the 'autokinetic light effect' is instructive in this regard. A person sitting in a darkened room who is shown a small stationary point of light will eventually imagine the light is moving. In group situations, Sherif discovered, nearly all feel compelled to believe they are seeing it move the same distance. Similarly, political communicators have long known how to use the 'bandwagon' (or 'reverse bandwagon') effect to win support. For example, a person will be led to believe that 'everyone' in the group to which s/he belongs is acting in a certain way. Rather than be the 'odd one out' individuals will often follow the majority and 'jump on the bandwagon' (Lee & Lee, 1939: 105). In essence, the pressures towards 'groupthink' (Janis, 1972) can be a powerful influence on how texts are read. A sense of belongingness, group solidarity and the desire to maintain existing relationships can significantly impact on how people (allow themselves to) interpret incoming stimuli, and so undermine their competence as readers. All of these factors influence not only the readers of media texts but also the producers of these texts, who have to read their environment in order to report on it.

The above discussion lends some credence to the notion that readers are simply 'positioned' by their coding systems (i.e. 'the prison-house of language' idea). The alternative perspective (articulated by Fiske, for example) is that readers are active agents. This tension between 'closed' and 'active' decoding (and closed and active encoding) is necessarily a core issue within communication studies and has consequently been an important tension throughout this book. Ultimately, if this book is to proffer any perspective on this issue, it is that instead of focusing on a binary opposition (i.e. 'active/open' encoding/decoding versus 'positioned/closed' encoding/decoding), it is more helpful to explore the notions of 'qualified closure' and 'qualified openness' and the complex relationship(s) between these.

Resisting versus promoting closure

Communication takes place within a matrix of shifting power relationships. This process is enmeshed with ongoing struggles to establish, maintain and/or resist power relationships. This can be at the level of power relationships within a small group or work situation or can be at the macro socio-political level. For the purposes of this book it is the macro (political communication) level that is of interest. It is in this regard that Hall's encoding/decoding notion becomes valuable. Using a combination of Gramsci and Hall, it is possible to conceptualize of the following communication 'positions':

- Encoders with power (those inside ruling hegemonies).
- Encoders seeking to build power (those seeking to establish and consolidate new hegemonies).
- Encoders seeking to overthrow existing power relationships (those

opposing hegemonic orders whether these be established, new or in decline).
- Encoders ambivalent about the outcome of power struggles.
- Decoders aligned to a ruling hegemony.
- Decoders opposed to a ruling hegemony (which may or may not imply an alignment to counter-hegemonic groups).
- Decoders ambivalent about a ruling hegemony.
- Decoders ambivalent about counter-hegemonic groupings (and/or hegemonic struggles).

These 'positions' will generate a range of possible interrelationships between encoders and decoders, encoders and encoders, and decoders and decoders. Some of these 'positions' involve players attempting to close and narrow discourse (in the direction of their own 'preferred' understandings), while other 'positions' involve a 'necessary' oppositional stance, that is a resistance to discourse closure. Because of the communicative complexity mentioned above, those seeking to bring about closure are never likely to meet with total success. However, this does not rule out the possibility that discourse closures can be (temporarily) achieved in certain contexts and with regard to certain groups and individuals. Good communicators are able to analyse contexts, individuals and groups in order to ascertain the likelihood (or otherwise) of achieving their communicative goals.

What is clear is that 'resistance' to meanings generated by encoders is always a *possibility* because individuals can think autonomously and read 'actively' – and so achieve Halls' oppositional or negotiated decodings. But it is a *possibility* that is not always *realized*. In political terms, the likelihood of oppositional readings seems to be greater when hegemonic orders are either new or old. This appears to occur because ruling groups in newly established hegemonies are still learning how to create and promote discourses appropriate to their needs. Further, in newly established hegemonies, decoders with oppositional readings are likely to be more numerous because the new hegemony has not as yet had sufficient time to promote and widely diffuse its preferred discourses. On the other hand, when hegemonies are old and crumbling, more communicative spaces will be available for dissent than when hegemonic orders still retain the capacity to 'police' the production and circulation of discourses in their spheres of influence. Hegemonies are struggled over and pass through periods of greater or lesser closedness, and through periods when hegemonic operatives display greater or lesser discursive competencies. As a result, the availability of 'spaces' for 'active readers' to engage in oppositional (or even negotiated) readings is contextually-bound. Revolutionary periods witness a growth in the 'spaces' for, and so a growth in, the 'availability' of oppositional readings, whereas periods of great conservative stability coincide with the ability of ruling groups successfully to promote their 'preferred readings' and/or to narrow the 'spaces' for 'oppositional readings'. Hence, the ability to engage in (and promote) a particular oppositional reading will vary according to the context.

The contextual parameters that open (facilitate) or close discursive possibilities are set by a range of variables, including the power relationships between the encoders and decoders at a particular point in time, the communication technologies available at that historical juncture and the competence of hegemonic and counter-hegemonic encoders and decoders.

Are we witnessing a new set of communicative struggles?

Many now agree that the end of the twentieth century witnessed the birth of a new form of socio-economic organization, which, in this book, has been termed global network capitalism. New information technologies (facilitating the growth of instantaneous global communication) are widely regarded as having been significantly implicated in the emergence of this socio-economic formation. From the point of view of conceptualizing the role of communication in building a new political order this raises a number of interesting questions:

- Are we witnessing the birth of a new hegemonic order (being built by global network capitalists)? And is a New World Order premised upon an era of global network capitalism now a *fait accompli*?
- Can we as yet discern the shape of global network capitalism's preferred or dominant discourses?
- If we are in a transition from one form of hegemony to another, does this equate to the opening up of a new 'revolutionary era' which will see the emergence of 'discursive churning', 'discursive openness' and 'discursive conflict' (until such time as the new hegemonic order firmly beds itself down)?
- Do the new information technologies necessarily create new 'spaces'

for communicative dialogue or debate? For example, is the notion of using the World Wide Web to build a new 'public sphere' a feasible proposition? (Ironically, as with the old bourgeois public sphere, a World Wide Web public sphere would similarly be confined to an elite – in this case the 'information rich'.)
- Alternatively, is the notion of a global public sphere a new mythology? Could it be that our societies have simply grown too big for us to even entertain the pretence that citizens can any longer participate in social dialogues within which they can exercise real influence? Maybe population size and socio-economic complexity now preclude anything but pseudo-participation. And so now all we are left with is power-elite decision-making and elite manipulation of communication flows. (In this regard, 'networked communication' has the advantage – for the networker elites – of being able to generate a greater sense of 'belonging' and 'participation' than does 'mass communication'.)
- What possibilities can be discerned for opposing the preferred discourses of global network capitalism?
- If a new hegemonic order does congeal, what will the shape of the new counter-hegemonic groupings, the new 'oppositional discourses' and the new sites of struggle be? (To what extent might the 1999 Seattle anti-WTO demonstrations provide an indication of the shape of a new counter-hegemonic set of discourses?)
- Will people growing up surrounded by information technologies be more likely to be highly 'information literate'? Will they become critical active decoders/readers of the discourses flowing through the proliferating range of channels available? Or will they become more susceptible to 'manipulative encoders' because of the highly 'informational' nature of their environment?

Presumably, the struggle between the forces for discursive closure and openness will remain a feature of human existence for the foreseeable future. But how the hegemonic and communicative struggles of the future play themselves out remains to be seen.

References

Abelson, R.P., Aronson, W.J., McGuire, W.J., Newcombe, T.M., Rosenberg, M.H. & Tannenbaum, P.H. (eds) (1968) *Theories of Cognitive Consistency: A Sourcebook*. Skokie: Rand-McNally.
Abercrombie, N. (1996) *Television and Society*. Cambridge: Polity Press.
Adhikarya, R. (1977) *Broadcasting in Peninsular Malaysia*. London: RKP.
Adorno, T. & Horkheimer, M. (1979) 'The culture industry: enlightenment as mass deception', in T. Adorno & M. Horkheimer *Dialectic of Enlightenment*. London: Verso.
Althusser, L. (1971) *Lenin and Philosophy and Other Essays*. London: New Left Books.
Althusser, L. (1979) *For Marx*. London: Verso.
Anderson, B. (1983) *Imagined Communities. Reflections on the Origin and Spread of Nationalism*. London: Verso.
Ang, I. (1985) *Watching Dallas: Soap Opera and the Melodramatic Imagination*. London: Methuen.
Arnold, M. (1957) *Culture and Anarchy*. Cambridge: Cambridge University Press.
Audley, P. (1983) *Canada's Cultural Industries*. Toronto: James Lorimer & Co.
Bagdikian, B.H. (1997) *The Media Monopoly*. Boston, MA: Beacon Press.
Bahro, R. (1981) *The Alternative in Eastern Europe*. London: Verso.
Berger, P.L. (1977) *Pyramids of Sacrifice*. Harmondsworth: Penguin.
Blumler, J.G. & Katz, E. (eds) (1974) *The Uses Of Mass Communications: Current Perspectives on Gratifications Research*. Beverly Hills, CA: Sage.
Boyd-Barrett, O. (1977) 'Media imperialism: towards an international framework for the analysis of media systems', in J. Curran, M. Gurevitch & J. Woolacott (eds), *Mass Communication and Society*. London: Edward Arnold.

Briggs, A. (1961) *The Birth of Broadcasting in the United Kingdom, Volume 1.* London: Oxford University Press.
Brivio, E. (1999) 'Soundbites and irony: NATO information is made in London', in P. Goff & B. Trionfi (eds), *The Kosovo News and Propaganda War.* Vienna: International Press Institute.
Brooks, B.S. (1997) *Journalism in the Information Age.* Boston, MA: Allyn & Bacon.
Buckingham, D. (1987) *Public Secrets: EastEnders and its Audience.* London: British Film Institute.
Burnham, J. (1962) *The Managerial Revolution.* Harmondsworth: Penguin.
Calhoun, C. (1992) *Habermas and the Public Sphere.* Cambridge, MA: MIT Press.
Castells, M. (1996) *The Rise of the Network Society.* Oxford: Blackwell.
Clarke, J. & Newman, J. (1993) 'The right to manage: a second managerial revolution', *Cultural Studies*, 7 (3): 427–41.
Clarke, T. (1950) *Northcliffe in History.* London: Hutchinson.
Cohen, A.A., Levy, M.R., Roeh, I. & Gurevitch, M. (1995) *Global Newsrooms, Local Audiences.* London: John Libby.
Cohen, B.C. (1963) *The Press and Foreign Policy.* Princeton, NJ: Princeton University Press.
Cohen, J.E. (1992) *The Politics of Telecommunications Regulation.* Armonk, NY: M.E. Sharpe.
Collins, R. (1990) *Culture, Communication, and National Identity: The Case of Canadian Television.* Toronto: University of Toronto Press.
Collins, R. & Murroni, C. (1996) *New Media, New Policies.* Cambridge: Polity Press.
Craik, J., Bailey, J.J. & Moran, A. (eds) (1995) *Public Voices, Private Interests. Australia's Media Policy.* Sydney: Allen & Unwin.
Crook, S., Pakulski, J. & Waters, M. (1992) *Postmodernization. Change in Advanced Society.* London: Sage.
Cunningham, S. & Jacka, E. (1998) 'Global and regional dynamics of international television flows', in D.K. Thussu (ed.), *Electronic Empires.* London: Edward Arnold.
Cunningham, S. & Turner, G. (eds) (1997) *The Media in Australia.* Sydney: Allen & Unwin.
Dahl, R.A. (1961) *Who Governs?* New Haven, CT: Yale University Press.
Dayan, D. & Katz, E. (1992) *Media Events. The Live Broadcasting of History.* Cambridge, MA: Harvard University Press.
De Beer, A. (ed.) (1993) *Mass Media for the Nineties: The South African Handbook of Mass Communication.* Pretoria: I.L. Van Schaik.
Deetz, S. (1995) *Transforming Communication, Transforming Business.* Cresskill, NJ: Hampton Press.
De Kock, W. (1983) *A Manner of Speaking. The Origins of the Press in South Africa.* Cape Town: Saayman & Weber.

Demac, D.A. (1990) *Liberty Denied. The Current Rise of Censorship in America*. New Brunswick, NJ: Rutgers University Press.
Demers, D.P. (1996) *The Menace of the Corporate Newspaper. Fact or Fiction?* Ames, IA: Iowa State University Press.
Derrida, J. (1976) *Of Grammatology*. Baltimore, MD: Johns Hopkins University Press.
Dwyer, T. & Stockbridge, S. (1999) 'Putting violence to work in new media policies', *New Media and Society*, 1 (2): 227–49.
Dyson, K., Humphries, P., Negrine, R. & Simon, J. (1988) *Broadcasting and New Media Policies in Western Europe*. London: Routledge.
Ehrenreich, B. & Ehrenreich, J. (1979) 'The professional-managerial class', in Walker, P. (ed.), *Between Labour and Capital*. Brighton: Harvester Wheatsheaf.
Emery, E. (1972) *The Press and America*. Engelwood Cliffs, NJ: Prentice-Hall.
Engelhardt, T. (1994) 'The Gulf War as total television', in S. Jeffords & L. Rabinovitz (eds), *Seeing Through the Media*. New Brunswick, NJ: Rutgers University Press.
Enzensberger, H.M. (1974) *The Consciousness Industry*. New York: Seabury Press.
Fanon, F. (1968) 'The pitfalls of national consciousness', in *The Wretched of the Earth*. New York: Grove Press.
Fiske, J. (1987) *Television Culture*. London: Routledge.
Foucault, M. (1972) *The Archeology of Knowledge*. London: Tavistock.
Foucault, M. (1977) *Discipline and Punishment*. Harmondsworth: Penguin.
Foucault, M. (1979) 'Governmentality', *Ideology and Consciousness*, 6.
Fox, E. (1988) *Media and Politics in Latin America*. London: Sage.
Franklin, H.B. (1994) 'From realism to virtual reality: images of America's wars', in Jeffords, S. & Rabinovitz, L. (eds) *Seeing Through the Media*. New Brunswick, NJ: Rutgers University Press.
Garnham, N. (1986) 'The media and the public sphere', in P. Golding, G. Murdock & P. Schlesinger (eds), *Communicating Politics*. London: Leicester University Press.
Garnham, N. (1992) 'The media and the public sphere', in C. Calhoun (ed.), *Habermas and the Public Sphere*. Cambridge, MA: MIT Press.
Gellner, E. (1983) *Nations and Nationalism*. Oxford: Basil Blackwell.
Golding, P. & Murdock, G. (1978) 'Confronting the market: public intervention and press diversity', in J. Curran (ed.), *The British Press: A Manifesto*. London: Macmillan.
Gorbachev, M. (1988) *Perestroika*. London: Fontana/Collins.
Gramsci, A. (1971) *Selections from the Prison Notebooks*. London: Lawrence & Wishart.
Guimaraes, C. & Amaral, R. (1988) 'Brazilian television: a rapid conversion to the new order', in E. Fox (ed.), *Media and Politics in Latin America*. London: Sage.

Habermas, J. (1971) *Towards a Rational Society*. London: Heinemann.
Habermas, J. (1974) 'The public sphere', *New German Critique*, 3 (Fall): 49–55.
Habermas, J. (1976) *Legitimation Crisis*. London: Heinemann.
Habermas, J. (1979) *Communication and the Evolution of Society*. London: Heinemann.
Habermas, J. (1989) *The Structural Transformation of the Public Sphere*. Cambridge, MA: MIT Press.
Habermas, J. (1992) 'Further reflections on the public sphere', in C. Calhoun (ed.), *Habermas and the Public Sphere*. Cambridge, MA: MIT Press.
Hall, S. (1980) 'Encoding/Decoding', in S. Hall, D. Hobson, A. Lowe & P. Willis *Culture, Media, Language*. London: Hutchinson.
Hall, S. (1981) ' The determinations of news photographs' recurrence', in S. Cohen & J. Young (eds), *The Manufacture of News*. London: Constable.
Hall, S. (1983) 'The problem with ideology: Marxism without guarantees', in B. Mathews (ed.), *Marx: A Hundred Years On*. London: Lawrence & Wishart.
Hall, S. & Jacques, M. (eds) (1990) *New Times*. London: Verso.
Hallin, D.C. (1986) *The Uncensored War. The Media and Vietnam*. Oxford: Oxford University Press.
Hallin, D.C. (1994) 'Images of the Vietnam and Persian Gulf wars in US television', in S. Jeffords & L. Rabinovitz (eds), *Seeing Through the Media*. New Brunswick, NJ: Rutgers University Press.
Hamelink, C. (1983) *Cultural Autonomy in Global Communications*. New York: Longman.
Hartley, J. (1982) *Understanding News*. London: Methuen.
Harvey, D. (1989) *The Condition of Postmodernity*. Oxford: Basil Blackwell.
Herman, E.S. & McChesney, R.W. (1997) *The Global Media*. London: Cassell.
Hobson, D. (1982) *Crossroads: The Drama of the Soap Opera*. London: Methuen.
Holub, R. (1984) *Reception Theory*. London: Methuen.
IBA (1997) *Community Sound Broadcasting Services. Position Paper on Four-year Licences*. Johannesburg: Independent Broadcasting Authority (10 June).
Ignatieff, M. (1998) *The Warrior's Honor. Ethnic War and the Modern Conscience*. New York: Henry Holt & Co.
Iyengar, S. & Kinder, D.R. (1987) *The News that Matters*. Chicago, IL: Chicago University Press.
Janicke, M. (1990) *State Failure*. Cambridge: Polity Press.
Janis, I. (1972) *Victims of Groupthink*. Boston, MA: Houghton Mifflin.
Jay, M. (1973) *The Dialectical Imagination*. London: Heinemann.
Karim, K.H. (2000) 'Covering the South Caucasus and Bosnian conflicts: or how the Jihad model appears and disappears', in A. Malek & A.P. Kavoori (eds), *The Global Dynamics of News Coverage and News Agendas*. Stamford, CT: Ablex.

Kay, P. & Kempton, W. (1984) 'What is the Saphir-Whorf Hypothesis?', *American Anthropologist*, 86, 65–79.
Keynes, J.M. (1942) *The General Theory of Employment Interest and Money*. London: Macmillan & Co.
Knightley, P. (1982) *The First Casualty*. London: Quartet Books.
Krasnow, E.G., Longley, L.D. & Terry, H.A. (1982) *The Politics of Broadcast Regulation*. New York: St Martin Press.
Kuhn, T.S. (1974) *The Structure of Scientific Revolutions*. Chicago, IL: University of Chicago Press.
Laclau, E. & Mouffe, C. (1985) *Hegemony and Socialist Strategy*. London: Verso.
Larrain, J. (1979) *The Concept of Ideology*. London: Hutchinson.
Lash, S. (1990) *Sociology of Postmodernism*. London: Routledge.
Lash, S. & Urry, J. (1994) *Economies of Signs and Space*. London: Sage.
Leavis, F.R. (1930) *Mass Civilisation and Minority Culture*. Cambridge: Minority Press.
Lee, A.M. & Lee, E.B. (1939) *The Fine Art Of Propaganda: A Study of Father Coughlin's Speeches*. Orlando, FL: Harcourt Brace Javanovich.
Lehmbruch, G. (1977) 'Liberal corporatism and party government', *Comparative Political Studies*, 10, 91–126.
Lenin, V.I. (1929) *Where to Begin*, in *Collected Works, Vol. 5*. London: Lawrence & Wishart.
Lipnack, J. & Stamps, J. (1994) *The Age of the Network. Organizing Principles for the 21st Century*. Essex Junction, VT: Omneo.
Louw, P.E. (1984) 'The libertarian theory of the press: how appropriate in the South African context?', *Communicatio*, 10 (1): 31–7.
Louw, P.E. (1989) 'The emergence of a progressive-alternative genre of media practice in South Africa with specific reference to Grassroots', *Communicatio*, 15 (2): 26–32.
Louw, P.E. (1993) 'The growth of monopoly control of the South African press', in P.E. Louw (ed.), *South African Media Policy*. Bellville: Anthropos.
Louw, E. (1997) 'Nationalism, modernity and postmodernity: comparing the South African and Australian experiences', *Politikon*, 24 (1): 76–105.
Louw, P.E. & Chitty, N. (2000) 'South Africa's miracle cure: a stage-managed TV spectacular?', in A. Malek & A.P. Kavoori (eds), *The Global Dynamics of News Coverage and News Agendas*. Stamford, CT: Ablex.
Louw, P.E. & Rama, K. (1993) 'Community radio: people's voice or activist dream?', in P.E. Louw (ed.), *South African Media Policy*. Bellville: Anthropos.
Lukes, S. (1974) *Power: A Radical View*. London: Macmillan.
MacArthur, J.R. (1992) *Second Front. Censorship and Propaganda in the Gulf War*. New York: Hill & Wang.
Manne, R. (1993) 'On political correctness', in D. Bennett (ed.), *Cultural*

Studies: Pluralism & Theory (vol. 3) Melbourne: Melbourne University Literary & Cultural Studies.
Marcuse, H. (1964a) *Soviet Marxism*. Boston, MA: Beacon.
Marcuse, H. (1964b) *One-Dimensional Man*. London: RKP.
Masmoudi, M. (1979) 'The new world information order', *Journal of Communication*, 29 (2): 172–85.
Mattelart, A. (1980) *Mass Media, Ideologies and the Revolutionary Movement*. Brighton: Harvester Wheatsheaf.
Mattelart, A. (ed.) (1986) *Communicating in Popular Nicaragua*. New York: International General.
McGuigan, J. (1996) *Culture and the Public Sphere*. London: Routledge.
McLuhan, M. (1962) *The Gutenberg Galaxy*. London: Routledge & Kegan Paul.
McQuail, D. & Siune, K. (1998) *Media Policy. Convergence, Concentration & Commerce*. London: Sage.
Mills, C.W. (1959) *The Power Elite*. Oxford: Oxford University Press.
Moran, A. (1995) 'Multiplying minorities: the case of community radio', in J. Craik, J.J. Bailey & A. Moran (eds), *Public Voices, Private Interests. Australia's Media Policy*. Sydney: Allen & Unwin.
Morley, D. (1980) *The 'Nationwide' Audience*. London: British Film Institute.
Morley, D. (1992) *Television, Audiences & Cultural Studies*. London: Routledge.
Mosco, V. (1996) *The Political Economy of Communication*. London: Sage.
Murphy, D. (1978) 'Control without censorship', in Curran, J. (ed.), *The British Press: A Manifesto*. London: Macmillan.
Murray, R. (1990) 'Fordism and post-Fordism', in S. Hall & M. Jacques (eds), *New Times*. London: Verso.
Neuman, W.R., Just, M.R. & Crigler, A.N. (1992) *Common Knowledge. News and the Construction of Political Meaning*. Chicago, IL: University of Chicago Press.
Nigg, H. & Wade, G. (1980) *Community Media*. Zurich: Regenbogen Verlag.
Nkrumah, K. (1968) *Neo-Colonialism*. London: Heinemann.
Noelle-Neumann, E. (1973) 'Return to the concept of powerful mass media', in H. Eguchi & K. Sata (eds), *Studies in Broadcasting*. Tokyo: Nippon Hosa Kyokai.
Noelle-Neumann, E. (1991) 'The theory of public opinion: the concept of the spiral of silence', in Anderson, J.A. (ed.), *Communication Yearbook 14*. Newbury Park, CA: Sage.
Nordenstreng, K. & Varis, T. (1973) ' The nonhomogeneity of the national state and the international flow of communication', in G.Gerbner, L.P. Gross & W.H. Melody (eds), *Communication Technology and Social Policy*. New York: John Wiley.
Ortega y Gasset, J. (1961) *Revolt of the Masses*. London: Allen Unwin.

Pavlik, J.V. (1998) *New Media Technology*. Boston, MA: Allyn & Bacon.
Pinsdorf, M.K. (1994) 'Image makers of desert storm: Bush, Powell and Schwarzkopf', in T.A. McCain & L. Shyles (eds), *The 1000 Hour War. Communication in the Gulf*. Westport, CT: Greenwood Press.
Poulantzas, N. (1980) *State, Power, Socialism*. London: Verso.
Price, M. (1995). *Television: the Public Sphere and National Identity*. Oxford: Clarendon Press.
Punter, D. (ed.) (1986) *Introduction to Contemporary Cultural Studies*. London: Longman.
Raboy, M. (nd) *Public Broadcasting for the 21st Century*. Luton: University of Luton Press.
Raboy, M. (1997) 'Repositioning public broadcasting', *Media International Australia*, 83: 31–7.
Reno, W. (1995) 'Markets, war, and the reconfiguration of political authority in Sierra Leone', *Canadian Journal of African Studies*, 29 (2).
Rock, P. (1981) 'News as eternal recurrence', in S. Cohen & J. Young (eds), *The Manufacture of News*. London: Constable.
Rosen, P.T. (ed.) (1988) *International Handbook of Broadcasting Systems*. New York: Greenwood Press.
Sadkovich, J.J. (1998) *The U.S. Media and Yugoslavia, 1991–1995*. Westport, CT: Praeger.
Said, E. (1981) *Covering Islam*. London: Routledge & Kegan Paul.
Saussure, F. (1974) *Course in General Linguistics*. London: Fontana.
Schiller, H. (1969) *Mass Communication and the American Empire*. New York: Kelly.
Schlesinger, P., Murdock, G. & Elliot, P. (1983) *Televising 'Terrorism'*. London: Comedia.
Shaw, M. (1996) *Civil Society and Media in Global Crisis. Representing Distant Violence*. London: Pinter.
Shawcross, W. (1992) *Murdoch*. London: Pan Books.
Sherif, M. (1936) *The Psychology of Social Norms*. New York: Harper & Row.
Sherif, M. (1937) 'An experimental approach to the study of attitudes', *Sociometry*, 1: 90–8.
Sinclair, J., Jacka, E. & Cunningham, S. (1996) *New Patterns in Global Television*. Oxford: Oxford University Press.
Smith, A. (1979) *The Newspaper. An International History*. London: Thames & Hudson.
Smith, A. (1980) *Goodbye Gutenberg*. Oxford: Oxford University Press.
Smith, H. (1989) *The Power Game. How Washington Works*. Glasgow: Fontana/Collins.
Smythe, D. (1981) *Dependency Road: Communications, Capitalism, Consciousness and Canada*. Norwood, NJ: Ablex.
Soley, L.C. (1992) *The News Shapers. The Sources Who Explain the News*. Westport, CT: Praeger.

Taylor, P.M. (1992) *War and the Media. Propaganda and Persuasion in the Gulf War.* Manchester: Manchester University Press.
Toffler, A. (1990) *Powershift. Knowledge, Wealth and Violence at the Edge of the 21st Century.* New York: Bantam.
Tomaselli, K.G. (1986) *A Contested Terrain: Struggle through culture. Inaugural Lecture.* Pietermaritzburg: University of Natal Press.
Tomlinson, J. (1991) *Cultural Imperialism. A Critical Introduction.* London: Pinter.
Tuchman, G. (1978) *Making News.* New York: The Free Press.
Tulloch, J. & Moran, A. (1986) *A County Practice: 'Quality Soap'.* Sydney: Currency Press.
Tunstall, J. (1978) *The Media are American.* London: Constable.
Tunstall, J. & Palmer, M. (1991) *Media Moguls.* London: Routledge.
Urry, J. (1990) 'The end of organised capitalism', in S. Hall & M. Jacques (eds), *New Times.* London: Verso.
Van Ginneken, J. (1998) *Understanding Global News.* London: Sage.
Van Schoor, M. (1986) *What is Communication?* Pretoria: J.L. Van Schaik.
Volkmer, I. (1999) *News in the Global Sphere. A Study of CNN and its Impact on Global Communication.* Luton: University of Luton Press.
Volosinov, V.N. (1973) *Marxism and the Philosophy of Language.* New York: Seminar Press.
Von Klarwill, V. (ed.) (1924) *The Fugger News-Letters.* London: The Bodley Head Ltd.
Wallis, R. & Baran, S. (1990) *The Known World of Broadcasting News.* London: Routledge.
Watson, A. (1992) *The Evolution of International Society.* London: Routledge.
Weber, M. (1978) *Economy and Society: An Outline of Interpretive Sociology.* Vol. 1. Berkeley, CA: University of California Press.
Westmoreland, W.C. (1980) *A Soldier Reports.* New York: Dell Books.
White, D. (1950) 'The "gatekeeper": a case study in the selection of news', *Journalism Quarterly*, 41: 383–70.
White, R.A. (1980) '"Communicacion popular": language of liberation', *Media Development*, XXVII (3/80).
White, R.A. (1983) 'Community radio as an alternative to traditional broadcasting', *Media Development*, XXX, (3).
Whorf, B.E. (1971) *Language, Thought and Reality.* Cambridge, MA: MIT Press.
Williams, G. (1960) 'Gramsci's concept of "Egemonia"', *Journal of the History of Ideas*, 4: 586–99.
Winkler, J.T. (1976) 'Corporatism', *European Journal of Sociology*, 17: 100–36.
Young, P. & Jesser, P. (1997) *The Media and the Military.* Melbourne: Macmillan.

Index

ABC *see* Australian Broadcasting
  Corporation
Abelson, R.P. et al, 210
Abercrombie, N., 49
ABT *see* Australian Broadcasting Tribunal
Adorno, T., 33–4, 38
  and Horkheimer, M., 14, 75, 95, 96, 97, 151
Africa, 42, 43, 56, 197
  informational 'dead spaces', 137, 138
  see also South Africa
African National Congress (ANC), 73, 202
Afro-Asian broadcasting, 76, 79–80
Aitken, M. (Lord Beaverbrook), 50
ALP *see* Australian Labour Party
Althusser, L., 10, 28, 115
Amaral, R., Guimaraes, C. and, 47–8
ANC *see* African National Congress
Anderson, B., 56
Anglo world
  alliance, 67, 127–8
  concept of newsworthiness, 160–1
  dominance, 139–40, 143, 144, 147–8, 194–5
  pattern of assimilation, 67, 171, 172
  pool of meanings, 3, 4
  regulation in, 71–6
anti-colonial elites, 140–1
Arnold, M., 44–5, 71, 75, 78, 83–4
Asia, 42, 43, 56
  Southeast, 135
  see also Afro-Asian broadcasting
Audley, P., 48
Australia, 44, 48, 49, 55, 56
  discourse closure, 114, 115
  public service broadcasting (PSB), 74–5, 78
  regulation, 72, 73, 74, 88
  Timor War, 180
Australian Broadcasting Corporation (ABC), 45, 56, 75, 88
Australian Broadcasting Tribunal (ABT), 73, 88
Australian Labour Party (ALP), 73

Bagdikian, B.H., 40, 49
Bahro, R., 32, 41
Baran, S., Wallis, R. and, 190, 191, 195
BBC *see* British Broadcasting
  Corporation
Beaverbrook, Lord, 50
Berger, P.L., 14
Berlusconi, S., 50, 82
Bertelsmann Group, 51, 52
binary opposition model, 196–8
Black, C., 50
Blumer, J.G. and Katz, E., 207
Boyd-Barrett, O., 139, 141, 142
Brazil, 47, 49
Briggs, A., 44
Britain
  Falklands campaign, 176
  newspaper groups, 55
  political 'middle ground', 115
  press 'censorship', 159
  public sphere, 93
  see also Anglo world
British Broadcasting Corporation (BBC), 44–5, 46, 56, 60
British Empire, 119, 123, 139, 161

British regulatory model, 72, 73, 74–6, 88
  vs. USA regulatory model, 72–3, 74, 76–84
Brivio, E., 172
Broadcasting Act (1990), Britain, 88
Broadcasting Standards Council, 88
Bunau-Varilla, M., 50
Burnham, J., 40, 57–60, 62

Calhoun, C., 94
Canada, 46, 48, 55–6
  public service broadcasting (PSB), 74–5, 78, 139–40
  regulation, 72, 74
Canadian Broadcasting Corporation (CBC), 74
capitalism, 125–6
  see also global network capitalism
Castells, M., 63, 125, 128
censorship, 43–4, 82–4
  'market censorship', 49, 51–2, 158–9
  'nanny state', 85
Chief Executive Officers (CEO), 157, 158, 165
China, 41, 66, 135
Chitty, N., Louw, P.E. and, 202, 203
CIM *see* computer-integrated manufacture
Clarke, J. and Newman, J., 60
closure *see* discourse closure
CNCL *see* Commission for Communications and Liberties
CNN, 200–1, 202
Cohen, A.A. et al, 194
Cohen, B.C., 19, 160
Cohen, J.E., 87–8
Collins, R., 74
  and Murroni, C., 70, 80
commercialization
  alternatives to, 100–3
  critique of, 96–100
Commission for Communications and Liberties (CNCL), 88
communication, 2–3
  distorted, 26, 27, 28, 98
  restricted, 26–7, 30
  role of global network capitalism, 213–14
communications professionals *see* intellectuals; journalists; media workers
communications technologies *see* technological developments
communist media, 40–2
community media, 53–4
computer-integrated manufacture (CIM), 128

conspiratorial elites, 141–2
consumption and identity, 150–1
context/meaning shifts, 23
contextualizing meaning-making, 3–5, 11–12
counter-hegemonic work, 23–4
Crook, S. et al, 62, 113, 128
cultural imperialism, concept of, 138–49
'cultural loss', 139, 142
cultural studies approach, 2–3
culture industry, 6–7, 55
Cunningham, S.
  and Jacka, E., 86
  and Turner, G., 47–8

Dahl, R.A., 6–8
Dayan, D. and Katz, E., 202–3
'dead areas', 137–8
deadlines, 164
decision-making over newsroom staff, 156–8
Deetz, S., 53
de-industrialization, 135–7
Demac, D.A., 71
deregulation, 85–9
Derrida, J., 4, 9–10, 10, 11
development elites, 42–3, 153
discourse, 29–32
  dominant, 22–3, 27
  management by hegemonies, 113–20
  resistances, 120–4
discourse closure
  intellectuals, 31–2, 34–5
  key factors militating against, 205–6
  of the reading process, 208–11
  resisting vs. promoting, 105, 211–13
distance and double misreadings, 190–200
dominant groups *see* hegemonies; power elites
Dwyer, T. and Stockbridge, S., 83
Dyson, K. et al, 80, 87, 88

Eastern Europe, 41, 53, 121, 137
ecclesia of ancient Greece, 101–2
Ehrenreich, B. and J., 59
EMBRATEL, 47
Emery, E., 47
encoding/decoding, 206–113
Engelhardt, T., 177, 181, 183, 184
Enzensberger, H., 15, 98, 102–3
ethnic minorities, 140–1
European Union (EU), 80, 135

Falklands War, 173, 174–5, 176
Fanon, F., 42

Federal Communications Commission
    (FCC), 71–2, 73, 81
  model in Japan, 80
film industry, 37–8
Fiske, J., 25, 206, 208, 209, 211
Foucault, M., 10–11, 23, 25
  and Gramsci, 28, 29–31, 32
Fox, E., 47, 53
France, 88, 93
Frankfurt School, 14–15, 18–20, 28, 35, 151
  commercialization critique, 96–8, 99
  communist- and state-run media, 41
  dialectical model, 33, 95–6
  hegemonies, 115–16
  pessimism, 38–9, 102
  public service broadcasting (PSB), 46
  sensationalism, 48
Franklin, H.B., 181–2
funding newsrooms, 158

Garnham, N., 92–3, 96, 100
gatekeepers, 157–8
  journalists as, 158–60, 169
Gates, Bill, 59, 68
Gellner, E., 56
Germany, 87, 93, 118
  East, 121
  Westphalia, 131
global cities, 134–6, 143, 144, 145, 149
  and 'global governance', 189–90
  second-tier centres, 153
'global culture', 3, 54
global network capitalism, 60–8, 102–3, 111–13, 126, 127–9
  communication role, 213–14
  and concept of cultural imperialism, 140–2
  and concept of media imperialism, 142–9
  and consumption, 150
  hegemonies, 130–2, 142–9
  new geography of power, 134–8
  reorganizing capitalism, 129–34
  vs. managerialism, 111–12, 119–20, 133, 146–7, 151–3
Golding, P. and Murdock, G., 159
Gorbachev, M., 133, 181
Gramsci, A., 7, 8, 11, 14, 15, 106–7, 113
  and Foucault, 28, 29–31, 32
  and Hall, 211–12
  ideologies, 28, 30
  intellectuals, 21, 22, 30–1
  meaning structures, 25
Grenada war, 174–7
'guilt discourses', 140

Guimaraes, C. and Amaral, R., 47–8
Gulf War, 173, 177–9, 180, 183, 184–7

Habermas, J., 22, 24, 102, 115
  public sphere, 69, 91, 93, 94–5, 98, 100–1
Hall, S., 11, 23, 166, 206
  and Gramsci, 211–12
Hallin, D.C., 175, 181
Hamelink, C., 139
Harmsworth, A. *see* Northcliffe, Lord
Hartley, J., 192
Hearst, W.R., 50
hegemonic-dominance model, 6, 7, 201–2
hegemonies, 20–1, 22, 106–7
  building domination, 8, 107–13, 149–54
  and counter-hegemonic work, 23–4
  discourse management by, 113–20
  see also discourse closure
  global network capitalists, 130–2, 142–9
  in news-making, 156, 159–60, 163–4, 165, 168–70
  and wars, 172–80
  weakening, 120–4
  see also power elites
Herman, E.S. and McChesney, R.W., 52, 53, 86
Hersant, R., 50, 51, 82
Holub, R., 207
Horkheimer, M., 14, 34
  Adorno, T. and, 14, 75, 95, 96, 97, 151
Hugenberg, A., 50

IBA *see* Independent Broadcasting Authority
identity, 146, 150–1
ideological state apparatus (ISA), 115
'ideology'
  Althusser's reformulation, 28–9
  Gramscian concept of, 30
  Marxist concept of, 27–8
Independent Broadcasting Authority (IBA), 73, 74
Independent Television Commission (ITC), 88
information revolution, 126
information technology *see* technological developments
informational economy, 128, 130, 132–4, 136, 137
  'information rich' sector, 92, 133, 135
'informationalism' principle, 145
informationalization of war, 182–3
'infotainment', 97

intellectuals, 11–15, 16
  discourse management, 30–1, 117–19, 120
  education/training industry, 14–15, 118–19
  and hegemonies, 22–3
    counter-hegemonic work, 23–4
  post-colonial, 43
  taming of, 14–15, 97–8
  tasks, 21–2
  traditional and organic, 21
  see also journalist; media workers
interest groups, competing, 7–8
Internet, 86, 107, 157–8
  and journalism, 157–8, 166
interpretation
  distance and double misreadings, 190–200
  and meaning-making, 206–11
ISA *see* ideological state apparatus
ITC *see* Independent Television Commission

Jacka, E., Cunningham, S. and, 86
Janicke, M., 81
Janis, I., 211
Japan, 80, 89, 118, 135
Jay, M., 33
Jesser, P. *see* Young, P. and Jesser, P.
journalists, 155–6
  contacts, 162–4, 198–9
  as creators of news, 160
  as 'data-inputers', 166
  as gatekeepers, 159–60, 169
  information-gathering formulae, 161–2
  misreadings, 193–200
  socialization of, 165
  symbiotic relationships, 167–70
  'tourist journalists', 200–3
  training programmes, 160–1

Karim, K.H., 193–4, 198
Katz, E.
  Blumer, J.G. and, 207
  Dayan, D. and, 202–3
Kay, P. and Kempton, W., 29
Keynes, J.M., 77
Kirch, L., 50
Knightley, P., 174, 175
Kosovo War, 174–5, 184, 187
Krasnow, E.G. et al, 71
Kuhn, T., 30, 152

Laclau, E. and Mouffe, C., 4, 9, 11
Lagarde, J.-L., 50

laissez-faire regulation, 70, 71, 76, 85
language approach, 8
language communities, 209
'language games', 4, 11
language, prison-house of, 25, 26, 211
Larrain, J., 27
Lash, S., 133
Lash, S. and Urry, J., 12, 13, 81, 86
  consumption and identity, 150
  de-industrialization, 136, 157
  nodal 'hubs' of power, 131, 134
  'reflexive production', 132
Latin America, 43, 46–7, 53, 56, 135
Leavis, F.R., 75, 78
Lee, A.M. and E.B., 210–11
Lehmbruch, G., 76
Lenin, V.I., 41
licensing/censorship model, 43–4
'linguistic struggle', 24
Lipnack, J. and Stamps, J., 63, 131
Louw, P.E., 49, 53, 114, 159
  and Chitty, N., 202, 203
  and Rama, K., 73
Lukes, S., 5

MacArthur, J.R., 175, 179, 180, 187
McChesney, R.W., Herman, E.S. and, 52, 53, 86
McGuigan, J., 64
McLuhan, M., 54, 69
managerialism, 40, 109–11, 121–2
  vs. global network capitalism, 111–12, 119–20, 133, 146–7, 151–3
Manne, R., 32
Marcuse, H., 14, 33, 41–2, 95
'market censorship', 49, 51–2, 158–9
Marx, K., 114, 125–6
Marxism, 25, 26, 41
  concept of 'ideology', 27–8
Masmoudi, M., 43
Mattelart, A., 139
Maxwell, Robert, 50
meaning
  control of, 25–35
  deliberately constructed, 15
  struggle over, 20–4
meaning-environments, 2
meaning-making, 1–2, 37–8
  contextualizing, 3–5, 11–12
  institutionalized, 16–20
  shifting nature of, 54–7
  intellectuals, 11–15
  power to influence, 5–12

media
  control of, 6, 9
    see also ownership of media
  production and circulation systems, 3, 4
  as source of power, 8–9
media imperialism, 142–9
media organizations, 52–3, 55–7
  socialization of journalists, 165
media workers, 30
  see also intellectuals; journalists
Mills, C.W., 5–6
Moran, A., 73
Morley, D., 25, 207
Mouffe, C., Laclau, E. and, 4, 9, 11
Murdoch, Rupert, 9, 51, 59, 68, 82, 89, 99–100
  see also News Corporation
Murdock, G., Golding, P. and, 159
Murray, R., 86
Murroni, C., Collins, R. and, 70, 80

Nationwide study, 207
NATO, 184, 186, 187, 189
Neuman, W.R. et al, 191, 192, 200
'new journalism', 47–8, 159
New World Information Order (NWIO), 43, 141
New World Order (NWO), 67, 101, 154, 171, 172
  and cultural imperialism, 140, 142, 144
  and development elites, 153
  and wars, 173–4, 187–8
New Zealand, 72, 73
  public service broadcasting (PSB), 74–5, 78
Newman, J., Clarke, J. and, 60
News Corporation, 50, 51, 52, 64–5, 86, 99
news-making
  routinizing, 159–66
  sites of, 156–9
  symbiotic relationships in, 167–70
newspapers
  corporatized chains, 55–6
  history of, 16, 37
  ownership, 49–50
newsworthiness, concept of, 160–1, 164–5
niche communication/media, 19, 65, 66, 99–100, 112–13
Nigg, H. and Wade, G., 53
Nintendo warfare, 179–80, 181–4
Nkrumah, K., 147
Noelle-Neumann, E., 34, 160
Nordenstreng, K. and Varis, T., 139
Northcliffe, Lord, 39, 49, 50

model, 39, 48, 65
NWIO *see* New World Information Order
NWO *see* New World Order

OECD countries, 153–4
  and distant places, 190–1, 196–7, 202
  resistance within, 149, 152–3
  'support' of wars, 173–4
one-dimensionality, 18–19, 33, 41–2, 51–2, 95
Ortega y Gasset, J., 75
ownership of media, 39–54
  and regulation, 81–2
  see also power elites

PACs *see* political action committees
Palmer, M., Tunstall, J. and, 40, 50
pariah groups, 196, 197–8
Pavlik, J.V., 86
PBS *see* public service broadcasting
pepperoni pizza organization model, 63–4, 131, 134, 145–6
Pinsdorf, M.K., 179, 186
pluralist model, 6, 8
political action committees (PACs), 164
'political correctness', 31, 32, 152–3
political economy approach, 2, 4–5, 6
post-structuralism, 9–10
Poulantzas, N., 8
power
  conceptions of, 9
  new geography of, 134–8
  sources of, 8–9
  to influence meaning-making, 5–12
power elites, 6–8
  changes, 57–68
  see also hegemonies; ownership of media
power relationships, 3–4, 11–12
  communication within matrix of, 211–12
  and discourse, 32
  intellectuals within, 30–1
PR *see* public relations
Price, M., 64
print technology, 54, 69
privately-owned media, 47–53
propaganda, 174
  'bullet theory' of, 25
public relations (PR), 163, 164, 165, 167–8, 169
  'public relations-ization', 172–3
  of war, 174–88
public service broadcasting (PBS), 44–6
  see also British regulatory model

public sphere, 69–70, 91–2, 98
  definition, 93–6
  and 'social dialogues', 101–2
Pulitzer, J., 39, 47–8, 50, 72

Raboy, M., 74
radio broadcasting, 70
Rama, K., Louw, P.E. and, 73
reading processes, 208–11
reception theorists, 25, 207–8
regulation, 69–71
  in Anglo world, 71–6
  and deregulation, 85–9
  key assumptions underpinning, 76–84
Reith, Lord, 44–5, 72
Reno, W., 138
resistance *see under* discourse; discourse closure; OECD countries
role labels, 195–6
ruling groups *see* hegemonies; power elites
Russia, 138, 198, 199
  see also Soviet Union

SABC *see* South African Broadcasting Corporation
Saddam Hussein, 178, 180
Sadkovich, J.J., 192–3
Saussure, F. de, 9, 10, 26
Scandinavia, 46, 83
Schiller, H., 138–9
Schlesinger, P. et al, 187–8
sensationalism, 48
Shaw, M., 179, 200–1
Shawcross, W., 9
Sherif, M., 210
Sinclair, J. et al, 144
Smith, A., 39, 44, 47
Smith, H., 107–8
Smythe, D., 47, 158
social conformity, 30
'social dialogues', 101–2
Soley, L.C., 167
'sound bites', 162, 167
South Africa
  censorship, 44, 83, 159
  community media, 53
  hegemonic changes, 109, 114, 118, 121
  media corporations, 55–6
  military PR, 176, 177
  'miracle discourse', 202–3
  news coverage, 197, 199, 200
  public service broadcasting (PSB), 74–5, 139–40
  regulatory system, 72, 73, 74, 82

South African Broadcasting Corporation (SABC), 75
  staffing, 157
Soviet Union
  collapse of, 63, 109
  digitalization of warfare, 181
  hegemonic changes, 121, 123, 133, 171
  communist media, 41
  'guilt discourses', 140
  see also Russia
spin doctors, 21, 112, 169, 200–3
Springer, A., 50
Stamps, J., Lipnack, J. and, 63, 131
state-licensed media, 43–4
state-subsidizing media, 46–7
Stead, W.T., 47–8
Stockbridge, S., Dwyer, T. and, 83
structuralists, 25
symbiotic relationships in news-making, 167–70

Taylor, P.M., 179, 180, 182, 183
technological developments
  hegemonic shifts, 60, 112, 132, 134–5
  new entrepreneurs, 58–9, 111
  news-making, 184–8, 201
  niche media, 19, 66
  Nintendo warfare, 181–4
  print, 54, 69
  regulation/deregulation, 80, 85–7
  see also Internet
telephony regulation, 87–8
television, 139–40
  and distant places, 191–3, 202–3, 209–10
  US network model, 48–9
  and war, 175–7, 183
Thatcher, M., 92
Thatcherism, 88, 91–2
Thompson, R. and K., 50
Timor War, 174–5, 180
Toffler, A., 86
Tomaselli, K.G., 23
Tomlinson, J., 139, 141, 148
Tuchman, G., 160, 161, 190, 210
Tunstall, J., 139, 140, 141
  and Palmer, M., 40, 50
Turner, G., Cunningham, S. and, 47–8

United States of America (USA)
  cultural imperialism, 138–9, 140
  and global governance, 135, 153, 189–90
  journalism schools, 161
  media corporations, 55, 56

United States of America (USA) *cont.*
  military PR, 175–6, 181–2
  network television model, 48–9, 60
  origins of global culture industry, 6–7
  perception of South Africa, 200
  political action committees (PACs), 164
  political 'middle ground', 115
  regulatory model, 70, 71
    vs. British model, 72–3, 74, 76–84
  television coverage of distant places, 192, 193
  see also Anglo world
Urry, J. *see* Lash, S. and Urry, J.

Van Ginneken, J., 193, 194, 195, 198
Van Schoor, M., 18
Varis, T., Nordenstreng, K. and, 139
victim–villain discourse, 140–1, 196
Vietnam War, 175, 176, 181
violence, 20–1, 22
Volkmer, I., 202, 203

Volosinov, V., 24, 31

Wade, G., Nigg, H. and, 53
Wallis, R. and Baran, S., 190, 191, 195
war
  and hegemony-building, 172–80
  'public relations-ization' of, 174–88
  and technological developments, 181–8
Watson, A., 131
Weber, M., 5
Westmoreland, W.C., 175, 192
Westphalia, 131
White, D., 159
White, R.A., 18
Whorf, B.E., 209
Winkler, J.T., 77
WWWWWH-formula, 161–2

Young, P. and Jesser, P., 173, 174, 175, 176, 177–8, 179
Yugoslavian conflict, 192–3, 195

Printed in the United Kingdom
by Lightning Source UK Ltd.
113849UKS00001B/226-288